ENERGETIC COACHING

BEING AND DOING WITH SPIRIT

JOHN COLLINGS, PH. D., M.C.C.
LEA HARPER, M.O.D.

KOLIMA
BOOKS

Title: *Energetic Coaching, Being and Doing with Spirit*
Second edition: September 2020
First edition: December 2007
© 2020 Editorial Kolima, Madrid
www.editorialkolima.com

Authors: John Collings y Lea Harper
Editorial direction: Marta Prieto Asirón
Cover phototypesetting: Sergio Santos Palmero
Book phototypesetting: Carolina Hernández Alarcón

ISBN: 978-84-18263-38-5

CONTENTS

FOREWORD

The doorbell rings. Opening it you see a delivery person peeking out from behind a huge refrigerator freezer that he claims you have just won. "This must be a mistake," you say, "I have no room for this."

Translated into coaching terms this story reads:

Your client, who sits near you or is on the phone, just finishes saying something. A snapshot of you during the past few moments reveals 1) your thoughts wandering and wondering which questions you might ask, 2) your ego fears that your selection will expose your lack of confidence, 3) your awareness of your stomach gurgling, 4) your judgmental self has been evaluating your clients words to be incongruent with your personal values, and 5) a gnawing sense you do not have enough time to turn this coaching conversation into something useful. Your ego is getting in the way; the energy of spirit has no room to enter.

The delivery boy is about to ring your doorbell, not with a refrigerator, but with this book, Energetic Coaching, along with the huge challenge to notch up your ability to coach.

THE LINK BETWEEN LEADING-EDGE THINKING AND ANCIENT WISDOM

The profession of coaching, discussion about energy and awakening spirituality are all active waves cresting. When asked to write this foreword I was reading E=mc2: a biographyof the world's most famous equation by David Bodanis (2000) and had just watched the PBS special on The Elegant

Universe (2003), based on Brian Greene's book of the same name. Through his explanation of "String Theory", Greene advances our understanding of the connection between macro universes like our solar system and the micro world of subatomic quantum particles and waves. The connection is vibration or energy. This kind of contemplation intrigues me as an intellectual hobby that might not seem to have much to do with coaching. When you read this book you will realize this has everything to do with coaching. Both the ethereal and concrete perspectives presented in Energetic Coaching go beyond—way beyond, the eleven key coaching competencies ICF claims as the crux of our profession. Think of this book as a bridge, offering coaching a link between leading-edge thinking and ancient wisdom.

FOUNDATION QUESTIONS

If you are an "open, receptive, learning seeker, traveling on the road to resolving the ultimate quest about what life is all about," you are probably considering buying this book or are reading it already and recognize yourself in these qualities that the authors use to describe the Energetic Coach. Seekers live in the question.

Have you, whether novice or seasoned coach, ever questioned how to raise your energy to a higher vibration or better yet, to help a client attain an "increasing frequency of a higher level of energy?" Are you familiar with processes and techniques to make tangible the intangible of spirit? Can you quantify your experience of spirit? Do you know how to grow energy?

This book has to do with these questions and the answers have something to do with familiar concepts: beliefs, actions, thoughts, attitudes, feelings, judgments, awareness, motives, values, choices, heart connection, intuition, natural physical laws and instinctive patterns. So what makes this book different from other coaching books or books about spirit?

WHY IS THIS BOOK DIFFERENT?

1. Whereas in my book, Coaching With Spirit: allowing success to emerge, I invite readers to consider the framework of spirit in the coaching process, I often documented observations without understanding why they were occurring. Energetic Coaching goes one step further and approaches the topic from the underlying dynamics to help you understand why we behave as we do and what to intentionally do about it.

2. The pièce de résistance, the most thought-provoking part of this book for me, was the chapter about the shadow side. No coaching book I am aware of has tackled this. Truthfully I am one of those people who would prefer not to spend time with shadow stuff. However after reading chapter 7, I know you will join me in appreciating the clearly written and compellingly useful coverage of this topic. The scenarios help us recognize when Shadow Teacher is present and ten ways show us how to enlist spirit to deal with these challenges. You will learn ways to confront shadows that show up in coaching relationships such as: ego, intensity of energy vibration, self and Self and attachment. I am now convinced about the necessity for us as Energetic Coaches to acknowledge and embrace the shadow in our work. This has taken me to a new level of integration in my coaching.

3. The authors entice and enrich us with so many learning possibilities from academic discussions, precepts, landmarks and models to the examination of expectations, values and qualities of Energetic Coaches. Their assessment in chapter 4 is one of the best appraisals of spiritual growth I have yet encountered.

4. Having spent the first half of my career in Human Resources (HR), I found the orientation guidelines in chapter 6 written by Energetic Coaches and for Energetic Members (the authors prefer that designation to employees) extremely refreshing, creative, vitalizing... and possible! For anyone in HR or Training and Development, this chapter is worth the price of the book. Also in the same chapter you will find excellent distinctions between Energetic Coaches and our allies, OD professionals.

A NON-INSTRUCTIONAL INSTRUCTION MANUAL

I thought chapter 7 had the most goodies until I read chapter 8. The authors profess there is no instructional manual on how to become or evolve as an Energetic Coach, and yet the chapter on the importance of practicing is packed with suggestions. Very often clients ask me how I maintain connection with spirit and I begin explaining my chosen ways and other possibilities. Each practice begs a different reference and seems like an extensive research project to the initiate.

All I need to say now is, "You will enjoy reading and experimenting with the concise and excellent descriptions of options all culled into one place and one book, Energetic Coaching."

PEEK INSIDE THE AUTHORS' PERSONAL JOURNALS, THEN WRITE YOUR OWN

There is something for everyone imbedded within the structure of the book. I found it well balanced to read an academic explanation followed by examples that come from John and Lea's actual internal and external realities. I felt as if they were giving me permission to read their personal journals, to roam inside the delicate lace of their musings and meander through the stripped fields of their brutally honest considerations. I know John and Lea and am touched with their authenticity and spiritual depth and their willingness to be vulnerable for the highest good of the evolution of all. Without this motivation this book would not have the impact it does.

Not only do you have the chance to dive into their world, you won't stay under the water too long because you will want to come up for breath to ponder the reflections and intentional imprints they offer you at the end of most chapters. This book will indelibly leave its own imprint in your memory as you read how to "seed, weed and feed the energy of spirit in relationship," or you reflect on their POW formula (Perception times Oneness equals Witness) in chapter 4. You can expect to add major installments to your journal.

Because both authors have expertise working with individuals and organizations, they take care throughout the book to apply the material and share coaching examples from both their individual as well as organizational work worlds. Very often people ask me how coaching can impact an organization. All I have to do is refer them to chapter 6. Lest you think you need to accumulate the decades of experience the authors have to be able to incorporate this information in your next coaching meeting, think again. This book offers a shortcut.

So when your doorbell rings, race to the door and don a smile because your bookshelf already has a space reserved for this book. When miracles seem to happen in your coaching meetings, smile again because you have read this book, discovered the magic of energetic coaching and successfully shared it with your clients.

With energetic coaching smiles,

TERI-E BELF, M.A., C.A.G.S., M.C.C.
January 16, 2004

Bodanis, David. *E=mc2: a biography for the world's most famous equation.* The Berkeley Publishing Company: New York, 2000.
Greene, Brian. *The Elegant Universe.* Vintage Books, New York, 2000.
PBS October 26, 2003 and November 4, 2003. www.pbs.org/wgbh/npva/elegant

For more information, you can visit www.energeticcoach.com

FOREWORD TO THE SECOND EDITION

We are very happy to share with you the second edition of *Energetic Coaching; Being and Doing with Spirit.* Thank you so much to our colleagues in Spain who undertook to translate the book from English into Spanish and publish it, and for offering to publish again in English for a wider audience. Along the way, we learned much more about the energetic spiritual principles already put into practice, such as through the Multiversity connections. We can barely comprehend how things have happened so quickly to easily fall into place. It's like energetic coaching breathed life into itself to grow and expand with the intentional assistance of many other coaching professionals who also turned out to be kindred spirits to shepherd through the process of studying, practicing and living energetic coaching.

Lea: *Little did I know that when I retained John Collings as my coach trainer to obtain my Success Unlimited Network™ coaching certification that we would becoming very close friends and write a book together. From the beginning, we recognized that our relationship was special and meant-to-be with a common desire to bring spiritual understanding and guidance into our lives. Because we deliberately sought spiritual connection in our relationship while coaching, and even more so, while writing this book, we experienced additional wisdom, guidance, perspective and validation of spiritual presence. Words fall short to convey our learning and experiences of spiritual connection with one another and with others. Despite that difficulty, readers often resonate with the book's concepts and recognize that something more is present and alive in relationships with intentions for betterment, such as a coaching relationship, and especially in the relationship a person has with self for self-improvement.*

Although this book was originally written for coaches, there are universal principles and practices to invite and increase spiritual connection that work for everyone. Coaching as a profession is especially suited to conveying and employing spiritual qualities and energy in the process of achieving dreams, and spiritual energy is often recognized in the coaching relationship as people tap into their authenticity and aspirations. So halfway through writing the book, we realized the principles and practices were enhancing our lives real time in very practical ways. The book transcended our initial intentions, writing it deepened our spiritual connection, and the living of it even more so. Spirit is present and accessible to all those seeking more out of life and who are looking within and waking up to inner knowing and a higher purpose in life, so it is not just for coaches, it is for everyone.

John: Lea and I first collaborated about energetic coaching 15 years ago. It took us five years of weekly calls in which the experience of being and doing with spirit become more real. Through focus and discussion about the reality of how spirit works in our lives, my vision of a book about coaching with spirit became a reality. Because we wanted to create living experiences of a close connection with spirit in our lives, the book relays what we learned and experienced in the process, which continues to this day.

Lea: It is amazing to me how 'Energetic Coaching' has burst into life! Who could have imagined that the book would be first adopted in Spain and that resulting collaborations would lead to a complete translation of the book into Spanish and a publishing contract overseas? The experience for me was pure enjoyment to see the reality unfold and flow along with it. As John and I continue to get to know the people who embraced 'Energetic Coaching' and made the effort to translate it and have it published in Spanish, we were honored to be a part of that special, spontaneous process. We realized the serendipitous qualities of the process. Apparently, the time was right for many others to want to learn about and apply the principles and practices. It was so easy to totally trust the process that unfolded before my eyes. In that process, there was a recognition that something else was going on that guided people to volunteer to translate and work on the book. We could see spirit in action to bring in the energy needed for this hefty endeavor. We were brought together for this purpose, no doubt, and it grows.

John: *Lea and I find it amazing what has happened in the evolving development of this book since its publication. At the outset, I found it difficult to find the words to describe the presence of spirit in my coaching and teaching work, even though I could see how it worked in daily practice. For the work of writing a book, I wanted a tangible human relationship to mirror my intangible relationship with spirit. I asked Lea to be my writing partner to translate our coaching relationship into a dynamic process that would go beyond working together into the experience of spiritual connection and energy in relationship. As a result, our relationship grew connected and congruent through the five years of writing and finally publishing this book. Even though it was a great deal of work, it was enjoyable with the effortless ease that comes from spiritual connection and expression with intention for the good.*

How 'Energetic Coaching' has become recognized and adopted is incredible. Once we self-published in English, I gave a copy of 'Energetic Coaching' to my client, Alfonso, and asked about the possibility of publishing it in Spain. He showed the book to his friend Elena, who was working on her PhD, and was willing to work with her many friends to translate the book into Spanish. The fit seen by Elena was to use 'Energetic Coaching' as a basic text for understanding and advancing spirituality in manifesting the integrative concept of the Multiversity and achieving her Ph.D.

A close friend, Marta, who was in the publishing business took on the task of overseeing Elena's work of translation. In time, Marta edited what they had done and 'Energetic Coaching' was published in Spanish. The translation work began as a team effort and the skill in maintaining the integrity of the book was outstanding.

This book you are reading has the bricks and mortar incorporating spirituality in a structure and pragmatic application for a person´s experience in relationships with self, self and others and individual relationship with community. This we have found 'Energetic Coaching' to be a very powerful force to bring forward each person's inner knower to foster congruence and empowerment to achieve life purpose and maintain integrity and authenticity to be completely true to oneself.

There is no formula that works every time or step-by-step instruction to bring spirit into experience and expression, but it is recognizable as real, especially in the relationship with others who are on a similar wavelength of spiritual connection and communication. We experienced spirit while writing this book as an expression of love. Spirit proved its validity and reliability and grew with conscious intention to manifest this love to bring more goodness and grace into our worldly experiences. Our egos receded, no longer needed for defense mechanisms or to achieve superiority or the external trappings of success. Through our relationship of respect, equality and love, spirit grew, and along with it, greater life satisfaction through the internal focus and prioritization on what is most important and eternal in ourselves and others.

Lea: *By getting more in touch with spirit through working with John on the book, I felt compelled and guided to advocate for justice and the protection of human rights, the environment and public health when the industry of fracking came to my family's doorstep. In the past ten years of advocacy, getting the truth out, organizing and building coalitions and keeping the faith during years of difficulty with opposition from well-funded individuals and groups, the energetic coaching principles and practices greatly helped to stay the course. Now that the truth is coming out about the industry's coercive tactics and lack of environmental regulation and oversight, my journey of truth and resistance has been recognized and validated. As a grandmother, I am keenly aware that climate change is here and the coming catastrophes our children will face if we don't right the ship in time. We are going to need a new world consciousness to bring a better future into reality sooner not later. I have seen in action time and again how energetic coaching has helped when I needed it the most, and this has enabled me to help others persevere in the face of daunting odds. Through internal guidance and validation, we find the sustainable energy and inner wisdom needed when external forces are stacked against movement toward the systemic changes needed now.*

I often would remark to John over these last ten years that I didn't know what I would do without energetic coach-

ing in my life as I work for human rights and environmental justice. As a bonus in our relationship, I see John practicing inner spiritual connection continually as inspiration. Now we are in the midst of a pandemic, and John is sequestered in his community living, and I am the primary caregiver for my 85-year-old mother with dementia. Such a learning experience life continues to be! We are finding the practices of energetic coaching even more essential than ever to navigate the choppy waters of uncharted territory seeking the change that must come for a better future! This is not an easy journey, but it is necessary and fulfilling, and we will be given what we need along the way as we remain congruent with our inner knowing.

John: *As I look back at my first understanding of why we were writing the book, to outline means to involve spirit in coaching, I thought mostly in terms of the coaching profession. What I found was that the real importance of working on the book is that it is a reminder of how important it is to choose thoughts and adopt principles and act accordingly. I was teaching what I needed to learn and practice every day, especially as I have faced many changes and am making a conscious transition into the next phase of my life, which at 92 years old is the death of the body. As energetic coaching became embedded in my life, I see how spirit creates a greater inner awareness and taps into guidance and creates good to attract even more good, and the positive spiral of energy grows. Seeing the book expanded to be shared throughout the world in another language shows me that energetic coaching has a life of its own, and I am the mere instrument to bring it forward and give it life to grow as my children have grown into its own being-ness. Energetic coaching will last long beyond my life, but I retain it as my legacy into the next world, which I continue to consciously create. I have no doubt that energetic coaching could be used as one of many ways to help usher in the new world consciousness that we need for human survival and transcendence.*

The fundamental concepts of energetic coaching are not new, of course. But we recognized the coaching relationship as uniquely suited to communicating spirit in words and descriptions for practical outcomes and experiences. To bring it to awareness through conscious choice and practice was something people were seeking and the coaching relationship could provide. There is a unique opportunity within the coach and client relationship to engage and integrate with spirit through accessing and listening to each person's inner knower. With greater intentionality and alignment with spiritual ideals, the inner knower comes forward as a personal conduit for spiritual connection and assistance.

Now that *Energetic Coaching* has been translated into another language and is published for the second time in English, we have had ten more years of practice to see how it works. The book itself remains the same, but the experience of it has grown to enhance our lives and the lives of many others. What we have seen in the years of energetic coaching practice are the benefits it brings for greater harmony, congruence, peace and authenticity. With intentional practice, the inner knower becomes one's own best coach in life. Coaching can make the introduction, but ultimately it will be up to the individual to choose to dance with spirit. Energetic coaching is not just for coaches; it is for all those who want closer experience of something more and much greater than the outer world can provide, which is within us at all times, and connects us with all that is. It is real, and through personal intention and experience becomes a force for good in the world. To intentionally bring the infinite eternal into the finite physical world adds an entirely new dimension to our human experience. To be an energetic coach is a calling. To be an individual instrument for spiritual energy and expression is a calling as well. We hope this book helps answer that call.

John Collings and Leatra Harper
Authors of *Energetic Coaching,*
Doing and Being with Spirit
www.energeticcoach.com/

A dream made true
Foreword from Elena Pérez-Moreiras

Three years after *Energetic Coaching, Being and Doing with Spirit* was first published in 2007, in October 2010 I met Alfonso (Medina) in the 1st Conference of Coaching and Psychology in Spain organized by the Professional Association of Psychologists in Madrid "by chance." When I saw him, I felt "this person and I have a special connection." In 2011, I asked Alfonso if he wanted to coach me to get the ICF certification and we began a mentoring process. In 2012, without knowing the existence of this book and boosted by my natural attraction to the energetic dimension of the human being (I am a development psychologist and an energetic coach for this reason), I invited Alfonso and other Spanish professionals to design and deliver the 1st Energetic Coaching Advance Program accredited by ICF. Two years later, in the final group retreat of this program (May 2014) that took place in Jaen (Spain), Alfonso gave me this book, *Energetic Coaching*, while saying: "Here you have, this is the first book of the bookshelf of our Multiversity."

Since 2011, I had the dream to contribute to build a Multiversity, a global, open and integrative space where professionals of every knowledge area meet to collaborate in building a better world (a dream that now, step by step is becoming true). I feel that there are a large amount of people all over the world that are connected by the desire to offer love and contribute to increase humanity in our society. I call it Improving Network Multiversity. In fact, I felt that all the team of coaches and facilitators of the Energetic Coaching Advanced Program represented the seed for this global movement. You can imagine how astonished I was when I realized that the master coach of my coach had written, seven years before, a book with the same name of the program that I had created with my colleagues as something new and unique. For me it was another manifestation of the serendipities and synchronicities that we live when the spirit acts through ourselves. I was absolutely positive about the importance of *Energetic Coaching: Being and Doing with Spirit* as a basic text for understanding and making spirituality advance in manifesting the integrative concept of the Multiversity, training energetic coaches and facilitators who would be attracted by the force and power of energetic coaching.

I had my first meeting with John in September 2015 in Bordeaux (France) in the retreat of our coaching school, Success Unlimited Network. It was a very important moment for me. As I expected, when I met him, I felt my deep connection with him. A beautiful morning, after a fantastic swim in the swimming pool of the hotel, I told John: "John, I promise you I will translate *Energetic Coaching, Being and Doing with Spirit* to Spanish." I felt that all the Spanish trainers attracted by spirit, energy, development of human being should have this book available to them.

This is thus the first book of our Multiversity (Improving Network), a place that attracts and welcomes professionals of all kind who want to "co-create the world we deserve and ALREADY IS." I began to summon people to translate the book in 2014 and 2015. The first team was formed by Eva del Olmo, Techu Arranz, Virginia González and Íñigo Elízaga, who translated some pieces, but other projects that had our attention at that time prevented the translation from progressing. In 2017, the SUN retreat was to be celebrated in Toledo (Spain). A day of July (today is July the 26th, 2020), I realized that John was coming in October and that his 90th birthday would take place some days later, in November. I felt the unavoidable force of the spirit displayed acting on impulse inside the deepest part of myself. I began to write to everyone who was part of the Multiversity and to more people to whom I had a deep connection in order to tell them: "John is coming in October, he is going to be 90 in November; imagine if we were able to translate the book in three months, invite him to stay in Madrid for some additional days and prepare a celebration to honor him and give him the gift of the book translated into Spanish." Like every time that love and spirit come to us, a lot of people reacted and decided to be part of the translation project. It was really amazing. The process of reactivating the book began easily and fast.

In October 29, 2017 we had an unforgettable day in Madrid when Alfonso and John received our draft copies of the first edition in Spanish. It was marvelous to see them so happy!

The days John spent at home sharing with me and my family his special conversation and wisdom were something that we will always keep in our heart. The 22th of that month, he wrote his: "For me, being an improving networker is…" It was so marvelous to feel and to see how the things that I had dreamed for throughout such a long time were becoming true little by little thanks to the action of the spirit!

In the Summer of 2017, I received another gift from heaven. I had begun my PhD in September 2015 on Energetic Intelligence. In Bordeaux (France), I had also met Carol O´Mear, a SUN™ coach and now one of my soul sisters. She participated in one of the body dynamics that I offered in the retreat and a very special connection appeared between us. We met again in Maryland USA for our SUN retreat 2016. When she knew that I was looking for a university in the USA to do my PhD stage, she suggested me to do it in Laredo (TX A&M International University-TAMIU), staying at her home. Do you imagine? My time in Laredo TX during the winter of 2018 was really unforgettable. Being in the States with the incalculable guide and love received from Carol and James (my "American parents") allowed me to grow as a professional and as a person, giving me energy to make large progress in materializing my life purpose.

In these months, we had the opportunity to meet Lea online sometimes. It was really important for me. I already had a very deep connection with John, but I never had the opportunity to meet Lea before. She was a very important part of all this framework. It was wonderful to meet her, to know her better and to share with her my vision of the Improving Network Multiversity. She also felt that she wanted to be part of it.

The spirit is wisdom. When the spirit acts everything is perfect. This "dream team" that we were creating with the spirit's guidance needed a very special additional piece, the piece who guaranteed the expansion of the spirit energy, and that is this book, *Energetic Coaching*. It couldn't be better.

Marta and her team of Kolima appeared in my life also "by chance" in October 2018 when I attended the presentation of a client's book. When I saw her, I felt the same that I did when I first met Alfonso, John, and so many people that I know and to whom I am connected with from the essence. When I first met her, I knew she was the perfect element we were looking for to complete this great team in order to do exactly what we were called to do: "Co-create the world we deserve and ALREADY IS all over the world with the guidance of the spirit." Thanks, Marta; thanks, John; thanks, Lea; thanks all the improving networkers who are now doing their job in their own spaces and countries. Thanks to all the people who will be coming to the Multiversity in the future, and also to all the people who, even without knowing that they are part of all this, they are. This is the place of "ANDs" where everything is possible, where everyone has a place from respect, deep listening, dialogue and authenticity. As John would say, we are together in the adventure of surrendering our egos to the happiness of the higher self, to carry out consistent actions in the now to achieve love, peace and happiness for all. From the deepest bottom of my soul, THANKS FOR BEING AND DOING WITH SPIRIT! If you are reading this and feeling the energy of love and happiness inside you, perhaps it is because you are part of this group of crazy multiversitarian people. Welcome! We would be delighted to have you in this boat that flows with love and spirit.

Majadahonda, Madrid, July the 26th, 2020

THE MULTIVERSITY IMPROVING NETWORK

The Multiversity Improving Network is a brotherhood, a place where old companions meet on the road. A place of respect, acceptance and joy for the encounter… This is how some of its members define it:

For me, "being an improving networker" implies coming from the place of genuine authenticity. "Improving" means incorporating and sharing my views in collaboration with like-minded people. It is surrendering my ego to the happiness of the higher self, carry out consistent actions in the now to achieve love, peace and happiness for all.

JOHN COLLINGS, author

For me, "being an improving networker is" to be the fullest expression of my authentic being in the Multiverse of Oneness, connected in Love with the Source of All-Beingness, expressing through doing the qualities of Spirit from where we came, to where we will return.

LEATRA HARPER, author

For me, "being an improving networker is" to create spaces of infinite possibilities where everything IS. I achieve this by placing my SOUL at the service of others and myself. When I am there, it is easy to BE and DO, what seemed impossible becomes possible; the powerful energy of the

SPIRIT that connects us and guides us, FLOWING, appears in the exciting adventure of CO-CREATING the world we deserve and ALREADY IS.

ELENA PÉREZ-MOREIRAS, energetic coach

For me, "being an improving networker is" an identity, how I am present and present myself. "Improving" for me means bringing my authentic and enthusiastic self into all connections for my advancement and the positive evolution of humanity. As a networker, I interact with, inspire, influence and embrace many people so we can encompass and intermingle our essence. For me, "improving" does not mean things are not good and need to be better. Improving means reminding myself and others that everything is perfect as it is and we need to honor, celebrate and be grateful for that. My role is to be aligned and open to receive and share the blessings already here."

TERI-E, coach

For me, "being an improving networker is" being a member of the improving network. As such, my life is blessed by a positive forward movement that occurs with ease and grace, serving Unity for the greater good."

VIKKI BROCK, coach

For me, "being an improving networker is" to live as a ray of light for others.

Alfonso Medina, coach

For me, "being an improving networker is" being part of a group of wonderful people who believe that there is something greater than ourselves that guides our purpose and helps us discover and be true to our essence.

Marta Prieto Asirón, editor

You can find more definitions of some other participants of the Multiversity Improving Network with the help of this code:

The "Multiversidad Improving Network" is a collective project that we put at your service and that at all of those who, as ourselves, are passionate about the human being ability to grow his energetic dimension and his spiritual nature. We are a network of promoters of people, teams, organizations and societies that are at the service of human development in order to contribute to the co-creation of the world that we deserve and ALREADY IS.

PREFACE

Remembrance of the One is still the best thing I know.
JOHANN WOLFGANG VON GOETHE

This book is the product of a collaborative effort by two people in relationship—a seasoned coach, John Collings, and a coach-in-training, Lea Harper. At the outset, with little knowledge of what was to come, we recognized one another as kindred spirits. I, Lea, sought coaching to know my inner self. I wanted to direct my life with vision, values, and purpose. I, John, am a master certified coach with more than 30 years of coaching and consulting experience. Although I had interwoven coaching with spirituality through the years, I had not realized that the pursuit of coaching excellence led to my spiritual growth. Through our relationship as coach and a coach-in-training, Lea and I quickly recognized a spiritual bond. At the same time, Teri-E Belf, the founder of Success Unlimited Network® "SUN," published her book Coaching with Spirit. It provided clarity about including the energy of spirit in coaching and catalyzed our desire to write. This book is for those who are seeking a close connection with spirit and who would like to express this connection in their personal and professional lives.

John: *Over the years of growing my coaching practice, I have deepened my work in spirituality. I continue to marvel at the synchronicity that has become a part of my daily life. I am acutely aware of the presence of spirit while I am coaching. I ask for guidance from spirit to transcend what might keep me from being fully present with my clients.*

In 2001 the leadership of SUN decided that Teri-E should conduct a coach trainer certification program to respond to the growing need for SUN Certified Coaches. Coaches, such as I, who were selected for the coach trainer role committed to using the triad of Results Game, Guidelines for Living, and the Well-Being Game. Those processes form the cornerstone of the Success Unlimited Network coaching program. In addition to practical tools, the coach trainers under the guidance of Teri-E are encouraged to use a spiritual base for their coaching.

On completion of the trainer program, I experienced two significant events that gave new meaning and focus to my coaching career. With the support of the SUN leadership team I undertook writing a spiritual coaching field book based on a model of coaching entitled The Potential of the Human Spirit. The second event was working as a SUN coach trainer to Lea Harper. Lea was attracted to the SUN coach program as a way to express her deep caring for people and her interest in integrity and pursuit of authenticity.

After a series of discussions and experiences in the working of spirit in coaching, I extended an invitation to Lea to partner with me in writing this book. Lea readily and humbly accepted. I understood the difficulty for me to find the words to describe the presence of spirit in my coaching and teaching work. I also appreciated the challenges of embracing spirit in my daily life. For the work of writing this book I wanted a tangible, human relationship to mirror my intangible relationship with spirit. I chose Lea as a writing partner to translate our coaching relationship into a dynamic process that would go beyond working together into the experience of spiritual connection and energy in relationship. Our relationship grew connected and congruent over the three years we spent co-creating this book. Our mutual respect and high regard for self and other evoked spiritual energy, guidance, and validation for our work together.

Lea: *One of the reasons I sought a new career as a coach was a gap between my life experiences and how I expected life to be by the time I was 50 years old. Even though I practiced continual inquiry and self-reflection, I wanted to fully express my authentic being. I wanted a close relationship with myself and with my soul and I wanted meaningful connections with others. I felt emptiness even after many successes and challenging experiences in life. I sensed there was a part of my being that was unbalanced and unclaimed. I had attended several churches and had participated in many New Age groups, yet my inner voice kept saying, "This is not it." I might have kept eliminating external possibilities forever, but I wanted to discover what did work and regain vitality and energy. I needed to communicate directly with my inner self, but I didn't want to do it alone. That was when my inner voice clearly directed me to find a coach who was spiritually inclined. I did what I often do, which is to make a wish, charge it with the knowing that what I want wants me, and let it go. That's the best I can describe how I found John Collings, my coach and trainer in the Success Unlimited Network certification process. As soon as I corresponded with John (after researching many different possibilities), I knew he was the coach I sought.*

The intellectual part of me (the one that I could always call on for my outer success and credibility) needed proof. The left-brained part doubted my intuitive "knowing." I felt the proof in my heart (the three years of practicing heart lock-in with my HeartMath® experience paid off once again). To this day, I still consciously weigh my heartfelt knowing equally with my intellectual evidence. Again and again, my heart demonstrates truth (even when it seems to contradict the logic of my rational mind). John was all I was seeking in a coach, mentor, and beyond, a real-life example of a spiritual person. He demonstrates a high level of inner and outer congruence that challenges me to do the same. Because of our relationship, I have received repeated validation to be who I am, connecting with spirit and others with authentic personal power.

What I had wanted, I found in my relationship with John and our work together. The labor of love this book required was hard, of course. I would not have agreed to such an endeavor without the inner knowing and experiential proof of spiritual connection and guidance that this work and my relationship with John have provided. By aligning my free will with my inner knowing, I experience the benefits of Energetic Coaching in my personal and professional pursuits.

Through the experience of a spiritual connection in our coaching relationship, we were energized to write this book. Because we shared a bond of goodwill for self and others, we experienced connection with spirit. Our relationship taught us what to write about. By seeking congruence through individually practicing what we preached, we felt spirit grow in other relationships as well. From the first recognition we were kindred spirits in coaching to the sustaining process of this work, we have felt the energy of spirit in our connectedness and appreciation for all of life. Love knows and grows.

We started this book as an academic, almost technical, discussion of the factors in relationship that create spiritual energy. But a description is only words and symbols that convey ideas but do not necessarily create meaning. What we wanted to portray were ways to invite the energy of spirit through a positive relationship such as coaching. How individuals experience spirit will be unique and meaningful on a personal level. To us Energetic Coaching became real and important as we deliberately created the qualities of our relationship based on spiritual values.

Raising spiritual energy is never-ending, forever challenging, and enlightening. We experienced spirit while writing this book as an extension of love going outside of itself, connecting with another outside of itself, then reconnecting with itself in an ever-increasing frequency of high-level energy. Spirit proved its validity and practicality in wonderful ways, which we offer as examples throughout this work. Spiritual energy grew with our conscious intention to experience spirit in relationship. Our personal spirituality morphed into a connected spirituality of relationship, which created a bond of friendship and love each of us felt internally and expressed externally with others. Through our relationship and this work, we experienced the being and the doing of coaching with spirit.

Lea: *John and I got together for our weekly coaching meeting and, as usual, began by discussing the book. We had completed nine chapters with much enthusiasm and enjoyment. One of the main reasons for our fine communication during years of working together was the quality of relationship we had built. Throughout our collaborative process our connection, goodwill, and sharing had created sustainable, lasting, positive energy for both of us. We often readily agreed with one another's viewpoints and worked to incorporate the other's perspective with what we had written individually. During the times that we differed, we communicated and reasoned with one another, often arriving at insights that enhanced our individual beliefs and tran-*

scended what we had known before. We operated together from increasingly high levels, which could best be described as a growing connection based on mutual respect and love. As our relationship became the tangible experience of our intangible values and goals, spirit demonstrated to us how the process of raising energy and connecting with our hearts produced results.

Energetic Coaching adds another dimension to the coaching profession in much the same way as Logotherapy added another dimension to the field of psychotherapy. According to the Viennese psychiatrist and founder of Logotherapy, Victor Frankl, "A psychotherapy which not only recognizes man's spirit, but actually starts from it may be termed logotherapy. In this connection, Logos is intended to signify 'the spiritual' and beyond that, 'the meaning.'" (The Doctor and the Soul). Frankl states that because the whole person consists of physical, mental, and spiritual aspects, to ignore the spiritual leads to "existential frustration," which is, he thinks, why some people seek psychotherapy. Logotherapy and Energetic Coaching acknowledge and invite spirit to relationship to aid in achieving coaching results that often surpass clients' initial expectation.

Logotherapy was developed to facilitate the discovery of what Frankl termed "will to meaning." Coaching specifically addresses will to meaning through the process of discovering life purpose, defining a personal mission statement, and by clarifying and choosing values and priorities. Through coaching, the client realizes that intrinsic qualities of character and personality are essential to success and well-being. Energetic Coaching focuses on the internal state as well as external goals to help the client achieve intrinsic satisfaction, growth, and meaning along with extrinsic results.

Energetic Coaching aims to balance and integrate internal and external worlds. Many who seek coaching focus on immediate goals to obtain external tangible outcomes. In addition, Energetic Coaching gives weight to the internal intangible energy as a precursor to external tangible outcomes. We emphasize the internal realm of thoughtfully chosen and cultivated individual values, and we strive to help clients narrow the gap between their inner being and outer doing.

We are human beings and not human doings. Through the process of Energetic Coaching, clients make choices congruent with their ideals and standards. We elicit the being aspect so that what people do reflects their inner self. Energetic Coaching intentionally deals with people's internal motives, values, attitudes, perceptions, feelings, judgments, belief systems, and thoughts to help them experience and expand their spiritual connection for positive external results.

Every relationship holds opportunity to grow spirit through close, caring connections. Each relationship is unique, and each person's experience of spirit is valid and important. There is no linear process, step-by-step guide, or instruction manual to go with individual paths of spirit, but there are metaphors, examples, landmarks, and milestones to use as guides. There are ancient teachings as well as new discoveries in science that Energetic Coaching employs in the process of describing spiritual connection. Metaphors become a framework for understanding as people derive insights to make choices and provide meaning to their lives.

In this book we will not attempt to prove the existence of spirit. Once experienced, it is proven. We describe the energy of spirit as we have experienced it and provide examples of how coaches and others consider their connection as a tangible personal relationship. Although spirit is always available, it eludes complete understanding. It lies beyond language, mental constructs, and conceptual ability. There is still the experience of it, however, that coaching can deliberately invite. This book describes some of the ways of inviting and experiencing the intangible and unfathomable energy of spirit.

We wrote this book to describe ways in which people can connect with spirit by intention and practice. It may come through a chance opening within them or upon invitation. *Because coaching invokes the positive and the good in relationship with clients, it provides the open invitation and space to experience spirit.* The coach acts as the compassionate witness, who reflects the ultimate compassionate witness of spirit. Without fully knowing, defining, or understanding what spirit is, anyone can invite the energy of spirit to work for the highest good. Energetic Coaching intentionally plants and nurtures the seed of intention to create awareness, connection, and integration through the inner knower in each person. With humility, openness, and appreciation, we embark on an unending journey into the inner self in connection with spirit for individual wholeness and collective oneness.

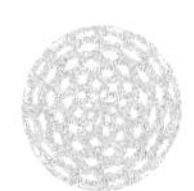

1. ENERGETIC COACHING

Erase the lines, I pray you not to love classifications. The thing is like a river, from source to sea-mouth, One flowing life.

ROBINSON JEFFERS

"Life is difficult," are the opening words simply and profoundly stated in M. Scott Peck's best selling book, The Road Less Traveled. The fact is life is not meant to be easy. The difficulties make people wise and powerful. In a society of seemingly isolated individuals with an overly external orientation, however, people can create even more difficulty. In all their seeking, they are driven to external consumption rather than internal consciousness. Indoctrinated into the social myth that idolizes the rich, beautiful and young, they fear the realities of loss and old age. Many seek perfection without knowing how to measure success. Sometime in life, they realize that in all their strivings, they are still falling short of something they want...without knowing what that "something" is. As nothing seems to satisfy their longing, they may begin to question what they were taught and the way they have operated. They seek self-knowing and self-acceptance, and internal peace that nothing external can take away. They want the feeling that they are okay no matter what. Many come to coaching wanting to identify their unique purpose—the life essence that is not derived from getting or going somewhere. They want to know and be who they really are. They want to experience the energy of spiritual connection.

Coaching as a profession is very good at defining different aspects of life, working on them, and then reassembling them into a more balanced and complete whole. With the scientific method, people can better understand a complexity by studying the parts. But where is that connecting force that makes the whole greater than the sum of the parts? Some people seem to seek the right answers and the right behaviors, just as those in authority had taught them right along. But what external system encourages internal individual authority? Where is the reward for being different—for being the fullest expression of authentic being, whether it fits the norm or not? Where is spirit? Viva d'etre! Viva la difference! Where is connection when people need also to express individual flair and uniqueness? Where is wholeness, and how can everyone create individual integrity?

"Energetic Coaching"...what is it? "Coaching with spirit"...what does that term mean? How could a process of spiritual connection be communicated in a book about coaching? How could coaches and clients increase consciousness and spiritual awareness through the coaching relationship? Those are questions encountered repeatedly while following a path of discovery.

As Energetic Coaches, we want to make the intangible real and to experience spirit in the coaching relationship. The process of writing this book on Energetic Coaching created for us the spiritual energy that we were writing about. Through this work we felt the power of our individual connection with spirit. We saw how internal beliefs manifested external reality for ourselves and for others and how some of our beliefs and actions disconnected us. Through attempting to quantify and describe the "heart," or "energetics," of the coaching relationship, we connected via positive energy. We verified our respective experiences in an effort to describe the essence of spirit. We captured our intuitive insights to communicate in metaphors, symbols, and language. Following emerging insights led us to goodwill for each other, which nurtured our individual identity and growth. We gained energy from our work together and meaning from our conscious choice to express and align our common values. The work of this book became increasingly meaningful as we expressed our shared inner values and vision.

Existence depends on relationships. Each human relationship is unique, and each individual's experience in relationship matters. The dynamics of relationship offer a direct way to experience spirit, which becomes manifest in positive relationships. Consciousness infused with good intentions toward others bestows blessings on the relationship. Spirit, as high-level consciousness, operates through relationships, starting with the relationship individuals have with themselves.

It is simple, but not often easy, to follow a spiritual calling, which is the inner calling of heart in equal relationship with mind and the hearts and minds of others. There are barriers—games, defense mechanisms, false projections, negative perceptions, ill will, and unconscious living that block the experience of spirit. Once recognized, however, people can learn to displace the deceptions of fear projected by the illusion of a disconnected self, known as ego. The sustainable energy of the intelligent heart-mind connection opens the channel to the source of heart-mind intelligence, creativity and energy. Whatever it is called—"God," the "Universe," the "Higher Self," "Atman," the "Tao," "Allah," "Wankan Tanka," "Brahman," "I Am," and many other revered names—the source of spiritual energy and connection is the same (beyond all religious or separatist generalizations of this energy, we choose to call the ultimate manifestation of spirit Source). Spiritual energy connects each person to the web of life. As people align heart and mind with good intention in relationship, they merge the internal intangible of being and external tangible of doing. They understand the holographic nature of the universe in relationship, the one found in all, and the all found in one. They dispel the illusion of loneliness, separation, inferiority, or superiority within themselves and in relationship with others.

Like an internal sun warming people's hearts, spiritual energy emanates from individuals into relationships. Spirit includes and co-exists with the shadow in self and others. As sunlight casts physical shadows, spirit reveals internal shadow aspects. Because each part of the whole is important, the dark as well as the light requires acknowledgment, acceptance, and integration. Energetic Coaching is a forum for wholeness, where individuals can turn on the light of their spiritual sun and integrate the darkness of shadow.

SPIRITUAL WORKINGS-THE ANALOGY OF THE SEED

Nature provides many examples of how spirit works. We found an apt analogy in the idea of seeding, weeding, and feeding the energy of spirit in relationship. By choosing to connect with spirit, people can enjoy its fruits within and without. Nature mirrors the maker of it. The analogy of plant growth to spiritual growth in human nature is a tangible example of spiritual principles.

In the cycle that represents the flow of life, we gather seeds at harvest from dying vegetation. When planting season returns ("To everything there is a time..."), through intention and choice we prepare the soil. Selecting seeds carefully, we sow what we want to grow. Planting illustrates cooperation and connection between people and spirit. Like the prepared soil, spirit awaits an idea, decision, or vision to co-create with the individual.

Humans co-create plant growth. Similarly, with nourishment, individuals co-create their life with spirit to receive the resulting bounty. Naturally, things we don't want grow too, representing the shadow side of life. Gardeners have to tend their crops to keep space for the desired plants. Weeds become compost for the next season's crop, demonstrating the opportunity to turn what becomes present but what is not wanted into fodder for the greatest good. Correspondingly, by successfully coping with difficulties and learning from challenges, people nurture growth and spiritual connection.

ENERGETIC COACHING NURTURES SPIRITUAL ENERGY

The existence of spirit may never be scientifically proven, but people can experience it. Unlike science that relies on objective, third party proof, spirit is subjective and personal yet impersonal and objective at the same time. Some people require externally validated data; which cannot be furnished but Energetic Coaching describes ways of understanding and experiencing the many facets of the intangible and unfathomable energy of spirit. Because coaching invokes the positive and good in relationship with clients, it is a natural forum to manifest and grow spiritual energy. Energetic Coaches invite spiritual energy by planting good intentions in relationship with clients. We foster a close relationship with spirit and provide the fertile soil for the experience of spirit to flourish for others and ourselves.

Energetic Coaching aims to integrate and balance internal being and external doing. Many who seek coaching have as their immediate goal external tangible outcomes. We give weight to internal intangible values to direct external actions. Energetic Coaching focuses on thoughtfully choosing and cultivating individual values and ways of expressing them. We support narrowing the gap between inner being and outer doing. Then clients can consciously choose language and actions consistent with their ideals and values. We encourage clients to be their authentic self, and we mirror their truth to them in relationship.

Energetic Coaches seek congruence between the being and the doing aspects. With congruence, people's doing emerges from their being. Their external state reflects their internal state. In Energetic Coaching we deal with internal motives, values, attitudes, feelings, judgments, belief systems, and thoughts to help clients experience their spiritual connection for positive external results. As they grow strong in the light, they can weed out barriers to spiritual energy. Like plants, people are naturally phototrophic. They grow toward the light of spirit for nourishment they cannot get in the dark.

Many people cultivate the energy of spirit by adhering to a practice. It can come through a chance opening within or by invitation. Spirit often appears in a positive relationship such as coaching. Coaches act as a compassionate witness, which equates to the consciousness and awareness of spirit. Without attempting an explanation where words fall short, we use stories, examples, illustrations, and metaphors to provide a seedbed for understanding how the energy of spirit works for the highest good. Energetic Coaching intentionally plants and nurtures spiritual energy through congruence, integrity, and authenticity. With spirit we create wholeness and connectedness with self and others through the expression of who we really are.

ENERGETIC COACHING HARVESTS SPIRITUAL ENERGY

John: *My coaching practice developed out of my Organizational Behavior Ph.D. dissertation, entitled "Later Life Career Transition." I chose to do a series of in-depth interviews with men who had gone through the stages of leaving their careers because of burnout or boredom. In my discussions with them I found other areas of their lives (family, health, relationships, etc.) had influenced their decisions to change careers. Their stories had a theme of discontent with their current work, trying a number of other careers with moderate success, and finally settling on a career that encompassed their experiences and passions in life. I included in my research a heuristic study of what was occurring in my own life.*

I came into coaching with a background in business and experience in operations, research and development, training, and organizational development. I kept telling myself as I progressed that I was preparing for an important role in life (as we all are). I am not sure if Energetic Coaching is that role; there may be other ones to follow. I do know that everything I have learned and practiced leading up to this point has made coaching one of the most satisfying and rewarding vocations I have known. It expresses my past experiences and present passions in a way that builds on who I am as a person, including spirit as well as mind and body.

Everyone is attracted to spiritual energy whether with conscious awareness or not. Spirit reveals our divinity within, the purest expression of our nature. The difference between accepting a powerful, good, loving, creative connection to the whole of humanity or denying it may be a reluctance to join. People may consciously or unconsciously block spirit's presence and power. Coaches can choose to work with spirit or they can work from an ego state. Blocking or ignoring spiritual energy limits coaching work with clients. Many within the profession are choosing to utilize all of what is available to them on behalf of their clients. One of the greatest strengths in relationship is the positive and powerful experience of spiritual energy and connection.

John: *As an experienced Life and Career Coach, I have many times found myself in a position with a client of putting my trust in something greater than my own intellect. At first I did not trust that intuitive source of information. I felt anxious about my coaching. My self-doubt blocked my creativity so that I offered my clients less than I could. When my ego dominated, I felt self-conscious and inferior. I wanted to demonstrate superior coaching, which a part of me knew was a charade. Over time I began to realize that if I ignored how I was performing in my coaching work and concentrated on my client, marvelous things began to happen. Empowered, clients quickly took responsibility for coming up with their own choices. And coaching became a joyful and effortless experience for me. As I have come to understand the role my ego plays as my teacher and how ego can block my creativity, I now consciously choose to work with spirit. My decision to open to spiritual energy has enhanced my role as coach and produced a close connection with my clients. I don't clearly understand how spirit works, AND I do know that it does work when I get out of my own way.*

ENERGETIC COACHING WEEDS BLOCKS TO SPIRIT

People grow spirit by preparing the groundwork with love, appreciation, and good intention. As coaches we choose to exchange positive energy with clients. We call our attitude "free will goodwill."

To nurture spirit in coaching, we first must appreciate and love ourselves. Every thought we have is a conscious or unconscious choice based on spirit or on ego. As we communicate, overtly or covertly, others realize or intuit our intent. When we choose loving thoughts and evoke positive feelings, we honor the values within ourselves that grow spiritual connection. We block spirit when we entertain egotistic thoughts, which separate us from ourselves and others. To open to spirit, we need to confront and acknowledge negative thoughts of separation, rejection, scarcity, and fear. Rather than judging ourselves and others, we can shift to contentment with the way we are now in connectedness and wholeness while remaining open to something even better.

John: *In 1989 when I began a new career, the term "coaching" was recognized primarily in the area of sports. I marketed myself as a consultant. I began to work with people invested in getting the most from life and living their passion, which often included their work. Many people I coached felt an inner stirring to seek out a partnership with a trained professional. They wanted to open the door to options in their lives. Some of my clients wanted to break free of dead-end jobs and express their creativity. Others wanted to manifest an elusive dream or vision. It was at that time that I met Teri- E Belf, owner of Success Unlimited Network® (SUN). Under her tutoring I expanded my roles to include SUN Certified Coach and Coach Trainer. My connection with Teri-E grew spiritually, adding a dimension to my coaching through our mutual respect and love. I felt I was on the right path, personally achieving what I was coaching others to achieve in their lives. By demonstrating to clients that I had done what I coached them to do, I gained personal congruence and connection with clients and with spirit.*

THE INTEGRITY OF A COACH

Individual integrity comes from inner authenticity and congruence in each moment. Maintaining conscious focus and commitment to be true to oneself can be challenging. Because chaotic external events appear to demand an external focus, there is a tendency to neglect the internal state. Unconscious or unaware of the internal state, fear and ego defense mechanisms can dominate. Energetic Coaches perceive external situations, relationships, and events as a mirror of clients' belief systems. When clients bring their inner state to consciousness, we can help them reframe with positive intention and purposeful action no matter what the external situation. Clients can meet the challenges experienced as weeds and turn them into fodder for continued growth and a bountiful harvest in the future. To have integrity, we Energetic Coaches must do our own work on an ongoing basis. We believe that individuals can align their thoughts, feelings, and perceptions with their stated internal values. Expressing their ideals and goals through external actions creates personal growth and power.

THE LIGHT OF POSITIVE INTENT

Spirit naturally grows when people choose positive intent. Coaching engages spirit through defining life purpose, discovering inner values, self-reflecting, and taking action congruent with values. The role Energetic Coaches consider vital is to hold the open space for clients to define and express their authentic being. Seeking self-expression starts with a conscious desire to clarify who they are and how they want to be. Energetic Coaching helps clients answer such important questions positively and decisively, no matter what the past has been or how the present or future appears to be.

At some level all people are working toward expressing their identity and purpose in life. As they live, they experience moments of joy, peace, love, and happiness, and spirit is profoundly present. For some though, such experiences (or even the possibility of them) seem foreign and frightening. They may sabotage spiritual growth and connection. They may become stuck. They may even back away from consciousness and connection. Some may justify their fear by saying that happiness and success are hard to come by. Some may feel undeserving. Without realizing their power, some people may sabotage themselves by acting like a victim. Instead of looking within, they weaken themselves by blaming external factors for perceived shortcomings, negative thoughts, or unconscious choices. Energetic Coaches redirect the focus within to where no external event or entity has influence.

We observe the internal state of our clients, the thoughts they state and the emotions they describe, to help them choose positive intent despite their external situation. We encourage them to hold a positive space for spirit to enter. They can bring their baggage into the coaching session, where they can test our ability to hold a positive energetic space for them. During such times we remember that spirit is ever-present, no matter how difficult the situation may seem. We remain open and inviting to spirit to aid in areas where coaching skills and techniques fall short. With positive intent, Energetic Coaches allow for shadow work and shine light on the dark aspects of the weeds, helping to remove and compost them for future growth.

Free Will Choice

Spirit operates within the universal law of free will. Coaches and clients can co-create results that improve the lives of all people involved. When we align our mind with the divine, our coaching work takes on energy of its own. Coaches who have connected with spirit attract clients who want the same. Both parties experience their relationship as positive and real. They build on each other's energy through a growing spiritual bond between one another and with other people. We create a relationship of equality as we choose to learn, grow, and create alongside our clients.

Through continued learning, coaches who have acquired skills and techniques of coaching may decide to work with spirit. The decision to align with spirit attracts clients who desire the same. The reason for coming together may not be obvious at first; yet, at a deeper level, such mutual desire opens the relationship to spiritual experience. Joining of free will between coach and client through conscious intention, choice, and invitation invites spiritual energy. A coach who is comfortable coaching with spirit exhibits free will goodwill while accepting the free will choices and intention of the client. With the energy present in the coaching relationship aligned with spirit for the highest good, Energetic Coaches co-create results with clients, often beyond the expectations of the either party.

Lea: *I learned about the profession of coaching during my certification as a HeartMath® one-on- one practitioner. Coaching intrigued me because it was described as tapping into the wisdom the clients already possessed for their highest good. Although I had earned my graduate degree in Organization Development, I did not feel comfortable in the role as an external expert change agent. I knew that lasting change had to come from within a person through free will choices. I thought that organizations as well as individuals had their own wisdom, often hidden and untapped. I wanted to find the spring and bring the water of wisdom to individuals and organizations. I wanted to encourage actions that reflected people's inner purpose. The field of coaching was my natural next step for empowering individuals and organizations to reveal innate wisdom and claim ownership of their self-selected results.*

THE IMPORTANCE OF CHOICE

In order to invite spirit into coaching, it is essential to recognize the importance of choice. Spirit does not gate crash. People have to invite it into the relationship. Just as focusing a beam of light creates a laser, the focus of coaches and clients to become more conscious and powerful invites spiritual energy. Always present, spirit awaits.

Why doesn't everyone invite spirit into their relationships? Some people are closed to spirit because they are separated by ego. Such separation causes the illusion of aloneness rather than all-oneness. When individuals separate from one another or spirit, which connects everything to everything, spirit waits outside. When they do not recognize how spirit connects, their ego is apt to take credit for what works or to place blame externally for what does not work. Separation and disconnection create difficult and superficial relationships.

John: *Harold sought my coaching services to guide him in a home business. He needed to hire additional people and lead them effectively. The employee in charge of product sales to the public sector challenged Harold's leadership. When he promised customers what their product line could not meet, consumers complained about the inadequacy of the merchandise.*

Harold wanted to build on the employee's strength as a salesperson without exaggerating the product to increase sales. Unfortunately, both men dug in their heels to justify their positions. Harold wanted to preserve the integrity of his business, while the employee criticized the product development efforts of the company. They could not identify a common vision. Their egos blocked the opportunity for spirit to create harmony and a win for all.

The more people open to spirit, the more that serendipity and synchronicity become part of their normal expression. They naturally proceed through their day with humor and light- heartedness. Once people decide to include it, spirit becomes increasingly operative in the external realm. Spirit creates positive energy exponentially because of the rewarding experiences it brings. Both coaches and clients benefit as relationships become more positive and rewarding.

THE ENERGY OF RELATIONSHIPS

Lea: *John and I were in one of our rare face-to-face collaborations on this book. Time had slipped away from us so that John had to hurry to make another commitment. Later my husband Steve asked me how our meeting had gone. I told him, "Great, as usual!" Then Steve said that he could not believe that we had not taken a break the entire day. I realized that even getting lunch would have been an interruption. John and I had been in a flow state. As I reviewed my notes that evening, I found some enlightening insights that I did not remember discussing. Where did they come from? We knew it was spirit. This dynamic happened repeatedly throughout the process of co-creating this book.*

People experience spiritual energy in connected and congruent relationships. The relationship may be internal among their thoughts and emotions and outer language and actions, or within a one-on-one relationship such as coaching, or with the larger community. Some clients are looking for something internally oriented in conjunction with achieving material goals. We use Energetic Coaching to supplement our coaching toolkit. Along with prioritization, goal setting, measurements, and inventories, Energetic Coaches look at the relationships clients have. We begin by examining the relationship they have with themselves. We invite them to explore gaps between inner desires and external outcomes. We seek congruence between inner being and outer doing. Energetic Coaches address the internal, value-driven, intangible results such as peace and harmony that many people seek in addition to their outward accomplishments. We back into the inner realm of values from the outer realm of results. What clients state they want or do not want indicates values and vision. The extent that they prioritize and pursue what they want is the extent that they maintain a congruent relationship with themselves. All other relationships stem from the relationship with self. Energetic Coaches focus on achieving congruence in relationships to open to spiritual energy and connection. Coaching naturally evokes spiritual energy by nurturing connected, congruent relationships.

It is important to differentiate Energetic Coaching from therapy, consulting, or mentoring. Energetic Coaches abide by this precept: Clients have the knowledge and ability to answer their own questions and define and achieve goals. As coaches, we elicit their internal wisdom and support it according to their wishes. We witness and facilitate clients in the coaching relationship, not as a guru, teacher, mentor, therapist, or outside expert. With Energetic Coaching we add the elements of goodwill and appreciation to become a compassionate witness for clients. We seek to bring out the inner wisdom of individuals and empower them to make choices. When we add goodwill and appreciation, spiritual energy rises spontaneously. Coaches benefit also because positive relationships reflect good intentions back to them.

WHY INVITE SPIRIT TO COACHING?

Lea: *Through the process of being coached, I felt called to be a coach. I sensed spirit as a part of the coaching process. I requested that John facilitate my getting a close connection with spirit. When I verbalized my desire, John told me that he had specifically expressed his desire to provide him with clients who were on a spiritual path. His next three clients also wanted a relationship with spirit in their daily lives. Spirit brought people together through their conscious choice to connect with it during the coaching process.*

Spirit works to manifest what people want in accordance with their highest good. Coaches who open a channel for spirit create and manifest desired results personally and in partnership with clients. Energetic Coaches recognize that spirit aids the coaching process. The energy of spirit is a tangible presence during coaching meetings and in the experiences between. Aiming to manifest the highest good helps coaches and clients co-create results that often transcend expectations. Even though the insights gained from the open channel with spirit can be challenging or confusing, spirit aids in discerning and acting on such intelligence. When people understand the message and accept the challenge to follow their inner promptings, spirit provides the resources and the support to follow a chosen path. Often, spirit manifests as a knowing of what to do and say in a particular moment.

Lea: *I was in the third of 10 scheduled meetings with my client Julie when she told me that she thought I was psychic. She said that I had offered insights and demonstrated intuition that had helped her become self-aware. She asked how she could learn to be psychic. I told that I had developed intuitive abilities and discernment by opening to my inner self and connecting with spirit. I also told her that I believed that everyone had the ability if open to such insights.*

Later, I asked John how he accounted for discernment. He said that he could tap into a place where all knowledge and truth were held. I asked him if the place was called the "collective unconscious." John said that he did not know what to call it, just that it was his connection with spirit that helped him in the moment reach inside and pull out necessary information for the benefit of his clients.

Spirit works for people's highest good without their knowing in advance what the outcome will be. They simply walk in faith as they receive promptings. The outcome, often better than expected, emerges in ways that could not have been orchestrated or predicted.

A Metaphor for a Process of Spiritual Growth

Imagine a continuum in which an individual moves from least energy to most energy. At one end lies the ego-motivated desire to be special, superior, and apart from others. At the other end of the continuum lies spirit, which manifests in a feeling of belonging, equality, and oneness with the all-in-All, or Source. Along the continuum, Energetic Coaches help clients clarify their values and life purpose in positive and meaningful ways. As the compassionate witness holding the sacred space for clients, we become the instrument for spirit to connect with clients. Spirit aids clients in creating external results congruent with inner desires. Coaches receive benefits from the relationship with clients and learn and grow along with them. The energy comes full circle with coaches and clients operating at a high frequency. Spirit acts in much the same way a catalyst accelerates a chemical reaction to excite electrons into higher energy states.

Congruence

Congruence removes barriers for spirit to aid in outer achievement. Congruence comes from the Latin word congruens, which means, "to meet together and agree." Energetic Coaching focuses on congruence between inner values and outer actions. Maintaining congruence builds relationships with self, others, and spirit.

We have excerpted the following from Genie Z. Laborde's book, Influencing with Integrity, to further illustrate the concept of congruence:

- Congruence occurs when all sub-personalities join together to work in a unified way.
- Each of us plays many roles; i.e., parent, business-person, athlete, leader, follower, etc.
- When our roles work in agreement, we are congruent; when they conflict, we are incongruent.
- Our way of behaving and the words we say are often incongruent. We say one thing and do another.

Examples of incongruence include:
- A quavering voice when speaking strong words.
- Shaking your head no while saying yes.
- Breaking out into laughter when making a serious point.

Ways to achieve congruence include:
- Being clear about what we want for ourselves.
- Role-playing our sub personalities and appreciating their occasional opposition to each other.
- Exploring our own polarities of judgment such as "nice person" and "bad child."

Energetic Coaching focuses on congruence. Incongruence blocks spiritual connection. When outer circumstances that people have created or accepted digress from their expressed inner desires, beliefs, and values, we know they have disconnected from their inner self. Energetic Coaching helps clients align with expressed values, purpose, and vision so that they create outer circumstances congruent with their ideals. We invite clients to use their inner wisdom (the part that knows and connects directly with spirit) to examine incongruence. We facilitate clients in reconciling inner process to form good relationships (starting with the one they have with themselves) to achieve what they want on the outside.

By aligning outer and inner worlds through choice based on inner ideals, people increase personal power. Spirit is always working for the highest good. Through Energetic Coaching people invite and experience spirit to achieve goals that benefit them and others in relationship with them. Individual decision-making with intentional purpose infuses relationships with a growing connection to spirit.

The choice to maintain positive intent is key to increasing energy for clients and coaches. Choice raises awareness, focuses actions, and concentrates thoughts, feelings, and perceptions for the highest good. Just as in harmonic motion, as waves synchronize, wavelengths of energy achieve a higher frequency. The difference between being powerless and powerful has to do with making intentional choices and aligning energy to build upon itself.

Lea: *Someone once said to me, "You are a shotgun. If you ever became a rifle, you would be dangerous." She meant that I scattered my attention and activities. I started my own business while I was still completing my graduate degree. I started a countywide Earth Day celebration. I was greatly involved with friends and family and had many hobbies and interests.*

I would read three books at a time rather than one. Until I decided what I wanted most and focused my energy in that area, I was fragmented and underachieving, busy but ineffective. Dissatisfied and disillusioned with little motivation for a career, I avoided the important deci-

sion: What do I want in my life? I began thinking in terms of what I wanted rather than what I didn't want. I found positive thinking difficult to do at first. I had been steeped in No rather than Yes.

When I realized that I wanted to foster good relationships between people personally and professionally, coaching became a natural path. It was easier to align my energy once I chose deliberately to express my values. Since then, I have received many external reinforcements that I made a good choice. Because coaching requires inner and outer congruence, the relationship that has become the most work for me is my relationship with myself. I strive to gain congruence and personal authenticity. Everything else flows from there. Coaching is something I have always done. Even though it comes naturally and easily to me, I have to remind myself that a path does not have to be difficult to be right for me for now.

The Coaching Relationship is Conducive to Manifesting Spirit

Through the focus on life purpose, personal mission, and inner values, people identify and direct their inspiration and passion. Coaching is a way to discover and direct energy. It provides the coach as a mirror to help clients use their inner ideals to drive outer goals. As the mirror of the compassionate witness Energetic Coaches reflect to clients any gaps between their ideals and reality. We observe their incongruence among thought, word, deed, beliefs, and outcomes so that they can examine the gaps. People create their external reality. They project what appears on the movie screen of their lives.

Energetic Coaching specifically seeks balance, congruence, and authenticity in individuals in order to achieve wholeness. Then clients can connect with spirit through their inner knowing. Coaching work is like spiritual work. We list similarities we have found in the appendix at the end of this chapter.

Because it creates positive relationships, coaching is a natural forum to experience spirit. Energetic Coaches co-create and channel spiritual energy with clients to manifest outer goals in congruence with inner ideals. To enlist spirit in the coaching process is a matter of client choice, aided consciously by the coach. As the compassionate witness and open channel for spirit, we invite the energy of spirit and help clients align with it if they desire.

Without inviting spirit, clients can still realize personal goals, but why would they or their coaches discount spirit as an aid to the growth and learning process? There are many reasons, but the small, separated ego self is the main one. External culture conveys a value system based on the cult of personality. Many people think in terms of being separate from others. They make comparisons and judgments as if they were inferior or superior to others. Energetic Coaching helps minimize dependence on external, ego-based desires and fosters spiritual connection through congruence with clients' inner knowing.

Energetic Coaching intentionally invites spiritual qualities in addition to the inherently positive qualities of the coaching profession by including principles such as:

- Everyone has an intrinsic desire to grow and live positively and energetically.
- Relationships manifest spirit through congruent connections; the individual with self, the individual with others, and the individual with community.

- People are all connected spiritually. We are hard-wired to seek the energy of spirit.
- As we are all connected, so individual thoughts, words, and deeds affect the whole.
- Spirit responds to congruence between inner being and outer doing.
- Our relationships and outer circumstances mirror our inner self.
- Our culture reflects the total of individual states of consciousness.
- The sustainable energy of spirit is invited through free will goodwill.
- Energetic Coaching seeks to incorporate spirit into the heart-mind and integrate shadow aspects to foster individual wholeness.
- We improve our relationships and inner-outer congruence through choosing to be our authentic selves.
- Spirit provides connective, sustainable energy; ego provides false, unsustainable pseudo energy based on judgments of separation and inferiority or superiority.
- Spirit works to manifest the highest good for the individual and the whole, which in turn benefits the individual and the whole as a hologram.
- Because spirit upholds the law of free will, people must make a conscious choice to invite and align with spiritual ideals.
- We all seek connectedness and wholeness, and alignment with high level ideals.

Energetic Coaches act as compassionate witness to hold the space for clients' inner knower to come forward. By doing so, we invite spirit into the relationship and act as a conduit to channel and focus energy for the highest good. We benefit by receiving in return what we put forth. We exemplify the power of positive and intentional choice to grow, align, and connect with the energy of spirit. Energetic Coaching is a life-long quest to achieve personal congruence and mirror it to others. Our commitment to authentic being and doing makes Energetic Coaching more than a career—it is a calling.

CHAPTER 1 APPENDIX

SIMILARITIES BETWEEN SPIRIT AND THE COACHING PROCESS

WHAT IS SPIRIT – AND HOW DOES IT WORK?	WHAT IS COACHING – AND HOW DOES IT WORK?
Spirit is energy	Coaching energizes clients through passion purpose
Spirit responds to positive intent	Coaching helps clients reframe to develop positive perceptions, language, thoughts,feelings, and actions
Spirit involves choice	Coaching helps clients develop options from which they make purpose-centered decisions
Spirit provides insights and guidance	Coaches as the unbiased compassionate witness partner with clients with their inner knower

Spirit works within the law of free will	Coaches take direction from their clients and sponsor clients' learning to use their personal will effectively
Spirit assists in achieving personal goals	Coaches do the same through goal setting, monitoring, mirroring, visioning, valuing, and defining life purpose
Spirit is experienced spontaneously	Coaching co-creates the experience of the positive energy of connected relationships
Spirit goes where invited, trusted, and wanted	Coaches do the same
Spirit is an internal experience	Coaching directs clients inward for internal congruence and decision making
Spirit is always present and receptive	Coaches listen and respond to clients' wishe
Spirit co-creates	Coaches and clients co-create from within and through the relationship between them
Spirit is experienced through love and appreciation	Coaches respect their clients and hold them in high regard
Spirit is freedom	Coaches identify barriers to freedom and help clients overcome them
Spirit is an internal manifestation	Coaches help clients identify their inner values and belief systems
Spirit connects to the highest self	Coaching supports growth from the small, egotistic self (small "i") to the larger, connected self (big "I")
Spirit is attracted to abundance, hope, and positive choices	Coaches help clients reframe negative thoughts, perceptions, and language to positive, hopeful statements
Spirit is infinite and powerful	Coaching empowers clients to listen to their inner knower and make purpose-centered choices to be self-empowered

2. COACHING WITH SPIRIT

*When people truly open their minds, and contemplate the
way in which the universe is ordered and governed, they
are amazed—overwhelmed by a sense of the miraculous.*
St. Augustine of Hippo

Writing a book with the expressed purpose of understanding spirit and inviting spirit into relationship is more conducive to internal individual experience than to communication to others. There is something about attempting to define spirit and how it works that defies explanation. Even for those who have experienced spirit often, language and cognitive abilities are limited to describe it. Because people experience spirit in positive relationships, Energetic Coaching creates the opportunity for spiritual energy and connection to arise in relationship with clients.

Relationships provide fertile ground for the seed of spirit to grow. Nurturing the seed must be done with faith and not knowing what exactly will grow. Energetic Coaches help prepare the ground with clients through openly inviting spirit into our relationship. Clients plant the seed, and we provide the tools, examples and support. Our stance of compassionate witness holds the space for spirit to appear. In Energetic Coaching we maintain openness and invite the presence of spirit. The seeds planted often bear fruit beyond what could be predicted. Clients often want to dictate the details of outcomes. Energetic Coaches remind them to remain open to the flexibility of "this or something better," that creates additional information and energy that elevates the coaching process.

Energetic Coaching helps lay the groundwork for a relationship with spirit that benefits the coaching process and client outcomes. Of course, clients decide to invite spirit into relationship and to practice what works for them to make a spiritual connection. We have no prescriptions; direct, linear approaches; singular model; or metaphors to completely describe how spirit works. Energetic Coaches provide the confidence and encouragement so clients can do their necessary work to co-create with spirit what they want from the inside out.

A DEFINITION OF SPIRIT?

To define the indefinable, were it possible, would inherently limit understanding of the energy that resides in everything, connecting all of life. Many wonderful religious and philosophical texts have been written to describe spirit. Theologians and scientists have attempted to define the mystery and to model spiritual energy. Each time people think they have a formula, another aspect appears, sometimes counter-indicative of what was originally understood. Energetic Coaching holds that all people can be right in their understanding of spirit, because spirit can be everything. No one can lay exclusive claim or copyright to spirit because it reveals itself uniquely in subjective individual experience.

Religion touches the field of science as quantum physics bumps up against what is called the "Source Force," the "God Particle," or Higgs boson (also called the "Adamantine particle," which appears to add mass to other particles in the quantum field). Scientists are discovering a vast connective energy in living matter that some speculate may provide proof of the existence of spirit. This energy is referred to as the "holographic universe," "Indra's Web," or Super String. Some have described the essence of spirit in the elusive energy of cellular memory and genetics. Others have speculated about a force outside the measurable electromagnetic field that conveys information to entrain and synchronize molecular and cellular processes. Some seek spirit at the Zero Point, which is the vibrational energy that molecules retain even at absolute zero. Still others believe that spirit resides in the mind and body through feelings that may be the beginnings of consciousness. Like light, both wave and particle, spirit defies objective identification, precise measurement or relative quantification.

We can choose open-mindedness, receptivity, invitation, and faithful action, without a guarantee that spirit will work as desired. Often, it joins in relationship to work beyond the wildest desires and finite expectations. When people experience it, they have an instantaneous transcendent knowing of vast and powerful forces. Some refer to their experience as an epiphany, a holy instant, or enlightenment. People may experience spirit fleetingly, leaving as quickly as it came. Spirit cannot be commanded or summoned. It coaxes people to get out of their own way to allow it to happen. Energetic Coaching invites spirit to produce positive energy and desired results, moving from intentional choice in the internal realm to co-creating desired results in the external.

As people associate thoughts with the brain, we associate spirit with the heart. Not the physical heart but the "sacred heart." The sacred heart entrains life through energy, such as the heartbeat of the earth, known to many indigenous cultures. Spirit gives life meaning, inspiring people to see beyond the physical senses and the small world of the egocentric self. It energizes those who seek the great beyond, beyond what is tangible and definable. People experience spirit as being known and unconditionally loved, through connection and meaningfulness, gifted by the grace of an incomprehensible Source.

Language provides understanding, meaning, and connection. It forms the framework for thinking and allows individuals to communicate about their common values, intentions, and understanding. Energetic Coaching seeks to provide a framework for conceptualizing and inviting spirit without religious connotations. We help clients integrate coaching with their existing religious beliefs. Their coaching experience can enrich their private religious experience. We also support integrating spirit into relationship for those who chose not to practice a formal religion but desire greater individual meaning and improved interpersonal relationships.

Spirit is the vital life force, omnipresent but not always perceived or experienced. People can decrease the gap between the egocentric self and spirit through physical practice, emotional direction, and mental intention. Individuals appear to be at different points on a spiritual continuum from low to high frequency. They tend to attract relationships and experiences that mirror their current vibrational level. Choosing to move toward spirit increases individual energy and power. People who increase their frequency through goodness and growth attract high-level relationships and experiences. The higher they attune, the more they perceive spirit and attract positive energy.

BEYOND MENTAL INTELLIGENCE

Energetic Coaching explores a common language and understanding to recognize and connect with spirit rather than to harness and direct it. Flowing with spirit leads to ease in being and doing. Energetic Coaches till, fertilize, and plant, and then wait expectantly and optimistically for what grows. Even though the harvest may not be what we expected, the bounty will be great. This organic way of living contrasts to modern day mechanistic thinking which fosters the illusion that the universe can be understood, harnessed, and directed through mental intelligence and effort.

John: : *I talked with a colleague, Mary Ann, a very successful coaching professional. She related to me that at the outset of her coaching career, she had sought to imitate her coach. She began by strictly utilizing the tools, methodically progressing through the step-by-step procedures with her clients. After wondering why her coaching business was limited, she decided to change. Mary Ann said that as soon as she allowed herself to be in the moment with her clients in openness and respect, her coaching business began to flourish. She became authentic by developing her own style, a combination of her coaching training and her connection with herself.*

Spiritual connection raises a person above the egocentric self and the limits of the secular world. It provides support for those who want to explore within and act from inner vision and values. Energetic Coaches, in congruence with spirit, help people to look, feel, and think beyond what they perceive physically. We enlist the whole person—body, mind, and emotions, seeking to balance the three aspects into oneness.

The experience of spirit has been described as a feeling of oneness and rightness, of being known and unconditionally loved. Serendipity abounds as unrelated happenings coincide. Over the long run, many people experience spirit as the peaceful, all-pervasive knowing that everything is in divine order. In relationship with spirit, individuals can integrate and connect with their inner self and with one another. Heartfelt connections result in a meaningful life and trust in unknown outcomes. People let go of the need to control or manipulate others or external events. Gauged by the intellect alone, spirit remains an elusive idea, a tantalizing thought, a preposterous notion. By going beyond the brain's processing of the five senses and random thoughts, individuals may experience spirit fleetingly as instants of profound knowing. To sustain the connection takes continuous preparation, planting, and nurturing. Instantly positive and validating moments of spiritual realization serve coaches and clients alike. This helps people commit to nurturing a lifetime garden. This gives promise to harvesting fruits of spirit even when the growing season has ended and a new one not yet begun.

People require faith and belief to understand spirit, which can only be known through individual experience. It is more of a feeling or intuition than an intellectual insight. Even when people experience what feels like spirit, such as a sudden, passionate impulse, it may be something else instead. If what people feel requires mental rationalization or extreme effort to sustain, it probably is not spirit. Spirit speaks to the inner knower, requiring no justification or rationalization. Spirit, like true love, embraces self and other for the highest good. Although it is seemingly impossible to describe spirit fully, individuals who dispel the illusion of separation can move beyond ego and the deceptive world of duality to gain spiritual understanding.

John: *Over the past few years I have found myself re-examining my attitudes and beliefs concerning my own spirituality. Just when I think I know what they are, spirit gives me a push in a new direction to look even deeper. Challenges and difficulties lead me to change. My coaching practice has become a spiritual training ground for personal growth. Clients show up to catalyze their spiritual growth, which catalyzes my own. Each one reveals the work of spirit in relationship. Building on past beliefs and attitudes, I form new beliefs that positively impact my life and work.*

Just as people grow physically, they also grow spiritually. In the spiritual growth process any dying off makes room for the new. There may be a few transcendent beings in the world who do not appear to have to search, try on, discard, build on, renew, or question their spiritual beliefs— but the vast majority do. In today's world of secular materialism and rugged individualism, many seek to use spirit as a commodity like money. Using spirit to satisfy egocentric desires may elicit some form of energy, but it will probably not be fulfilling, connecting, or sustainable. Any attempt to separate from, judge, or condemn others disconnects a person from spiritual energy. A belief that spirit can be used to advance individual desires is incomplete. Once people open to spiritual guidance from within, their outcomes align with their highest good for self and others in relationship with them. When individuals try to force attitudes or beliefs about spirit on others, they automatically negate the very energy that they are attempting to convey. Spirit holds steadfastly to being integrative and inclusive.

PURPOSE OF ENERGETIC COACHING

There is an axiom in Neuro-Linguistic Programming: The map is not the territory. This text cannot be the entire territory called "Energetic Coaching." Perception at a given moment focuses experience. Because spirit encompasses the personal and impersonal at the same time, some of our illustrations may evoke only inner knowing. With time and practice, language, symbols, and description may transpose to facility. Energetic Coaches like to take what comes and continually open to what may manifest.

Teri-E Belf's book, Coaching with Spirit, describes the process and dynamics of welcoming spirit into the coaching relationship. We realize that spirit is a phenomenon of inner dynamics responding to positive relationships. Coaching is often a forum for experiencing spiritual energy. With Energetic Coaching we deliberately aim to practice positive intention in relationship as a means of engaging spirit.

John: *Now that I practice Energetic Coaching, I can see that spirit has been present and available throughout my coaching career. In the past, I may have taken personal credit for the work of spirit (ego likes to do that). At the very least, spirit was working, and I did not recognize, nurture, or optimize its energy in ways that I might have for the greatest benefit to my client. The more I experience spirit in the coaching relationship, the more I relax and let go. I marvel at the outcomes that clients achieve by going within for answers and acting congruently from their essence, which is their connection with spirit.*

Energetic Coaching is for professional coaches and others who desire to join the energy of spirit for the highest good of themselves and their clients. In a quickly and dynamically evolving profession, coaches often find that they deliberately or accidentally experience spiritual energy through relationships with their clients. The positive connection between coaches and clients

John: *Being open to spirit through the process of writing Energetic Coaching, I have had many transcendent experiences in relationship with myself and with others. For instance, I had been at odds with my fellow coach, Carole, over coaching styles and philosophy. I had thought her dogmatic and entrenched. During a recent SUN coaching retreat it so happened that we were to do an improvisation illustrating what happens in coaching when roles get in the way. I was not happy about being put in that situation with her. However, when I opened to spirit, it allowed a marvelous outcome. I had a peak spiritual experience of connection with Carole that I most likely would not have been open to receive. In that moment I knew and accepted her completely. By giving over to spirit, I received a deep understanding of how and why my fellow coach was as she was, which added to my coaching abilities. Our experience provided the basis for a solid relationship between us.*

An evolution in spiritual consciousness is taking place. Because spirit is common to all, it transcends differences among people. Many are now discussing and writing about spirit in relationship with individuals and their communities and organizations. Increasing popularity of this "soft" realm makes it acceptable to talk about spirit in business and science. Many now seek to capture the energy of spirit to advance their visions and achieve satisfaction in life. When aligned with spirit, which crosses all boundaries and knows everyone as equal and complete, individuals are realizing new possibilities in relationships that help them achieve their personal desires. Success compels them also to want to advance the dreams and desires of others. At the same time, it is important to modulate the pendulum swing. Spirit cannot be conjured, faked, or contrived—thank goodness—or a close connection with it would be a hollow goal. Spiritual connection requires each individual to strive for congruence. Energetic Coaches challenge clients to enunciate their visions and values and act in accordance with them to create congruent outer doing from inner being.

The field of coaching is a likely place to identify a new paradigm in human relationships that involves spirit directly. Science increases understanding of the physical world; Energetic Coaching directly and intentionally advances spiritual understanding and connecting through the process of helping clients align their inner and outer selves. Congruent individuals integrate their physical and spiritual worlds. Coaching integrates the scientific secular world with the realm of human passion and desire.

An outcome of the Energetic Coaching relationship is that people recognize the voice of their inner knower. Their results can be provocative and life changing. Having learned to delve into their being and strive for congruence, they grow from the coaching relationship. As clients evolve according to their own inner direction, they have the tools to act as their own best coach in the continuous process of achieving wholeness and oneness.

John: *As I reflect on the purpose of a book on Energetic Coaching, I realize that the seeds go back to my work in a group of seven people who founded the Spiritual Learning Community in 1999. "Coincidentally," that was when I took a greater spiritual orientation in my coaching practice.*

Our vision is "A community committed to creating an atmosphere of openness to our spiritual connection that allows for sharing and integration of our human experience with our spiritual learning." The principles of the commu-nity are...

- *Inclusion of all, providing many and any avenue for self-discovery and spiritual growth.*
- *Learning in an environment of love with the experience of being empowered to be in connection with the truth.*
- *Free choice around what to learn and what to believe and know.*
- *The experience of being both teacher and student within the same situation.*
- *Presence of spirit in family, career, and all other areas of life always.*
- *Open and truthful dialogue between self and spirit (congruence).*

Energetic Coaching results from advancing and living the foregoing precepts. I have transitioned from the Spiritual Learning Community into something new, and my thirst for working with spirit has expanded. I have experienced a direct connection with spirit that has enhanced my coaching and the heartfelt desires of my clients. As I write this I realize that I can play a key role in bringing spirituality into the coaching profession due to my experience of spirit and the importance of it in my life and career. I must respond to this call while feeling ill-equipped to do so. I know spirit will provide the validation of the process as I go along.

WHO ARE ENERGETIC COACHES?

Energetic Coaches embark on a sacred quest (question). Rather than answering questions, we question answers. We explore what clients want without knowing the landmarks or limits of where their search will lead. We are propelled by seeker energy—an open receptive learning orientation that invites the unknown and the unfathomable. We know that there is more to life than external orientation and that even though we sometimes feel uncomfortable in the process, we are willing to travel into the mystery—oriented inward, seeking to experience truth and connection that results in wholeness and oneness.

Those who enter the field of coaching expect to engage in important relationships with clients. Energetic Coaches know that such relationships often lead to more meaningful experiences than what clients may have expected. As the coaching relationship reveals deep levels of knowing, we can provide the experience and perspective needed to support clients in their individual exploration. It is only through our personal and sometimes difficult travel into the quest(ion) that we can light the way for clients. As they search and ask questions, they open to new ways of being and doing.

Because Energetic Coaches have tamed the dragon of the egocentric self (little i), they find coaching with spirit rewarding as a process rather than as outcomes. Once emptied of self-serving desires and motivations, we become the vessel for spiritual expression. As an instrument of spirit, we serve the clients in their quest for connection with their big I, their true self. Energetic Coaches act as the compassionate witness to create safe, open, nonjudgmental contexts for clients to experience confusion, ask difficult questions, listen to their inner knower, and receive insights to act on.

Energetic Coaches are an instrument for spirit to play its wondrous music; we are not the conductor, player, or audience. To the extent we connect with spirit in our daily life, we vibrate as instruments clear and melodic. Energetic Coaches aim for congruence in thoughts, words, and deeds in relationship with self and with others. Those who are closest to us find honesty, connection, and consistency within our relationships. As authentic people with integrity, Energetic Coaches seek a close connection with our inner knower. To communicate with us is to know who we are. We desire to speak and act consistently in truth with kindness.

John: *I was meeting with a client who became interested in this book about Energetic Coaching. As I relayed to her what an Energetic Coach was, she stated, "John, you are not just writing about coaching with spirit—you are a coach with spirit!" The spiritual aspects of my coaching had clearly come through all along; she had realized spiritual energy and qualities even though we had not discussed them.*

Energetic Coaches act authentically and create success as doers in the external realm. Like everyone else, we want to function well in life. Connecting being with doing makes a difference in how we do the doing. For instance, we certainly have to market ourselves to gain clients, but we stay open to the outcome. By allowing spirit to operate and direct the effort, often mysteriously, clients find us. In searching for answers for themselves, those clients use Energetic Coaches as mirror and witness to their process. We happily serve them. Humbly and appreciatively we support their efforts to attain congruence between their inner and outer selves to achieve desired outcomes.

Even when clients stop short along the process, Energetic Coaches demonstrate the ability to release, knowing that everything is in divine order. Sometime later, clients may renew the relationship. We honor their choices, so we support their decisions. We know that clients are continually undertaking the necessary lessons for personal growth and advancement. By pointing out positive ways they can appreciate their struggles and strengths, Energetic Coaches encourage clients to believe in themselves. As they begin to engage their inner knower, clients need us less and less. Energetic Coaches give credit to clients for doing their own work.

Lea: *Three of my coaching clients dropped out of the coaching process. Because I know the three clients personally, I have been able to follow their progress. In almost every case, the former clients were able to achieve their goals in their own time and way. They had been growing and learning right along. From time to time, I have been contacted to coach on a specific issue, but overall, the clients are continuing to follow their inner guidance. Coaching helped them to define what they wanted; the clients decided how to get there.*

THE PATH OF SPIRIT

A good coach does not desire dependence. Rather, we want to help clients to coach and mentor themselves. Ultimately, the path of spirit is an individual one. It appears solitary because congruent people go within for answers and no longer seek them on the outside. Energetic Coaches shine the light of knowing in not knowing and hold witness along the way for clients to discover their own connection with spirit. We cannot walk the path for them, but we do have confidence in unknown outcomes because we have walked our own human path. We as compassionate witness hold a confident objectivity. Our perspective can be very empowering, especially for clients who have not known such a relationship. Lovingly encouraging others to appreciate and believe in themselves is often all it takes for them to look within to grow.

Energetic Coaches provide clients positive reinforcement for hope, vision, and confidence to venture into the void of the hidden unknown, at first with us as a guide and then increasingly in relationship with themselves. By operating successfully in the external world, we want to live courageously as examples of high-level principles. Our words and deeds reflect our value system. Our doing exemplifies how to be and do congruently with inner values and visions. Because complete congruence is rare, Energetic Coaches are often tested to see if we are "for real." We welcome such testing, seeing it as another opportunity to demonstrate the peace of knowing who we are. Energetic Coaches provide the light and landmarks for those who are taking the journey within to discover who they are and what they want. Ours is the path to authenticity— the path of congruence and spiritual connection to oneness.

THE MIRROR OF THE COACH

Circumstances do not make the man, they merely reveal him to himself.
UNKNOWN

Relationships are mirrors for individuals to see who they are. People usually attract others whose energy is similar. Through their relationships, they can determine their own frequency. If not satisfactory, they can decide at what vibration they want to live, without blame or rejection of the other.

There is a saying "It's hard to soar with eagles when you're running with turkeys." When clients realize they are attracting discordant relationships, they can choose to change their own frequency. A disconnection invites individuals to examine what part they played to create it. Sometimes, to keep a relationship in rapport, they have to decide to increase or decrease frequency. Individuals can choose to surround themselves with people on the same frequency or higher, letting go of those relationships with people of lower, draining energy who do not choose to grow. The mirror of Energetic Coaches helps clients choose how they want to be and who they want to be with.

Energetic Coaches maintain a high frequency of energy to provide a channel for spirit. Even if we attract clients on a low frequency, we recognize the potential that they themselves may not see. The mirror of spirit reflects a reality to clients that they may have only imagined for themselves. The goal of Energetic Coaching is to provide unconditional support and safety to help clients get where they want to go. Despite fears of separation that may come with authenticity, Energetic Coaches know that we all are part of the one. We honor clients' process, even in the midst of their most arduous questioning. Through our knowing, we resist providing external answers for clients. Instead, by staying in the quest, we empower clients in the process of discovery with faith in the unknown.

Trusting the innate wisdom (inner knower) of clients and intentionally creating an environment of open acceptance (compassionate witness), we invite the energy of spirit. Positive energy brings out the best so clients can know themselves as worthy, complete, and acceptable as they are.

There is no necessity for clients to change, but success creates a desire for more learning. Clients see their own potential in the mirrored reflection of coaches. For some, coaching is the first relationship in which the other encourages them to be themselves. We provide the support and the mirror for clients to see themselves as powerful co-creators of what they desire. Living fully requires sustainable, renewable energy of self-knowing and acceptance, which increases spiritual connection. The ultimate reward for us is when clients graduate to self-coaching. We aim to help them empower themselves to the level they no longer need us. As the energy in the coaching relationship amplifies, we coaches gain inner knowing and empowerment in return.

Of course, there will be some clients who choose to stay at their familiar frequency and resist going to their inner knower for guidance. They drop out of Energetic Coaching. We are able to release them, holding the space for their return through positive intention and accepting that their sense of timing is accurate. We have tended the seed.

Energetic Coaching provides language and understanding to open channels for spirit to fill. The coaching relationship is ideal in many ways for helping clients step into the sometimes murky waters of their inner world. After they test their being, they can learn to swim in the vast spiritual ocean within. Because we know how to swim, we can help others learn.

It is said that you can give people fish for a day or you can teach them to fish for a lifetime. Energetic Coaches teach clients to fish and encourage them to fish for themselves. Even though people know the answers or the best course of action, they may need support for many reasons. By connecting with their inner knower, they will feel a compelling desire for congruence. By acting as a mirror for the inner knower, we shine the light on what clients may need to see. They may delay claiming what they want because they fear that they are not good enough to deserve it, or at a deeper level, that they cannot handle the responsibility of their great goodness and power. People can maintain a close relationship with spirit to the extent they want what is best for them. Energetic Coaches aim to help clients remove barriers to spiritual connection by identifying and transcending internal blockages.

As children learn by example from their parents, Energetic Coaching clients can learn by the example of their coaches. Motivation to act comes from within clients as they choose positive energy, create a supportive environment, live in unconditional acceptance, tackle challenging situations, and gain confidence in their abilities. We reflect their new behaviors and beliefs back to them. The challenge to bring out the personal best in others becomes, in turn, a modus operandi for coaches. As we gain energy to do what is best ourselves, we create examples of how we succeed. The mirror becomes the reflection, the two merge into one, and clients grow to be their own best coaches.

The Challenge of Energetic Coaching

Energetic Coaches help others experience spirit because of the goal that we share with clients. Seeking spirit brings many people to coaching and many of us coaches want to help others help themselves. We desire to help clients discover their life purpose and realize their personal best. The decision to be coached means clients want personal improvement. The choice to fulfill potential is fertile soil for spirit to grow. We hold the space and offer witness and support to the process of others walking their own path. Finding the way may sometimes be arduous, so Energetic Coaching provides provisions for the journey into the inner unknown.

People cannot understand others unless they have sojourned a similar path. The Success Unlimited Network (SUN) coaching protocol practices that principle by insuring that all SUN coaches have themselves experienced the coaching process before entering the coach-in-training program. Similarly, we who coach with spirit knowingly and willingly do so from experience gained by allowing spirit to work through us for ourselves and in relationship with others.

As Energetic Coaches, we hold ourselves accountable to maintain connection with our inner knower. The calling to work closely with spirit to achieve oneness is not entirely altruistic. Energetic Coaching provides the gratifying opportunity to grow and learn from spirit along with clients. The rapport we enjoy with clients is congruent and reciprocal—whatever we do for others, we do for ourselves as well. The learning process never ends; there is always growth and mutual enhancement available through spirit. We know that we can be beacons of light along the path but not the path itself. Ultimately, the path always leads to the same source of energy and creativity, goodness and love—the all in All.

Energetic Coaching Requires Trust

Coaching is a process that requires us to be one hundred percent present for clients. We make it safe for them to explore what they want and what they don't want for themselves. In a safe environment clients can afford to take risks to experience positive energy, hope, authenticity, and power. Their willingness to take a good look at themselves is the first step toward growth and personal freedom. By accepting clients as they come, we demonstrate trust in them during the coaching process. Trusting clients builds their self-trust. Trust creates openness and acceptance, nurturing the seed of spirit. Spirit's emergence helps clients acknowledge, explore, and integrate their hidden shadow self as well as their public persona. By including the many dimensions of clients in the purview of Energetic Coaching, we help them integrate different aspects of themselves. As they become aware of who they are, they may realize why they have encountered and created difficult life lessons. Understanding helps clients identify what they want to achieve in life and how to integrate themselves into their real, larger-than-life essence. At times, coaches may need to demonstrate trust when clients doubt themselves. To reap the most benefit from the inner work, clients have to commit to changing for their own good. In relationships, trust makes a safe space for truth to be acknowledged for people to grow.

People experience spirit as positive and powerful energy. The relationship of respect and trust between coaches and clients provides an opening for spirit to enter. The coaching process can remove barriers that clients have erected and reinforced, sometimes over many years, so that they can feel spirit flowing freely. With spirit they can dispel the illusion of separation and superiority or inferiority promoted by the ego.

Lea: *While John coached me as a coach-in-training with SUN, I started to question my abilities and my direction. I knew that I needed coaching, and I thought I was innately suited for the profession. However, I doubted my abilities to market myself, and I did not like to "brand" myself, identify a niche, or over-promise to attract clients. My marketing efforts detracted from my desire to coach because I did not feel authentic in the process. I judged the marketing aspect of coaching as a waste of time and energy. John never bought into my negativity. As John questioned my resistance to marketing, he held the space for me to question myself to decide if I was being congruent.*

John relayed personal stories of how he would "find" clients, which seemed to happen with ease and enjoyment. Never before had I considered that marketing could be fun and effortless. It took awhile for me to see that coaching, including marketing, was working for John. Staying open and accepting my doubt, John answered my questions. Because he had no doubts regarding my ability to market myself, I began to see things I wanted to do. John continues to gently encourage me in my marketing efforts, knowing that I am working in my own time and process to do what it takes to establish a successful business in my terms of success. I may do it differently from John, but because he respects my ways and trusts my abilities, he helps me believe in myself. John showed in every way that he had no attachment to the outcome of our process together and respected my best judgment. This has allowed me to promote my coaching business in a more unusual way that may be less lucrative but more reflective of my values.

Energetic Coaching is not a teacher-student, guru-follower relationship; coaches and clients are equals. We know that clients have the answers within themselves, so we provide a safe place for the answers to emerge. We ask questions and provide feedback or feed-forward when the client requests information. We trust the process of spirit. We realize that the amount of trust clients maintain reflects the amount of trust they have in themselves. Both partners in coaching grow, which is the best reward for being a coach. To coach with spirit means to have opportunities to plumb our own depths, connecting within for wholeness and achieving oneness.

Energetic Coaching is a servant-leader role. As successful leaders, Energetic Coaches can authentically choose the role of servant. We know that no one person has all the answers and that the process of connecting to wholeness is different for everyone. Through asking questions rather than acting as an expert, we allow clients to come to know, trust, and respect their own inner guidance. They design their own outcomes. Clients desire different results at different stages of their growth. Connecting with spirit never ends. Once clients recognize and trust their own knowing, they can coach themselves along their chosen path.

Energetic Coaches eschew the separate and superior or inferior egocentric self so that trust grows. Coaching requires credentials of an intangible nature, such as humility, self-respect, self- love, self-esteem, wisdom, and faith. As soon as clients register an aha and we know we are staying in the question, spirit provides reinforcement to catalyze self-knowledge and growth. For Energetic Coaches who recognize ego, lessons come with humor instead of humiliation. Aware that we are growing and learning along with our clients, we resist small egocentric urges to demonstrate superior expertise, experience, or knowing. We trust ourselves and our clients, knowing all things work together for the good.

ENERGETIC COACHING—NOT ONLY FOR COACHES AND NOT FOR EVERY COACH

Energetic Coaching provides information on coaching with spirit for practical applications that can be useful for any relationship in which people desire spirituality and positive energy. People can use this book to coach themselves in building congruence between their inner and outer worlds. Also it can help in one-on-one relationships to remove barriers and explore ways to foster mutual growth. Teams and group members who want the energy of spirit to assist them in accomplishing their goals can follow Energetic Coaching precepts. People do not have to be experienced coaches to be Energetic Coaches. There will be many who are called to the coaching profession specifically by spirit. Although they may be novice coaches, their connection with spirit will energize them to help others connect with spirit too. The practices and principles found in Energetic Coaching help communicate in tangible terms experiences of an intangible nature. We intend this book to build a bridge between people's physical and spiritual experiences, incorporating both worlds for balance and wholeness.

John: *I invited Lea to write this book on coaching with spirit with me because I could sense her connection with spirit and natural coaching abilities. Although some may wonder why I did not invite a seasoned coach, I knew that Lea would be a perfect partner in the process. In acknowledging our mutual connection with spirit and one another, we used our relationship to create this book using ourselves as examples and experimental subjects. I had been open to working with someone who possessed Lea's spiritual qualities, and somehow I knew that Lea and I were to write this book together. Lea knew it too. We both have been amazed at how smoothly the process has worked for us to increase spiritual connection through our relationship within ourselves and with one another. What has been created together is larger than either of us could create without our positive, respectful and supportive relationship.*

There are coaches who have encountered spirit time and again who want to know more about how to open to its energy to enhance their coaching effectiveness. There are coaches who are skilled in other areas of practical application who are not interested in coaching with spirit. Those who seek to coach with spirit will find clients who are seeking the same. Often, clients choose the best coach for where they are at the time. Those who want to build relationships with spirit will use their seeker energy to find others on the same journey. Energetic Coaching is one path that can be useful for those who want a closer connection with spirit. There are many.

HOW OPPORTUNITIES FOR COACHING WITH SPIRIT ARISE

Potential clients may contact coaches for the express purpose of developing spirituality in life. Or the subject of spirit may arise during the process of coaching. By looking closely at the outcomes of the coaching experience, we may find spirit already present. At any point in the coaching process we may notice a charge of energy, a well of emotion, a profound insight, an inner knowing or message from spirit. Then the course of the meeting as well as the overall result of the coaching relationship often transitions to an exploration and integration of inner knowing. As questions arise, clients begin to weigh answers, understand, and grow concepts. As they discover personal truth, they may tentatively begin to apply it. The congruence between their inner and outer worlds and the immense power of choice over thoughts and emotions give clients positive feedback to stay the course.

Some clients seek a coaching relationship because of a prompting from spirit. Such a spiritual wake-up call may have been triggered by many causes—an emotional upheaval, a personal tragedy, a growing awareness that there must be more to life, a desire for inner satisfaction and strength, or a sense that something important is missing. Searing questions, which must be answered sooner or later in life, often arise during the coaching experience. The most important ones are answered through people's inner knower opening to spirit; such questions as:

- Who am I?
- What do I want?
- How shall I live my life?
- What is most important to me?
- How can I arrange my time to experience what is important to me?
- How do I get rid of what I don't want?
- How can I create greater creativity, goodness, and love in my life?
- What is success in terms of what matters to me?
- How can I integrate myself into an outer world that does not seem to support me?
- How can I express who I am?

The outcomes become secondary as the process reveals the ways in which clients can discover answers within for deep questions. Energetic Coaches provide the mirror of knowing for clients to see that they have their own answers if they go within to find them.

CHAPTER 2 APPENDIX

WHAT ENERGETIC COACHING IS	WHAT ENERGETIC COACHING IS NOT
Inner-outer congruence	Separation
Inclusive and integrative	Rules or dogma
Servant leadership	Conversion of belief systems
Humility	Right or wrong way
Authenticity	Egocentricity
Integrity	Prescription
Compassionate witnessing	Imbalance
Letting go	Control
Trusting and trustworthiness	Denial
Equality	Neediness
Respectful	Demand
Caring	Attachment
Acceptance	Judgment
Growth orientation	Expert persona
Unconditional love	
Positive intention	
Free will goodwill	

ENERGETIC COACHING PRINCIPLES

- We are co-creators with others and spirit in our day-to-day living.
- We can come from a place of spiritual connectedness (love) even when we don't feel it in the moment.
- We learn especially as we offer learning to others.
- We have an inner knower who recognizes truth even when we harbor doubt and confusion.

- We know there is no one way to spirit; many individual paths lead home.
- Connecting and empowering others connects and empowers us as individuals.
- Because the divine lives in everyone and every situation, we are inclusive and equal with all others.
- We have a mindset of inclusiveness and equality even when we are challenged by a differing perspective.
- We acknowledge that spirituality is present in all areas of life, including work, family, friends, acquaintances, the natural environment, our organizations, and our cultural systems.
- We can choose to live in harmony with ourselves and the belief systems of others with acceptance for all avenues of self-discovery and inner knowing.
- We know that our relationships are mirrors for us to see and know ourselves. We project what we expect and choose to expect the best.
- We know that truth comes from within from our connection with Source through spirit.
- We are powerful co-creators of what we want or don't want in life.
- The more congruence we achieve between our inner being and outer doing, the closer our connection with Source in oneness.

EXPECTATIONS OF ENERGETIC COACHING

1. There are many different paths to spiritual growth. Energetic Coaching can help with the decision and hold the light on the path, but the choice of path and outcome belong to clients alone.

2. Energetic Coaching takes place without a formal religion, but people can apply universal principles derived from religious teachings and incorporate religious beliefs as they choose.

3. Energetic Coaching is based on developing qualities and attributes of love and appreciation within the individual, including love and appreciation for self, others, nature, life, and the Source of life.

4. Energetic Coaching seeks to integrate and balance physical, emotional, and mental aspects of individuals in inner and outer ways for a closer connection with spirit.

5. Energetic Coaches commit to personal growth, including connecting with spirit as a continuous process rather than as a final result.

6. Energetic Coaching emphasizes the importance of the inner world to create outer circumstances. It develops congruence between intent and action, which leads to self- knowledge, consistency and authenticity.

7. Energetic Coaches use personal practice to grow spiritual energy. We support clients in adopting their choice of personal practice.

8. Energetic Coaches encourage clients to provide direction for the coaching process based on their unique sense of inner guidance.

9. Energetic Coaching develops an awareness of habits of thought to replace negative counterproductive mental

processes with positive and self-empowering perceptions and beliefs.

10. Energetic Coaches hold a safe space to allow the inner knower of clients to emerge, including the shadow aspects that they may not know or that they may reject.

11. Energetic Coaches facilitate as a servant leader to help clients develop a connection with spirit, the ultimate life coach.

12. Energetic Coaches expect our clients to do the necessary work for their personal growth.

13. 1Energetic Coaching can be an adjunct to psychological, psychiatric, or medical interventions, but will not be used in place of needed medical attention.

3. FRAMEWORK FOR ENERGETIC COACHING

The moment you begin your sacred quest, you will be joined by a special inner energy. You might call it a guide, a guardian angel, a golden wind, or an inner voice. It is a holy and sacred energy that is older than time and comes to you from another world. It will awaken within you the knowledge and resources you need as you begin your journey into the inner worlds of your Infinite Self.
STUART WILDE

Quantum mechanics has demonstrated that the world is built of interconnecting relationships with outcomes based on probabilities that appear to manifest when they are observed. Likewise, people experience spirit in relationships due to choices that create outcomes from all the possible probabilities. There are as many possibilities as choices, and spirit co-creates according to individual intention and invitation. Just as the laws of physics create the context for everyday life, so the properties of spirit demonstrate laws that either release and direct its energy or block its potential. Energetic Coaching seeks to discover and apply spiritual principles to provide a common language for people to co-create what they want with spirit. Even though no one knows exactly how spirit works, we want to stir people to consider their individual choices to select from probabilities. Through intention to connect in wholeness, people can align with spiritual principles to experience a transcendent integration into oneness. Energetic Coaches seek to align and connect with spirit through the inner knower. We want to use spiritual energy to support clients in building positive relationships.

In her book Coaching with Spirit Teri-E Belf provides stories, examples, citations, and analogies to describe how spirit works in the coaching relationship. Energetic Coaching emphasizes the underlying dynamics to foster spirit in relationship. Because it is infinite and indescribable, there can be no inclusive model or finite formula to define spirit or how it works. No singular way invokes spirit or utilizes it. Open-mindedness, receptivity, invitation, and faithful action help. Often, spirit works beyond people's wildest desires and limited expectations. Spirit cannot be commanded; it compels them to get out of their own way to allow it to enter. When people experience spirit, they have an instantaneous knowing of how positive and powerful it is. Those who practice the art of positive thinking will normally have a few examples of when the outcome did not arrive as they expected. The subconscious mind is a great field of unharnessed energy. Spirit at large moves and manifests in its own time and in a seemingly impersonal but purposeful way. Energetic Coaching seeks to develop a common language and understanding of an organic process, effortless and open to being guided by spirit from within rather than seeking to direct it.

This organic way of achieving results contrasts with modern day mechanistic thinking, which fosters the illusion that humans can understand and control the universe. Although there are those who seek to do so, the magic and mystery of something greater than the self would be lost, and humans would be reduced to manipulative automatons with nothing but self-centered will to motivate them. By embracing the mystery, Energetic Coaches act as examples and facilitators for clients to discover and align themselves with spirit. We sponsor openness and equality in relationship. We explore with clients inner being and outer doing to achieve congruence. People increase energy when they balance the two aspects of human experience and align themselves with authentic language and action that express their inner values and vision.

THE METAPHOR OF THE TRIAD AND THE SPHERE

Our objective in working with spirit is to connect and integrate spiritual energy with individual intent and choice so that the separate one can integrate with the whole one. In spiritual terms, anything other than oneness is an illusion. The ego in the deceptive world of duality fosters separation and aloneness. To go beyond apparent separateness and relate everything to a common point, we use an overarching metaphor for connecting with spirit: a triad that can spin in all directions on the axis of the centerpoint to create a sphere.

Picture a triad within a sphere. The metaphor of the triad in the sphere may be useful to depict how spirit works in the coaching process.*

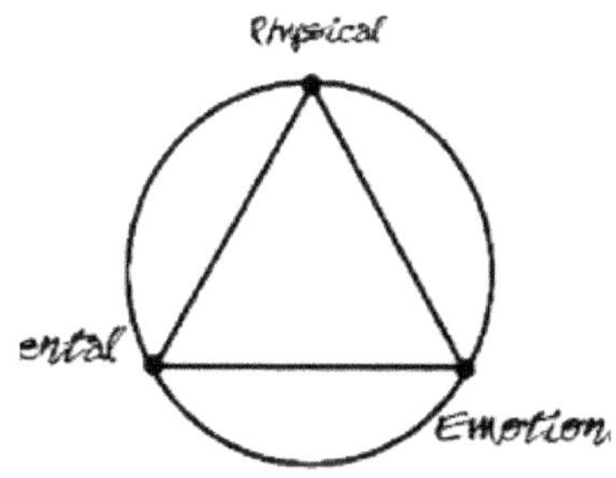

The triad represents the mystery of the three-in-one concept. Embedded in the sphere and rotating around a common axis, the triad represents the inner and outer aspects of the three areas of human experience: physical (perceiving), mental (thinking), and emotional (feeling). To integrate each aspect into the whole, people need to give equal importance to their conscious physical, mental, and emotional states as well as their inner perceiving, thinking, and feeling states. Perceptions affect emotions; emotions affect the physical body; the physical body affects feelings; thinking affects the mental, back and forth, in and out, all in a connected way. It is rare to have the inner and outer aspects and all three dimensions of experience balanced and integrated without some incongruence among them. Although we consider balance and integration as the optimum outcome of Energetic Coaching, probably no one achieves it once and for all. There is always work that can be done to achieve balance and a higher frequency of energy.

When thoughts align with feelings, which align with perceptions and so on—each aspect congruent with the others, the triad becomes the three-in-one sphere by rotating around the centerpoint. The centerpoint is the seamless connection of inner and outer, conscious and unconscious, spirit and inner knower No need for ego; the two become one.

Within the sphere the separations among perceiving-physical, thinking-mental, and feeling- emotional bodies disappear. Thinking manifests in the physical, physical manifests in the emotional, mental manifests in the feeling, and so on, in equally interchangeable ways. The triad rotating around the centerpoint of Oneness creates the sphere. The sphere encompasses, connects, and balances the duality of the three aspects of human experience, incorporating them into the whole. The common core represents connection with Source through spirit in Oneness in which inner and outer unite and integrate.

THE PERCEIVING-PHYSICAL BODY

To see the world in a grain of sand,
And a heaven in a wild flower,
Hold infinity in the palm of your hand,
And Eternity in an hour.
WILLIAM BLAKE

The physical world reflects the spiritual world. Just as the planets rotate around the sun, spiritual energy rotates around a common core of Source. Nature reflects the characteristics of the creator. That people are spiritual beings in a physical world does not mean that the physical world is separate and somehow less than the spiritual world. The outer mirrors the inner. Nature holds many clues to discover the characteristics of the creator of it.

The physical body, often portrayed as a heavy vehicle with severe limitations and handicaps, does not have to be a barrier to people's connection to spirit. Overemphasizing the five physical senses may create an illusion that only the external world is real. The human state of wholeness balances and connects spirit with matter. People perceive the external, tangible world through the five senses as they receive different energy vibrations. At one time many believed that unless something could be seen and measured, it did not exist. Now, although some still limit their reality to sensing and focusing, most people know that an incomprehensible expanse of energy vibrates beyond our five senses. At the subatomic level, the human body is part of all that is. The physical body, rather than acting as a barrier to spirit, can convey it through actively and consciously perceiving energetic information through the inner knower or what can be called the sixth sense or intuition.

Lea: *When I want to connect with my spiritual self, I open the channels of my chi energy through exercise and dance. If I feel bogged down or disconnected, I know that I need to move my body or breathe consciously. Thoughtful movement provides me a literal means to access a virtual state. A song may come on the radio that calls me to dance. Dancing helps move me to the spiritual realm. Increasing my physical energy increases my inner energetic state, and I feel more alive.*

To discover what is happening during the coaching process, Energetic Coaches can tune into our own frequencies and those of our clients. Sometimes we pick up a deep knowing about how to respond. If we scan our body for physical signs of inner knowing, our inner voice can bypass ego with its agendas, judgments, and limits. Then we clear the way to understanding and connection. Spirit will lead us to effective coaching beyond what might have come by way of skill or experience alone.

Lea: *I remember a coaching situation in which I became increasingly confused. Among the mixed messages I was receiving, I could not determine the real message. Suddenly, in exasperation, my client made a sweeping gesture across her throat. At that moment I realized that she was exhibiting a disconnection between her head, her logic, and her heart, her feelings. When I pointed out what her physical gesture portrayed to me, my client understood her confusion. We worked together to reconcile her conflicting thoughts and emotions. By resolving them through acceptance of her feelings rather than rejection, I saw my client clear her throat, which opened the channels between her head and her heart in order to speak her truth.*

John: *Over my years of coaching I have tuned into the information my physical state shares with me about the quality of the work I am doing. Two years ago I was conducting a live coaching demonstration before 25 people on the role shadow plays in coaching. A fellow coach volunteered for the 20-minute demonstration. To add to the safety of the demonstration, I requested that she keep her coaching issue to herself. We were sitting face-to-face for the demonstration. Even though our coaching work seemed to be going smoothly, about seven minutes into our work I began to notice tension building in my neck and shoulders. I wondered what my body was telling me. As we continued, I realized my client was dealing with a very sensitive issue. My ego feared that I was going to fail in front of my peers. Working with my inner voice, I got up from my chair and asked my client to join me. Moving my body brought me calm and clarity. I also observed that as my client moved through her issue, her posture shifted from tense to relaxed and her voice from harsh to soft. In the end, my volunteer client expressed gratitude for the coaching we had done together. My recognizing and acting on physical cues enhanced our coaching results.*

In an attempt to build spiritual connection people often ignore or disregard the perceiving physical body. But ancient sages recognized the physical breath as correspondent to the spiritual breath of life. They used breathing to open up the channels of chi to create energy and consciousness. By deep breathing and relaxing muscles, people can release stress and resistance and open the body to spiritual energy. Practicing yoga, tai chi, qui gong, and other disciplines creates spiritual energy through the physical body. Once we include the body in our decision- making process, free of judgments based on appearance and other external criteria, we and our clients can tune in to each other. Energetic Coaches help clients become aware of physical sensations and identify incongruent gestures and postures, facial expressions, shifts in position, eye contact, and other unconscious behaviors. Becoming aware of such behaviors helps connect with spirit so that clients can listen to their own inner knower. We act as a mirror to help clients observe what is going on within that is being expressed externally. Acting as a compassionate witness, we do not speculate about what that would be. We encourage clients to seek insights using their inner knower to achieve inner/outer congruence.

Because the external is a reflection of the internal, the physical body is affected by the perceiving body. The perceiving body has thousands of messages from the external world bombarding it on a moment-by-moment basis. It is not possible to consciously consider all incoming information, so the perceiving body has to choose what to focus on and what to filter out. People mostly filter unconsciously, greatly influenced by habit. With awareness and practice they can choose what to perceive without judgment. The perceiving body affects the physical body in positive ways to achieve congruence and a high-energy state connected with spirit. Perceiving what is positive and good from the incoming messages has a positive effect on the physical body.

Two people can be in the same situation and perceive it very differently. For example, observe the body language of the spectators of opposing teams. Some demonstrate positive energy (whose team is winning) and some who favor the losing team show very different, more negative energy. Same game, different energy because of the different way of perceiving.

The Feeling-Emotional Body

There can be no knowledge without emotion. We may be aware of a truth, yet until we have felt its force, it is not ours. To the cognition of the brain must be added the experience of the soul.

Arnold Bennet

Emotions are energy in motion. Energy compels expression, but people do not always use emotions for channeling and directing their energy. Many seem unaware that they can choose their emotions. Emotions that are experienced consciously often come from feelings that are hidden. For instance, a person may experience anger that comes from a feeling of hurt or jealousy, which in turn, is coming from insecurity. Connecting the inner feeling with the outer emotional body leads to congruence.

Through socialization and self-judgment people lose their connection with their feelings. Often spirit is experienced through feelings such as love, peace, and harmony. Children have a wonderful way of showing their feelings without constraint, before they become socialized to deny or downplay them. Rejection may lead to disconnection from feelings. The intellect may take over and judge them inappropriate or too strong to handle. Over time, many learn to subordinate the innocence and energy of feelings to cues from others and cultural expectations. Adults, especially men, feel the pressure to detach from feelings. Then they can experience emotions unrelated to their true feelings.

Feelings cannot be judged because they are never right or wrong. They just are. Negative, draining emotions are signs that feelings need to be brought to the surface. Otherwise, people may explode with an emotion of unknown origin and inappropriate to the situation. Witness road rage or depression resulting from dismissed or buried feelings.

Feelings link us directly to spirit, which many associate with positive emotions and the experience of belonging, rightness, and reverence. Spirituality provides a sense of meaningfulness and importance, connecting the individual with universal energy, transcending the temporal and mundane to reveal passion and purpose. Lack of emotion or passion in life may signal a lack of spiritual connection. Negative emotions such as anger can signal alienation and incongruence within self and with others.

Lea: *In coaching, clients talk about what they want or don't want in life. I find that by focusing on what is wanted, positive energy is increased. If I allow complaining about what is not wanted, the positive energy is canceled. As clients become more focused on their vision and values, I look for signs that they are emotionally engaged in the process. It is not enough to speak intellectually about goals and desires. It appears there must be a head-heart connection to create more effectively. Once a client actually feels what it would be like to accomplish what is wanted, they appear to create on a certain level which means it won't be long until that creation is manifested in the physical. I would describe the emotional connection with what is wanted as a "gut feeling," and sometimes wonder if it has to do with precognition.*

Without spiritual connection to feelings through the inner knower, people are subject to stimulus-response reactions to external events. Lack of emotion causes them to feel lifeless and helpless. When they rollercoaster through waves of ungrounded emotional energy, they feel at risk and out of control. Lack of emotion or strong, overwhelming emotions indicate unbalance away from the still centerpoint.

Energetic Coaches explore signs of disconnections from the inner knower by following clients' strong emotions or exploring lack of excitement and enthusiasm for life. We do not give negative emotions such as fear or anger extra energy. We stay clear of judgment or resistance to what is. Instead of increasing melodrama, we provide a mirror of objectivity and acceptance so clients can experience, explore, direct, and integrate their feelings. Energetic Coaches support opening to spirit as clients experience authentic feelings without judgment or rejection.

Through the compassionate witness, Energetic Coaches recognize and acknowledge feelings. We hold a safe space for clients by accepting strong emotions. If clients lack enthusiasm for what they want, we address the incongruence between stated desires and the energy to pursue them. In the Western world the culture gives greater weight to intellect than to emotion. The neck-up approach emphasizes linear, logical, external, rational thinking. Energetic Coaches connect intellect with heart. Information must pass through the limbic system, the "heart" of the brain. Even though people state that they know something, unless they integrate their truth into their inner knower, they retain an abstract concept and not the congruence needed to act authentically in the moment. People will not experience wholeness until they accept emotionally the voice of their inner knower.

John: *As I embarked on a coaching career, after spending a number of years doing training and consulting, I challenged myself to be myself differently. I had been rewarded for my clear logical thinking. During times when I lived by my wits, I was unaware of the stress in my body. Working with a mentor, I started tuning in to the signals my body was giving me in the absence or presence of physical well being. The soreness in my neck and shoulders indicated I was operating from the neck up and shouldering a burden. I have come to appreciate how fine an instrument my body is for letting me know when negative emotions are tying me in knots and blocking the flow of spirit. Now, I choose to acknowledge my body's signals and allow my heart-mind connection to flow with spirit through acknowledging and accepting my feelings as equally as my intellect.*

The physical body provides keys to connection and balance of emotional energy and feelings. It receives and sends messages that might otherwise be ignored were they not accompanied by emotion. If there is incongruence in emotions, feelings, and thoughts, the physical body may express the mismatch as disease or physical discomfort in order to get attention. Significant discomfort from energy blockages can be what it takes to get people to turn within to listen to their inner knower.

To experience wholeness, people need to express and direct their highly charged feelings. Often, it is much more acceptable to individuals and to society for people to express only positive feelings. Negative feelings, though unpleasant, require acknowledgment and expression as well. People create inner imbalance when they suppress their undesirable feelings. And they convey their imbalance to others as mixed messages.

When people acknowledge negative emotions, they strengthen their connection to spirit. Their body language matches the words they state. Uncovering and nonjudgmentally acknowledging negative feelings is necessary for unleashing the inner knower and connecting with spirit. People grow when they can experience and express feelings honestly without judgment, and others read their outer, emotional body as spontaneous and real.

The external world seldom condones negative emotions. Companies reward executives for maintaining optimism even when the stock market plummets. Those who grieve may wear black yet refrain from sharing their grief with others. Children are told to stop crying over spilled milk. Negative emotions breed separation and alienation even though companionship may be what the griever needs most. When those who are disappointed keep a stiff upper lip, they alienate from life. They may find it less energetically draining to be alone than to try to be positive around others. yet when they try to express negative feelings, they may find no forum. Once again, people need a balance. We are not speaking about those who are consistently pessimistic. We are encouraging people to express their feelings authentically so that they can discharge energy appropriately without alienation in order to integrate and move forward.

Energetic Coaches accept negative and positive feelings equally without judgment. Both are elements of becoming whole. By holding the space as the compassionate witness and allowing clients to emote, we reflect how to experience unwanted and unpleasant feelings as well as pleasant feelings without giving value to either. Knowing that there are elements of good in every bad and elements of bad in every good, we seek the centerpoint of nonjudgment.

By allowing feelings and emotions to be without judgment or rejection, clients can explore the origins of them. Instead of responding or reacting, clients can connect with their inner knower for guidance. Energetic Coaches help with the connection through positive intention. We find great opportunity for growth especially in difficult or challenging situations. When we hold the space for unwanted feelings or emotions with positive intention, clients have a real life, real time example of how to follow suit. Despite the human urge to resist, deny, or act out negative emotions, clients learn to accept them along with positive emotions as part of becoming whole.

Feelings affect people's worldview and core value systems. Old values may no longer apply to a current situation. Beliefs from childhood can be released when they have been outgrown. Energetic Coaches help clients to discover their worldview and core value systems and their origination. If not wanted or appropriate, we encourage clients to consciously create new paradigms that serve them better. Clients may be surprised to know that feelings can change with conscious intention. Spirit through the inner knower aids the change process for those who desire to adopt a worldview that creates more positive and powerful feelings. No matter what has happened in the past, the future can be created anew.

Everyone knows people who thrive on melodrama. They behave incongruently and erratically, creating chaos for themselves and others. No one can count on volatile emotions disconnected from the real feelings to create and sustain relationships and spiritual connectedness. To create and sustain emotions aligned with spiritual values, people need to channel energy in productive and positive ways, dealing with difficult feelings rather than denying them or hurting others.

Combined with bad intention or no intention, negative energy depletes and destroys. Unfortunately, the media, society, and even human nature tend to focus on the negative rather than the positive. By concentrating on problems, tragedies, and fear, people create addictive pseudo energy. The outer negative drains energy from the inherent positive. Dispirited, people separate from others and fragment inside. This conflicting duality pervades the energy field in subtle ways below consciousness with a cloud of malaise and malcontent. As innocuous and innocent as it may seem, consuming inner junk food saps our emotions. Watching soap operas, which show the worst qualities in people, the news that only reports tragedies, pornography that exploits and trivializes sex, and horror films that graphically portray the most heinous violence disconnect with spirit. Ingesting negative thoughts, emotions, and images anesthetizes and alienates people from the inside out. Absorbing negative outer input deadens and dulls the senses, blocking consciousness and isolating people from spiritual energy and one another.

People can replace negative emotions with positive feelings through conscious focus and practice. They can mitigate the influence of the external world by making the internal decision on which kind of external input to ingest: negative draining input or positive energizing input. Even though the external world bombards them with seductive, desensitizing messages of deprivation and despair, their inner knower has the power to choose where to focus and what to absorb. Just as food affects physical health, thoughts affect mental health and feelings affect emotional health. Perceptions, thoughts, and feelings affect all aspects of human experience from within. Ultimately, people choose what feelings to carry and what emotions to convey. Spirit lives in the space of choice between positive and negative. People connect with spirit by acknowledging the negative and choosing the positive.

The researchers at the Institute of HeartMath® in Boulder Creek, California, have studied the effect of replacing emotions of upset and stress with positive feelings. Through practice of the Freeze Frame Technique™, they have demonstrated that people can replace the automatic stress response with the intention and choice to breathe positive feelings into the heart. Their studies have shown the technique leads to balanced mental and physical states. By replacing the unwanted, negative emotion with a desired, positive feeling, they achieve a sense of coherence and well being. Over time, people can mitigate their automatic stress response through practice of conscious breathing into the heart with positive feelings.

Choosing to experience positive emotions does not mean burying negative emotions. Instead, as people hold negative emotions up to the light for introspection without acting on them, they gain inner power and strength, and the negative emotion loses the driving energy it once had. People can free themselves to feel without acting on emotions. Even if they do experience a negative feeling, over time they can gain energy and power by creating congruence between their inner and outer states of feelings and expressed emotions. They can feel the hurt rather than expressing the anger.

Energetic Coaches stay open to clients by accepting negative emotions and releasing barriers to spirit so our clients can grow positive feelings. Through our example, clients can begin to notice different perspectives and acknowledge their power to choose the positive over the negative. The compassionate witness of the Energetic Coach allows feelings to surface into a safe space of acceptance. The compassionate witness does not get caught up in the drama of either negative or positive emotions expressed by clients. Seeing and experiencing emotions as low- to high-level vibrations of energy, accepting positive and negative alike without judgment, we remain at the centerpoint to reach integration and wholeness. By dealing with and releasing negative feelings, we create more space for positive emotions to be experienced.

The Thinking-Intuitive Mental Body

If you are distressed by anything external, the pain is not due to the thing itself, but to your estimate of it; and this you have the power to revoke at any moment.

Marco Aurelio

Energetic Coaches focus on thoughts while integrating and balancing intuitive and rational aspects of thinking. We help clients think about what they think about. Awareness in the moment of what they are thinking helps people examine the quality and the contribution of thoughts to their overall well being. By examining thoughts, clients can discover the connection between thinking and their physical and feeling sensations.

For many, the rational mind is more developed than the intuitive. This is out of practical necessity to deal with the physical world. Children learn to turn off the intuitive daydreaming mind to focus on the external cues more than internal insights. Balance comes from attending to intuitive insights as well as rational thoughts. By doing so people can overcome the tendency to dismiss intuition because it does not make logical sense.

People construct their worldviews and belief patterns by what they think. To operate at a high frequency, Energetic Coaches decide what thoughts to transmit and what thoughts to receive. We explore mental processes with clients to shift negative thinking to positive in the same way that we encourage positive feeling-emotional energy—through conscious choice and practice.

Clients' mental processes create the focus, direction, and drive to pursue what they want. Energetic Coaching focuses awareness and makes practical application of rational and intuitive information. Life is not only about the external aspect of doing; living emanates from integrating heart and mind and body of inner being. As a result of conscious decision-making, clients gain clarity and direction. Their rational mind integrates intuitive insights and tests such input to determine if the insights are true.

People tend to rely on the rational mind at the expense of openness that comes from living within a question. Intelligence is not all that is needed for understanding and achievement. When dealing with inner matters, the inner knower speaks through intuition. For the most part, people like to know, to predict, and to figure things out. Society rewards intelligence and proof. Energetic Coaches are able to stay in the present moment no matter how uncomfortable and keep the faith no matter what the temporary external state. Our holding a space of not knowing allows clients time to slow down and integrate their rational and intuitive thoughts. They learn to keep their mind open and engaged. They learn to tolerate an internal state of confusion without acting until their inner knower provides direction, often through intuitive insight.

To live fully, people need to subordinate their habituated mind to an open mind. Children open up to daily life with curiosity. For awareness and inclusiveness, those with child-like receptivity and wonder can connect rationality with perception and feeling. By remaining in the present moment, they free themselves from past prejudices and future projections. Energetic Coaches challenge clients to examine and discard unproductive, ingrained thinking patterns, worldviews and beliefs in favor of open mindedness. The habituated mind slowly gives way to allow creative sparks of insight to think outside of the box.

Individuals who consciously observe their thoughts, such as in a meditative state, often find their thinking to be undisciplined, unintentional, distracting, and negative. Some use meditation to calm the "monkey mind," as the chaotic mental state is sometimes called. Once people observe their thoughts with detachment, they can make conscious choices to reframe negative thoughts and resist wasting energy on them. Energetic Coaches provide an example for clients by observing habits of thought that go behind the words, feelings, and physical reactions of clients. In the coaching moment, we flush out distracting or negative thinking patterns for examination and possible revision.

Through conscious choice, people increase their personal power. They connect with spirit by only observing negative thoughts, creating positive thoughts, or letting go of thoughts entirely. The space between thoughts, where spirit awaits, is the experience of integration and oneness. Observing thoughts without attachment to them makes room for the inner knower to come through. People connect with spirit when they give attention to their inner knower.

The thinking body contains the story or subtext people have about themselves as an individual. For many the subtext is negative or egocentric. They may say about their physical body, "I'm not attractive." An example of a negative emotional subtext is "That's too risky. It frightens me." A negative mental subtext might be "I'm not qualified to take on that subject." People can use the thinking body to create positive subtexts instead, inviting spirit as an ally to reframe self-defeating thoughts into possibilities. Energetic Coaching taps into guidance from spirit through the inner knower to create more powerful and positive perspectives. Energetic Coaches recognize negative thinking and share positive energy with clients. Because coaching seeks to diminish negative belief patterns and emphasizes positive constructs and language, clients gain energy. As they identify mental blocks to spiritual energy and power, clients can choose to replace them with constructive, valid, and productive thought patterns of both a rational and an intuitive nature.

Energetic Coaches pay attention to client language to discover underlying thought and belief patterns. They address expressions of negative thinking and invite clients to change their language when they speak to themselves. At every opportunity, we reflect negative self-talk and encourage clients to reframe it. Even though we focus toward the positive, we do not operate from a Pollyanna perspective. Difficulties and challenges require acknowledgement and empathy as well as appreciation for the opportunities for improvement they present. However, if clients speak and act from a negative self-perception and worldview (one is usually a reflection of the other), coaches can help them to choose positive thinking instead. Changing negative thought patterns, the way they perceive a situation, or the attitude toward it may be all clients can do about a certain situation. But in this change, they take a huge step since the inner intent is much more powerful than the external influence. By exercising their thinking body with conscious choice, clients can turn their focus to where it can do the most good—within as a positive intention.

PHYSICAL-EMOTIONAL-MENTAL INTEGRATION

The mental, emotional, and physical bodies operate together to create human experience at the micro level. Spirit joins at the macro level of interaction in which physical-emotional-mental bodies become whole. Energetic Coaches, aware of the concurrent micro and macro levels, help clients tap into all levels at once. We give equal weight to the inner and outer aspects of each of the three bodies. Connecting the sides of an equilateral triangle that spins congruently in all directions creates the spiritual sphere. If we discern that the three sides are disconnected or unequal, we can encourage our clients to balance and integrate the three levels into oneness.

Lea: *I am what is called a "neck-up" person, someone with a strong intellect nurtured and rewarded from early on. I became aware I was out of sync with my physical and emotional aspects when I enrolled as a coaching client. There were meetings in which emotions would sweep over me. Even though I was caught off guard, my coach John kept me grounded. He knew to go to my intellectual safe place and then return to my emotions and physical sensations. Had we explored my emotions and physical reactions without my intellect, I could not have integrated the whole of my experience. I had been leaving parts of me out of awareness. Energetic Coaching provided an opening for me to leverage my inner knowing so I could remove the blocks I had created with my outer orientation and denial of feelings.*

Physical practice provides fertile soil for spirit to grow. Such practice may include meditating, prayer, deep breathing, focused bodywork, and any other actions that create high-level energy. Emotional practice involves loving—acting and speaking congruently with intentional love. Seeds that people plant with love bear spiritual fruit. Mental practice grows spirit through choosing thoughts. Especially during difficult times, turning thoughts from negative to positive creates personal power. Through appreciation of the way things are, people gain balance and perspective. Weeding out negative thought patterns helps people connect and grow with spirit. People often embark on well-intentioned actions to improve themselves and the world. However, without love for what they are doing, they tend to lose energy for their endeavors. In like manner, without the personal practice to nurture and renew, some may find it difficult to sustain love and appreciation. Creating love and appreciation with physical practice builds energy. Choosing physical, mental, and emotional means to align with spirit creates congruent and authentic language and action.

People's physical, emotional, and mental subtexts affect one another. Their experience on the physical level affects their mind and emotions. Thought affects the physical and emotional bodies. Emotion affects the physical and mental bodies. People can choose what affects them and how. Energetic Coaches help their clients integrate the three states into one by finding ways to balance each aspect as the opportunity arises. Just as the energized electron leaps from a lower shell to a higher one, a person who never stops learning and growing increases energy. Personal congruence, integration and balance are an ongoing process that create authenticity and integrity for greater wholeness.

THE INDIVIDUAL IN RELATIONSHIP

Imagine three layers of concentric circles containing the embedded triad of physical, emotional, and mental aspects within the overall sphere of oneness. The three levels of interactions that take place in relationship are:

1. The individual in relationship with self (inner and outer).
2. The self in relationship with other (inner and outer).
3. The self in relationship with community (inner and outer).

congruent relationships

The three levels of relationship interact concurrently. Physical, mental, and emotional experiences are aspects of each of the spheres of relationship. There are also aspects of inner being in relationship with outer doing. As people integrate each dimension of physical, mental, and emotional with self, other, and community from inner and outer perspectives, the different aspects become reflections of one another. As the reflections come into congruence and balance, all aspects form a hologram, mirroring and reflecting one another.

Oftentimes, people do not know their relationship with themselves. Even though there do not appear to be two entities, a closer look reveals that vital and important relationships exist between spirit and ego and between inner and outer selves. People's relationship with themselves is the most important relationship of all. Depending on how well they balance conflicting relationships within self and in relationships with others, they create or dissipate energy.

Reflective of the individual in relationship with self is self in relationship with other. One-on- one relationships provide the best mirror for people to know themselves. Self-knowledge is often the area of greatest individual difficulty and the most opportunity. Whereas people can operate singly or in the community without challenges to self-image and egocentric desires, their close one-on-one relationships provide the mirror and reflection needed for growth and spiritual connection. The quality of one-on-one relationships serves like an oscilloscope to measure frequency levels. If people need to work on themselves in order to grow (and we all do), the place to start often shows up in the problems and challenges of their closest one-on-one relationships, which most readily reflect their relationship with themselves.

The outer concentric circle is self in community, which encompasses all relationships that reflect and define a person within the tribe. People tend to identify themselves by their family unit, their organizations, their village, and their nation. Social constructionists hold that the external community creates individual identity through socialization and upbringing by the tribe's individuals consciously or unconsciously subscribing to behavioral norms and customs. People can best assess the pervasive effects of their culture after they encounter a different tribe with diverse customs and culture. Depending on their willingness to learn, they expand their worldview to include the entire human community. To achieve greatest personal knowledge and power, individuals can become aware of what is or is not authentic for them without rejecting the community or trying to change it. They can take responsibility for personal inner change and growth as the first step to creating relationships with others they desire.

RELATIONSHIPS MIRROR AND REFLECT SPIRIT

When people's relationship with others mirrors and reflects the same qualities that they want for themselves, they create congruent relationships. Through congruent relationships, people's connection with self and with others becomes seamless so that each is both separate and connected. Finite boundaries blur into infinite inclusiveness. Individuals experience what it is like to be one and One. The holographic nature of individual experience manifests as relationships mirror and reflect the people in them. Without losing their identity, people can experience close connection. In words attributed to Chief Seattle, "What is done to the web (of relationships) is done to the self." What benefits or detracts from the self benefits or detracts from the other and vice-versa. The Golden Rule becomes not just a law to be obeyed, but a way to experience personal growth and fulfillment.

Through congruence and equality in harmony with good intention, individuals create spiritual energy. When they choose positive relationships with self, other, and community, they align their centerpoint for spirit to spin the triad into an all-encompassing sphere. As they integrate and blur the boundaries among their emotional, mental, and physical bodies, their inner and outer selves, and their relationships with self and others, they experience the congruence and energy of oneness.

Coaching as a profession utilizes the mirror of relationships to serve clients by challenging disconnection between self and other and between inner and outer being and doing. Energetic Coaches know that the individual is not separate from context, so we focus on congruent relationships at various levels. The three parts of the triad represent the connected individual. Once individuals have achieved wholeness through inner and outer integration and congruence, they can connect with others in balance and congruence. Through oneness, each experiences equality with every other individual. Congruent Energetic Coaches serve as examples of such integration (although difficult to maintain as a static state). To the extent that clients listen to their inner knower (which sometimes shows up as their conscience), they remove barriers to balance and congruence.

To expand on the metaphor of the three-in-one, acting and interacting to form a sphere of oneness, imagine separate drops of water for each relationship—individual with self, individual with other, and individual with community. Next, imagine concentric waves emanating as each droplet falls into the ocean (Source). At the point of overlapping patterns from the separate drops, a "node" forms. If the droplets are not aligned, one wave will cancel another. If the drops of water land at exactly the same point, they compound their energy. Wave energy from a common core results in the exponentially magnified energy of harmonics.

Individuals with a common, cohesive intent (core values and vision) gather power from their relationships with self, other, and community. They experience the greatest force by targeting Source as the core, the origin of free will goodwill. Their "droplets" of good intention manifest through increased energy and congruence. By uniting the energy of good intention expanded into relationships with all others, people can create a huge waveform. Harmonic spiritual energy from the individual combines with the whole. Through connected relationships individuals have greater positive impact than each could create or experience alone. When people come together and dispel the illusion of separation from Source and from others, they increase their energy exponentially.

Individuals release exponential energy through common intention (being) and combined action (doing). On micro and macro levels they form strong connections in congruent relationships. Physical, mental, and emotional aspects unite through individual intention to align with core values. Inner being and outer doing reflect each another. In external relationships people experience others as reflections of self, not separate or superior or inferior. Relationships formed from a common core connect people and invite spirit. Having created harmonic energy, people become more powerful to make individual, institutional and worldwide changes for the better.

Through closely connected positive relationships, especially with the self, the inner knower comes forward. The small i of the ego recedes as self-identity, self-knowing, and self-respect replace doubts and insecurities. People emerging from the small, separating world of egocentric desires gain energy to form relationships with others on the same wavelength. It is no longer important to be the separate and superior rugged individualist to feed the small ego. Such an identity can never be complete. This becomes obvious when compared to the connected wholeness of being the one in One in a community of the all in All.

THREE LEVELS OF RELATIONSHIP

The qualities of relationships people have with themselves and others reflect the quality of their relationship with spirit. Energetic Coaches support positive and enhancing relationships with others and encourage clients to do the same. Because some may find it threatening to examine their relationships with themselves and others, Energetic Coaching offers a safe place to explore. We help clients build a positive relationship with themselves through examining gaps between what they desire and what they manifest. Then they examine gaps in relationships between the inner and outer self, the one-to-one other, and the community. In the process clients listen to their inner knower to guide them in reaching congruence and authenticity.

Even though the quality of a relationship is intangible, it is vitally important. The quality of relationships with self and others affects every aspect of human experience and contributes or detracts from personal well-being. In order for Energetic Coaches to aid clients in safely examining their relationships, we use qualitative measures. Martin Buber in his book I and Thou discerns that there are three kinds of relationships: I and it, I and you, and I and thou. In the "I and it" relationship people use each other solely for egocentric desires. Relationships progress to "you" when those involved see the other as separate and equal. The highest form of relationship with the other is "I and Thou," in which each treats the other as equal, connected, and respected.

- I and it: Separate and disconnected – egocentric – I-object
- I and you: Separate and equal – ego/spirit-centric – I-other
- I and thou: Separate and connected – spirit-centric – I-One

Correlating to Buber's description, Energetic Coaching describes the three relationship qualities as the I-object, I-other, and I-One. The three levels exist dynamically, often without conscious awareness. Once people have a framework for observing the qualities of their relationships with self and others, they can explore the gap between what they have and what they desire. We seek to help clients achieve more of the I-One quality of relationship with self and others.

Lea: When John and I first met for coaching, I sought a business relationship. I saw John as the object of my desires to achieve goals and obtain my purpose and satisfaction in life. Through the growth of our relationship, John and I learned to respect and value one another as individuals and see one another as part of the one. A feeling of connectedness evolved in which John and I received spiritual energy from our relationship. This dynamic can happen whenever people practice free will goodwill in relationship. Our relationship continues to grow in energy and connection as a result of our conscious intent to operate through the I-One relationship.

Creating the I-One relationship requires continual awareness and decision to act congruently. The closer people are with another, the more challenging for them to assess the quality of their relationship. There are employers who view employees only as objects to achieve profits and employees who use employers just for a paycheck. There are marriages in which the husband and wife see themselves as separate with no common ground, cohabitating but living in isolation. There are individuals who have little regard for their own life, spending it recklessly and without purpose. Once people discover that a relationship is less than the I-One relationship of equality and respect, they can act to improve it. They may have to make tough choices to bring congruence between what they say they want and what they do to get it or who they say they are and what they do to be that way. We act as compassionate witness for clients struggling to achieve the authenticity they desire in relationships through greater self-knowing.

Those who deliberately build relationships of oneness through congruent being and doing learn to subordinate self-centered desires for the benefit of the whole. They stop using political behavior and selfish manipulation as tactics. They have no egocentric compelling need to do so. Energetic Coaches serve others by shining the light on the superficial nature of external differences and focusing the laser within to the common ground of universal desires—to respect and be respected in relationship—to experience integration and oneness.

SPIRIT IN RELATIONSHIP

The path to spirit is the path of I-One in relationship. This I-One relationship creates a powerful energy that integrates all aspects of the individual, from within to without and then back within. Congruence among thoughts, feelings, and emotions manifests to integrate the self into the whole. The individual becomes the one-in-One. The person becomes spirit in action— "God doing." There is no discrepancy between who an individual is and what he or she says and does. Personal authenticity fosters trust in relationships, which grow in secure affinity almost effortlessly. When there is a discrepancy from the outside, the individuals can reconcile it by knowing themselves because they have connected inner knowing and outer doing. Whatever occurs on the outside they perceive realistically through their mirror within, which they use to grow and to act. Through Energetic Coaching clients increase their flexibility and decisiveness. they move consistently and congruently between internal being and external doing to invite spirit to their relationships.

Spirit arises most readily in the relationship with self. People who allow a discrepancy between who they are and what they want, and what they say and do, experience little of spirit. Internal struggle and incongruence between intention and action block spirit, producing feelings of separation, alienation, and loneliness. Even though spirit is in everything always (all ways), people struggling with themselves or with others, tend to disconnect from it. To the degree that people maintain congruent relationships—with the inner and the outer self, with significant others, and with the greater community—they flow with spiritual energy.

HUMAN "KIND" IN RELATIONSHIP

First there must be order and harmony within your own mind. Then this order will spread to your family, then to the community, and finally to your entire kingdom. Only then can you have peace and harmony.

CONFUCIUS

Energetic Coaching seeks to bring congruence to relationships, starting with the relationship people have with themselves. As the triad of inner-outer relationships with self, other, and community forms a sphere, the separating distinction between inner and outer and self and others melds. Energy radiates from inner congruence, reflected in relationships with others. Authenticity creates strong connections with self, others, and spirit. All become one in wholeness. Acceptance, respect, caring, and oneness naturally ensue. Energetic Coaching is a vehicle through which spirit can be expressed and experienced in relationship to put more kindness in human "kind."

CHAPTER 3 APPENDIX
SUMMARY

I believe in the absolute oneness of God and therefore also of humanity. What though we have many bodies? We have but one soul.
MAHATMA GANDHI

Individuals create spiritual energy from within through choice manifested in experience. The three levels of experience consist of the physical/perceiving, mental/thinking, and emotional/feeling micro and macro levels. Envision a triad embedded in a triad embedded in a triad. Each triad represents the individual in relationship from the micro (individual in relationship with self) to the macro (individual in relationship with others and with community). As people integrate inner intention and outer experience, they achieve wholeness. The sphere around the centerpoint within the individual in congruent relationship with self forms a common core of sustainable energy of I-One.

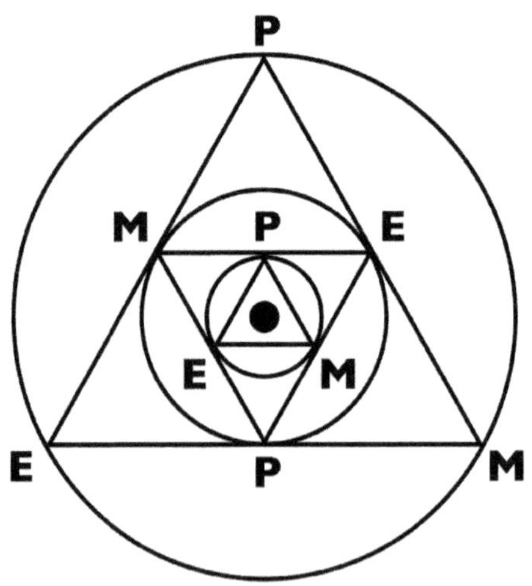

As individuals achieve congruence throughout relationships, from within and without, their embedded triads become embedded spheres.

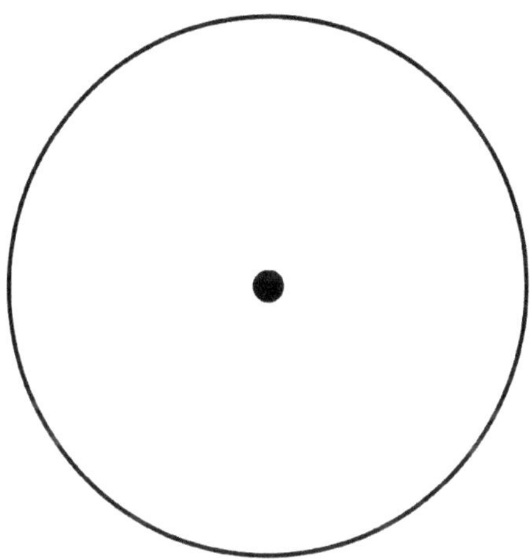

The embedded spheres become one around the common core. As individuals create energy by centering on spiritual values and vision, they experience congruent relationships with themselves, others, and their community at large. They increase their energy as they narrow the gap between themselves and others. The choice to create the desired inner invisible world of thoughts, feelings, and perceptions causes the outer visible world to align with what is wanted.

●

The sphere and the inner core, like a wave and a parti-cle, are separate *and* One. They appear different according to a person's focus. The sphere can contract to become a singular point of individual vision and values or expand to encompass all of the whole. Relationships mirror and reflect one another. People increase the sustainable energy of spirit with positive thoughts, feelings, and perceptions. Spirit is experienced through increasing energy and connection created by the physical, mental, and emotional experiences of I-One relationships. By integrating individual identities into inclusive Oneness, people create wholeness and connectedness. The one becomes One.

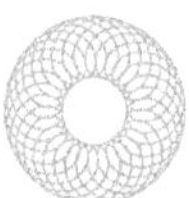

4. THE INDIVIDUAL IN RELATIONSHIP WITH SELF

Trust thyself: every heart vibrates to that inner string.
Ralph Waldo Emerson

We carry within us the wonders we seek without us.
Sir Thomas Browne

Energetic Coaching holds that the quality of relationship with self is the most important. It supports self-knowing, self-love and self-respect, affecting the quality of all other relationships. The relationship with self is most important and is also the relationship over which individuals have the most power. Many people subordinate their relationship with self to relationships with others because they tilt toward outer orientation. Energetic Coaches may ask clients to describe the relationship they have with themselves. Depending on their level of self-awareness, clients may reply with confusion, resistance, or amusement. The question may strike some as the most vital consideration of all. There is great benefit for people who are willing to self-reflect to get to know and love themselves. A positive, congruent relationship with self is as vital to the growth of human spirit as water is to the planted seed.

Because all other relationships mirror the relationship people have with themselves, the relationship with self is key to achieving wholeness. It may be, also, the most difficult to observe and discern. Because of socialization and learning through external cues and the intangible nature of the self, many people tend to focus on their relationships with others. Unless they maintain the type of relationship with self that they desire with another, they can readily lose themselves or subordinate their values and visions to the will of others. When people focus on the relationship with themselves, they put first things first to know themselves so they consistently express their authentic self in all relationships.

The period we live in has been called the Relationship Age because a giant leap in human understanding is taking place. People have begun to question the systems they belong to. They are no longer satisfied with answers to life's difficult questions offered by established institutions such as church, family, legal and political systems, and the media. When they desire healing, they find incomplete and unsatisfying the medical model that deifies the outsider as expert. Now, many are taking charge of their own health and well being. Putting their greatest faith in themselves, they are realizing that they can use external experts as instruments but the final authority comes from within.

As adults, people resist being told what to do. They want to live fully through conscious intention and choice. Those who desire growth relish the challenge of leaving their comfort zone. They realize the power that comes from taking charge. They decide how to respond rather than allow others to pull their strings. They are the cause and not the effect of life.

The seeking and finding taking place now is coming from within. Many people have discovered that there is more to life than their jobs and whatever else is taking place in the external world. Those who look for external validation in relating to others and the universe are coming away frustrated. They find little meaning on the outside. Some experiencing the shift in awareness and understanding are turning to Energetic Coaching for validation and reinforcement of their quest for self-empowerment, healing, meaning and wisdom.

The path to spirituality is a personal path. Those asking tough questions such as "What is life about?" and "What do I want?" can be pulled between external rewards and reinforcements and an inner voice saying, "This isn't it" or "This won't last long" or "This doesn't satisfy what I was seeking." Whether people achieve worldly success or not, if they disconnect from self, sooner or later they will have to acknowledge that something is missing. The external world is temporary; nothing in it lasts forever. Awareness of mortality reveals that the most important things cannot be wholly encompassed by earthly life. To the extent people do not choose to be guided by their values and visions, they lose energy through the gaps in wholeness created by the split within. Some will seek Energetic Coaches to listen to questions, hold the space for inner conflict, reflect their own voice of inner knowing, and challenge them to be true to themselves. We support and encourage clients' effort and struggle to help them build a close relationship with self.

Coaching usually involves focusing intention and energy on achieving external goals. Energetic Coaching includes visioning, goal setting, personal accountability, and commitment for outer accomplishments, but our main focus is on achieving inner satisfaction and sustainable energy. We know that satisfaction and sustainable energy come from within as people find identity, meaning, and connection. With purpose and values bigger than self, clients gain inner knowing and outer accomplishment.

Because of outer influences and pressures to assimilate, socialize, and conform, it is natural to experience a split between external demands and internal needs. That dichotomy can bring on inner conflict and self-denial. The tendency to seek answers to life's tough questions and personal satisfaction on the outside widens the gap. People need balance. Connecting with spirit to narrow the gap requires a subordination of outer answers and external explanations in favor of listening within. It is not enough to seek spirit; there must be a personal experience of it. Energetic Coaches can provide an external validation of clients' experience of the intangible. We support the close connection between self and spirit to create authentic relationships with others. Some people experiencing a disconnection between who they sense they are and what they experience externally think the world has gone mad. Often, to make sense of it means they have to sacrifice what they want. They feel pressure to compromise their ideals to fit an exterior mold. Those who question the rules are sometimes ostracized, labeled, and marginalized as troublemakers. Relationships with others reinforce the disconnection because those disconnected from self attract others in the same state. Such dynamics create a vicious cycle, where people lose energy by resisting. When a person turns inward to find personal power, detaching from the illusion of outer chaos, others in relationship may resist because their egocentric desires go wanting. Energetic Coaching provides the space and the perspective to remain on the path to individual wholeness and self-empowerment despite outer appearances and constraints and the selfish or manipulative desires of others.

THE I-ONE RELATIONSHIP WITH SELF

The intention of Energetic Coaching is to achieve congruence so clients have an I-One relationship with themselves through the inner/outer two becoming one. As the client's inner knower provides guidance to build congruence in being and doing from the inside out, spirit and ego cohabitate. There is no longer a need to judge others or resist what is, so ego is no longer a barrier to spiritual energy.

People have an I-object, I-other, or I-One relationship with self. In I-object or I-other relationships they experience a disconnection with the inner knower. When Energetic Coaches observe gaps between who clients are internally and what they present externally, we ask questions like these:

- If this is a priority, how much time during the week do you spend on it?
- If this relationship is important to you, what are you doing to show it?
- If this is what you want, what is keeping you from getting it?

By addressing inconsistencies between stated intentions and outer behavior, clients begin to challenge themselves to be authentic. Inner congruence closes the gap between the inner knower and the presenting self. As clients resolve internal and external conflicts, they regain lost energy to achieve their most valued objectives.

The I-One relationship provides a personal standard for congruence and integrity. As people align their outer presentation with their inner intention, others begin to notice a difference. Their outer actions represent their authentic inner being. The tree is known by its fruits. Energetic Coaches, through the compassionate witness, provide clients a safe, nonjudgmental reflection of inner and outer incongruence between being and doing. As clients address incongruence, they resolve the paradox for themselves. Clients empower themselves by realizing that what they experience outside, they have created first within.

I-One represents the ideal, never completely achieved once and for all. There will always be conflict with human nature, the limits and demands of the external world, and struggles with ego and the egocentric expectations of others. At times, such conflicts may appear overwhelming. Some may tire of seeking consciousness and congruence. Externally, the effort may create hardship and turmoil before the seed sprouts and bears fruit. To align with the inner self is the path to human growth and wholeness, but it is not usually the easy path.

The path may appear solitary and frightening if there is little support on the outside. Institutions and individuals who are vested in incongruence sense when others have stopped buying into their messages and influences. Even though Energetic Coaching itself is an external influence, the purpose is to support the client's inner resolve to seek personal congruence in the face of hardship and opposition when that happens.

While the external world applies pressure to conform, congruence beckons from within. Seekers have to focus on their goal. To help, their intention provides the invitation to connect with spirit. Energetic Coaches hold the space for clients' inner knower to remain congruent rather than succumb to external agendas. We help clients let go of unwanted influence so they can weigh options. Clients overcome resistance through acceptance. They free themselves to decide what to do from the balanced centerpoint of personal power guided by their inner knower.

The pseudo energy of resisting attracts some people. They criticize and condemn, don't like this and don't like that. They seem to thrive on battles, but theirs is only ego-energy. The I-One relationship means that people move beyond resistance to recognize what is on the outside. They see the false sense of superiority or control created by rejection and judgment. People in the oneness of congruence do not waste energy in rejection and resistance. Instead, they ask, "What can be done about this situation?" or "What good does that do?" They derive no satisfaction by feeling superior to others. From that perspective, the inner knower comes through, and those who listen find true power and control within.

The I-object and I-other relationships are based on separation in which the individual perceives another person or situation as a thing removed only objectively or subjectively in relationship with self. The I-One relationship perceives no separation of objectivity and subjectivity, only the oneness of mirror and reflection. Without separation people transcend outer influences to create their own powerful world within, choosing what to think, feel, and perceive to create more of what is wanted.

Over time with conscious intention, clients come to appreciate congruence between inner being and outer doing. External difficulties and tests prove commitment to I-One. As they determine their own path and maintain their purpose, clients realize that they choose how the outer world affects their inner self. To resolve ego conflicts, they conserve energy and achieve freedom and self-empowerment by opening to spirit. Unruffled by outer influences and circumstances, those with the greatest congruence have the greatest power because they close energy-draining gaps. Harkening to the voice of their inner knower, they move past their inner battles to a place of calm resolve.

SELF-EMPOWERMENT

There is nothing, no tragedy too great, no malady so incurable, that we cannot find something to counteract it if we do not forget to go within.

PARAMANANDA

Self-empowerment means people operate from within with choice over thoughts, emotions, and perceptions of the physical world. Those who operate from the separated I-object or I-other relationship allow themselves to be manipulated by external appearances and conditions, expectations, fears, and misperceptions. The puppeteers of unchallenged thoughts, emotions and perceptions triggered by external observations and events cause individuals to act in a stimulus-response mode. The saying "The mind is a wonderful servant but a terrible master" reflects the importance of directing inner thoughts with conscious intention and choice.

No one from the outside can bestow personal empowerment. There is a great deal written and discussed about empowering individuals and employees, but empowerment is something people choose for themselves. The best that the external world can do is to remove barriers, allowing people to create self-defined growth and empowerment. Energetic Coaches observe the level of personal power clients claim. Then we use every opportunity to turn their focus within to develop even greater personal power.

People achieve self-empowerment by consciously choosing authentic attitudes and perceptions and through refining inner thoughts and feelings. They can consciously create their thoughts and feelings to perceive and experience the outer world as a reflection of the inner. As Abe Lincoln observed, "Most people are about as happy as they make up their minds to be." Through a congruent I-One relationship with self, people invite spirit to inspire positive, high- level standards of behavior and values. They plant the seeds of positive intention for their external outcomes to reflect their internal desires.

Thoughts are things. Nothing is created without a prior thought. People can send their energy via feelings in any direction they desire. Because they are spiritual beings in a physical world, the connection of the inner self with spirit through the inner knower leads to wholeness. Ego ceases its boundary battles. Eventually, with practice and patience, what people experience in their inner and outer worlds reflects each other. As individuals resolve the gap between their sense of self and what they experience, they grow, bloom, and bear fruit they have co-created with spirit.

Thinking and feeling are subject to inner choice. Certainly, people tend to think positively or negatively based on external events and circumstances. Likewise, they can allow their connection with spirit to be influenced by their outer world. It is easier to experience spirit on a good day than a bad one. Different people perceive the same event differently. Despite the situation or the degree of difficulty, their commitment to keep the spiritual connection in each moment makes the difference. People need spiritual energy and connection most when circumstances seem difficult. Through consciously choosing a positive perspective in the face of adversity, people can test and strengthen their spiritual connection. Even though the current external situation may not be subject to immediate change, they create self-empowerment by choosing inner reactions.

Connecting with spirit means deciding to make thoughts and feelings congruent with the positive, sustainable energy of spirit. People align with spirit by aligning with their inner knower. Releasing egocentric desires to be separate and superior, they guide themselves by spiritual values such as goodness, appreciation, and love. Consciously connecting with spirit removes energy blocks. Despite outer circumstances, people experience self-empowerment through inner direction and decision.

The inner knower conducts spiritual energy. People separated from self have difficulty getting in touch with the inner knower. They struggle with internal issues. Sometimes they seem unaware of their own motives and intentions. Personal congruence between self and inner knower strengthens the spiritual connection. Those connected and integrated in an I-One relationsip with self experience their spiritual nature. People energized through spiritual experience and oneness experience authentic personal power. No one can influence or direct their thoughts, feelings, or perceptions without their conscious choice to allow it. Paradoxically, because they hold their power, they know how to allow the external to inform them without capitulating to its influence. They maintain the choice to incorporate what feels right to their inner knower. They don't need negative experiences to learn from; they can learn from observing the outcomes of decisions consciously or unconsciously made by others.

Personal empowerment begins with conscious choice. Free of external influences, people can choose to do something out of the desired being state. Empowered people no longer have to do anything. They know that they choose to work at a particular job, comply with society's laws, pay taxes, and even fulfill the expectations of others. They have replaced feelings of victimization, powerlessness, blame, and weakness with authentic personal power. These individuals are not a captain without a ship or a ship without a captain, neither able to navigate anywhere. They choose to live as captain and ship, able to travel unknown waters because the compass of the inner knower points the way.

ENERGETIC COACHING: THE INDIVIDUAL IN RELATIONSHIP WITH SELF

The world is a looking glass and gives back to every man the reflection of his own face.
WILLIAM MAKEPEACE THACKERAY

As we illustrated in Chapter 3, the common element in the metaphor of the Triad and the Sphere is the individual in relationship with others. The triad comprises mental, emotional, and physical aspects. The triad exists within the duality of the inner and outer selves, which people bring into congruence through their inner knower connecting with spirit. Choice in congress with spirit replace the little i of the isolated, egocentric individual with the large I of the congruent, integrated individual. Energetic Coaches continually seek inner-outer congruence in order to coach others to do the same. The I-One relationship transcends the conflict of duality and leads to integration. Energy is released.

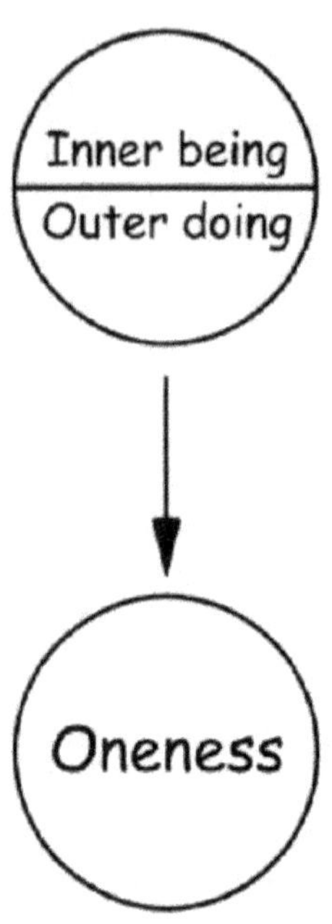

Inner being
Outer doing
Oneness
Inner Knower
outer self
inner self
being
doing
congruence
oneness
inner/outer
being/doing

We use the infinity sign, the reflective image of two circles joined at the center, to illustrate congruence through the centerpoint of the inner knower. People experience inner and outer worlds differently. Their"locus of control" indicates whether they tend to look inward or outward for how to behave or explain what has happened. A distorted infinity sign shows imbalance between the inner being and outer doing. Most overemphasize outer doing at the expense of inner being, probably because the five physical senses orient outward and society makes demands. Opening to the inner knower provides perceptual abilities beyond the physical senses. Spirit speaks quietly and does not oppose individual free will or impose its own will. People have to choose to give the inner being weight to balance outer doing. In balance, the inner and outer reflect one another so that the infinity sign can fold into itself as a single sphere, rendering each person an individual and a part of the whole One.

Here is an example of achieving balance in the realm of healthcare. People can consider the externally oriented healer of the medical model and the internally oriented healer of their inner knower. Though relatively new to the Western world, Easterners have used the combination for ages. An integrative approach engages and empowers people to take responsibility for their own healing, using external experts as consciously chosen instruments. The internal expert of the inner knower makes the call after weighing input from others.

People experience spirit internally through thoughts, emotions, and intuitive feelings and externally through synchronistic and meaningful events. Because the external self reflects the inner self, individuals create and attract experiences that match their inner state. The point of greatest individual power is in creating the outer reflection of experiences through inner intention. Energetic Coaches help clients choose congruence to unblock energy channels. Inner emphasis counterbalances the outer influence of the external world. Most people perceive the external as something separate and powerful. Those who orient toward the external world risk stimulus/response behavior. Giving weight to outer influences reduces the intrinsic power of the individual. We redirect focus on the inner, intangible being. Then clients can act in accordance with inner values and vision. They remain stable yet open to learning even as the external world changes perpetually.

THE LARGE I OF INTEGRATION

Out of clutter, find simplicity. From discord, find harmony.
In the middle of difficulty lies opportunity.
ALBERT EINSTEIN

Intention, which arises consciously or unconsciously from within, can serve ego or spirit. Energetic Coaches help clients determine whether their intentions connect, equalize, and empower (spirit-centric) or separate, judge, and deplete (ego-centric).

People issue an invitation to spirit when they choose to align with their values guided by the inner knower. Spirit awaits invitation because it cannot oppose or impose.

When people transition from the internal to the external, they turn intention into action (doing). When they act in congruence with their essence, they invite a connection with spirit and experience integration. Through spiritual connection and self-empowerment, they grow from responders to initiators. As they dispel the illusion of separation, they dissolve duality into the reality of oneness. When the power of intent to invite spirit and initiate action result in integration, the individual universe within connects to the universe at large. The three Is of intent, invitation, and initiative move the little i of the egocentric self to the large I of the spirit-centric self. In Energetic Coaching we use the following formula to illustrate the integration process:

INTENT (ALIGNED WITH INNER BEING) X INVITATION (TO SPIRIT) X INITIATIVE (CATALYST FOR OUTER DOING) = INTEGRATION (ONENESS)

THE CONTINUOUS PROCESS OF INNER-OUTER CONGRUENCE

When the inner knower connects people with spirit, the process leads to wholeness (holi- ness). In the mode of compassionate witness, Energetic Coaches maintain objective awareness of the present with clients. We invite spirit by being open to wisdom that we can bring to bear on any situation at any moment. Openness is the state of being that accepts the way things are. We know that clients have the answers within. Because we accept what they bring to the surface, clients can listen to their inner knower safely to gain congruence.

John: *My primary mode for accessing information is visual. I see spirit perched on my right shoulder in the role of observer-compassionate witness of all that is taking place in a coaching meeting. While I am fully engaged in discussion, the observer part of me is catching every nuance of my client's actions and state. As long as I keep that channel of information open, I have a steady flow of insights to work from. I can interact from my compassionate witness through my inner knower free from judgment or self-monitoring. I have come to respect the integrity of spirit acting through me, especially at those times when my rational mind starts to search for the right thing to say or do. The neat aspect of the compassionate witness meta-cognitive state is that it works in harmony with the rational mind by balancing input without ego. Spirit automatically arises as I think objectively, feel compassionately, and behave congruently with the wisdom and guidance of my inner knower.*

Through coaching, clients visualize and realize their life purpose. Living on purpose creates energy, which they can convey and share with others. They increase their upward spiral of energy as they choose to connect with others and spirit. Energetic Coaches exercise choice over thoughts, emotions, and actions. We aim to select what to think, feel, and do. Slowly and imperceptibly, the exterior illusory world and the egocentric self become less powerful and imposing as we experience strength and integrity. The vast internal world expands and evolves into oneness within and without. The process never ends. People ever and always grow or must wither and lose life energy, for that is the dynamic of nature.

In the infinity sign analogy, the centerpoint of the inner knower connects inner and outer worlds equally. Complete integration results in coming so enveloped with spirit that the individual cannot be separated from it: individuals join something huge. Ending duality, incongruence becomes congruence, inner and outer worlds come together, self-consciousness merges with spirit, the one becomes the One.

Both sides of the infinity sign expand from the centerpoint of the inner knower, the conjunction with spirit. In order to experience spiritual connection, people choose balance at the center. Achieving inner and outer balance reconciles the duality of apparent opposing forces. Inner and outer selves turn inside out. As the inner and the outer reflect each other, individuals interact with others with personal authenticity. The infinity sign melds into a single sphere as they balance at the centerpoint of inner knowing. From their balance point people can observe the wild pendulum swings of polarity created by egocentric separation. Congruent people free themselves from passing judgment to transcend the polarity that hides the reality of oneness. The pendulum stills at the balanced center.

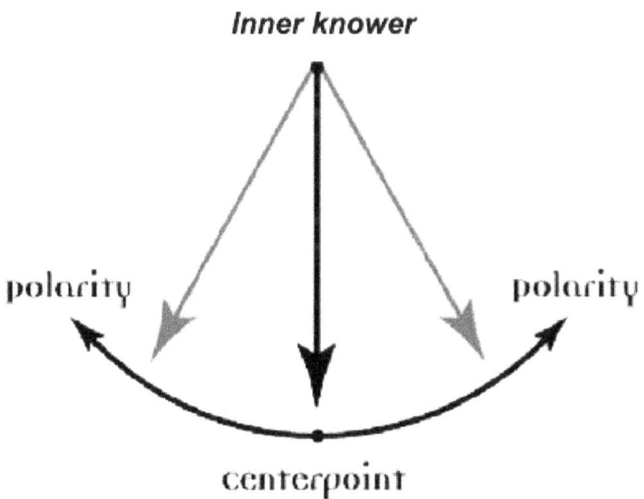

POLARITY: CHOICES AWAY FROM SPIRIT	CENTERPOINT: CHOICES CLOSE TO SPIRIT
(Negative energy low vibration)	(Positive energy high vibration)
Ego	Spirit
Fear	Love
Separation	Connection
Condemnation	Forgiveness
Judgment	Nonjudgment
Superiority/Inferiority	Equality
War	Peace
Unconscious or Bad Intent	Good Intent
Hurt	Healing
Stimulus-Response	Initiator
Scattered	Integrated

Lea: *In grade school, we learned about opposites. I thought opposites were totally unrelated. Now I realize that opposites are part of a continuum of energy, where darkness is the absence of light and contrasts of black and white morph into shades of gray. How can there be duality when one aspect of experience cannot exist without the other? Now I see that even though the coin has two sides, it is the same coin whether it shows heads or tails.*

THE PUSH/PULL OF POLARITY

Yin and yang, male and female, strong and weak, rigid and tender, heaven and earth, light and darkness, thunder and lightening, cold and warmth, good and evil...the interplay of opposite principles constitutes the universe.

CONFUCIUS

In the external world of duality there appears to be a conflict of opposing forces. As a result, people tend to label and categorize things and situations with evaluations such as good/bad, like/dislike, love/detest, care/don't care. For openness and acceptance of what presents itself in coaching meetings, Energetic Coaches seek balance in the push/pull of polarity. When people take a polarized stand and pass judgment on a particular trait, characteristic, situation, or value, they dissipate their energy by separating and disconnecting. For instance, if taken to the extreme of polarity, each of the polarities below has positive and negative aspects. Integrated, they are two-sided coins:

- Objective/Subjective
- External/Internal
- Male/Female
- More/Less
- Growing/Burning
- One/Many
- Outer orientation/Inner orientation
- Sorrow/Joy
- Difficulty/Ease
- Individual/Other
- Macrocosm/Microcosm

Most people tend to attach to enjoyable states or traits such as pleasure and to reject others such as sorrow. Holding things as opposites creates an artificial separation and tension between the elements. Releasing judgment allows valuation of each to equalize and incorporate both. The poles depend on each other for existence. Both have value, although one state may be easier to live in than the other. Holding similar views about worldly matters allows people to transcend the ego-dominated state of separation and duality. As they resolve apparent dichotomies to integrate the push/pull of polarity, individuals lose the resistance of judgment and open to spiritual connection.

It is a natural human tendency for people to separate and judge until they realize that what they reject on the outside reflects what they reject on the inside. Through perceiving the unwanted situation or characteristic as an opportunity to self-reflect and grow, they can transform old dualities into new concepts. Accepting opposites as equals leads to the inclusivity of wholeness.

Acceptance and appreciation of the way things are balances at the centerpoint. Resistance wastes energy. Accepting apparent dichotomies of life releases energy for what people want. Redirecting energy is like turning up the heat in an atom; it increases the vibration. At the activation point the electron jumps to a higher shell. When individuals balance at the centerpoint, they create an activation point for jumping. Experiencing life at the centerpoint, or"middle way," establishes a dynamic balance of potentially polarizing forces. Without judgment of the way things are, Energetic Coaches encourage clients to envision what they want. By the act of envisioning without judgment, clients raise their energy to attract what they want. Like vibrating electrons, they become energized and leap to a higher energy state.

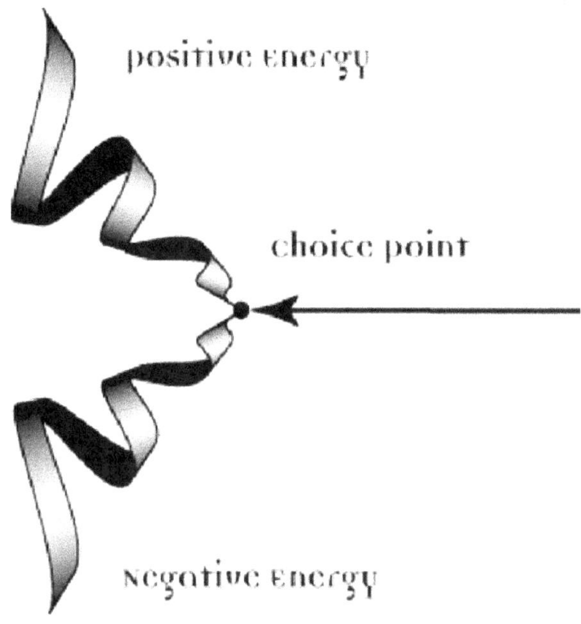

Consciously choosing inner thoughts, feelings, and perceptions creates the *POW* in POWER, which originates from within. We use the acronym *POW* to illustrate the process of choosing to align with the inner knower.

PERCEPTION (ACCEPTANCE AND APPRECIATION OF APPARENT OPPOSITES) X ONENESS (RESULT OF RESOLVING DUALITY TO REMAIN AT THE CENTERPOINT OF INCLUSIVENESS) = WITNESS (SEEING AND BEING IN THE META-COGNITIVE STATE) = POW

Energetic Coaches use their being as a tool. We project equality, acceptance, and appreciation for how things are. With the spirit of oneness to transcend duality, we automatically take the stance of witness. We model what it is like to be free of the push/pull polarity of apparent duality, free from judgment and separation. Inviting spirit with the stance of the compassionate witness, we help clients connect and open to their inner knower. The acceptance and authenticity we model helps clients gain balance and integration through letting go of judgment and separation.

LETTING GO

In the end these things matter most: How well did you love? How fully did you love? How deeply did you learn to let go?
BUDDHA

John: *"Letting go" is a term most of us are familiar with. In a recent coaching meeting a client asked me how letting go could be positively stated in coaching. Her concern was that if she let go, what would she have? I shared that I let go of my attachment to the specific result while holding on loosely to my visions of desired outcomes. This allows the work of spirit to be present in the form of creativity and openness to new ideas. Letting go allows something more to happen, often beyond my best expectation.*

Resistance focuses energy on what people don't want. When they oppose, they lose energy that could be used to attract what they do want. To activate energy, Energetic Coaches use powerful questions as catalysts, such as "What is your payback for staying stuck?" and "What do you want instead?"Answering truthfully allows clients to let go of their resistance and redirect their energy. Even though the current trait or state may not change noticeably immediately, clients gain energy by visualizing and co-creating possibilities with spirit.

People can transform their reality by learning how to be an open witness. Oneness is not a static state that can be achieved once and for all. Oneness is a dynamic balance continually available by reconciling opposing forces and ascending to the next level of vibration. In oneness the individual achieves identity and connection within (through the I-One relationship internally as authentic being) with individuation and connection without (through the I-One relationship externally as authentic doing).

To achieve wholeness, people must embrace all aspects of life experience, especially the push and pull of polarity. When they still the pendulum, they release energy to vibrate up. The illusion of being separate and unconnected comes from the egocentric belief system that this or that is either good or bad. Disconnection by making judgments creates the downward spiral of diffused, depleting energy. People create positive energy by letting go of estimations of good or bad and remaining with how things are. The lessons and opportunities for growth lie in the painful as well as in the joyful experiences of life. Most often the painful experiences offer more opportunity to grow. In nature, shadow and light achieve perfect cohabitation. Both pain and joy have benefits, but pain usually offers the larger lessons and serves as the greater catalyst to higher energy if it can be used in a positive way. Of course, reframing pain can be challenging.

Lea: *My friend, Michael, is the happiest person I know. He has a zest for living a long life (he says he is older than dirt). You wouldn't think he would be so joyful. Orphaned as a child, he was abused by his caretakers. He lost his wife, the love of his life, and I know he continues to miss her after many years. Still, Michael remains cheerful. He admitted that he was so consistently positive and upbeat that some people thought he was daft. When I asked him what the key was to his deep-rooted happiness, he said, "Ahhh...when you learn how to turn pain into joy...there you have the key." I continue to struggle to apply this truth that, little by little, I am only beginning to understand.*

To become whole and to experience fully requires letting go of ideas of perfection, attachment to outcomes, resistance to what is present, and desire for the static state of the comfort zone. To experience and accept the continuum of opposites with a willingness to change moves the inner state of the individual into dynamic balance at the centerpoint. Wholeness requires a state that is free of judgment and rejection or desire and attachment. Connecting with nonjudgment and acceptance for all that is releases positive energy. People create openings for spirit when they let go, accept, then let go again.

NON-ATTACHMENT

It is human nature to want. Motivation stems from desire but wanes when the desire achieved is external, such as money, status, or power over others. Everything that is external is temporary and ultimately unsatisfying. Once achieved, people must want something else to keep the pseudo- energy moving. Once gratified, they require more and more to maintain their sense of satisfaction. However, Energetic Coaching does not aim to help clients free themselves from desires for external outcomes. External outcomes are byproducts of internal intention and choice. Spirit desires for individuals what they desire for themselves. The inner knower leads the way. To co-create with spirit, people hear, feel, and visualize their desired outcome internally without needing external proof. Spirit does not need the details, only the purposeful intention. For instance, spirit does not respond to wanting money; whereas, those desiring to experience abundance with good intention (vs. selfish desire) move with spirit to create prosperity.

If people have an attachment to exactly what they want externally, their attachment limits spiritual energy. Through the push/pull polarity of the outer world, people tend to attach to specific externals. Out-of-balance external orientation and attachment can result in over- consumption, depression, addictions, extreme competitiveness, and other separating and self- destructive behaviors.

Non-attachment is choosing to allow "this or something better." Non-attachment means that people invite spirit to co-create and then open to what manifests. While they may have desires, they consider life an opportunity to grow in spiritual connection. Detachment, on the other hand, means abdicating personal responsibility for visioning and co-creating what is desired. Those who detach disconnect the flow of spiritual energy. They often appear lifeless, uncaring automatons, unaware of their potential as powerful conduits of energy.

Helen Keller observed that too often people focus on the door that is closed rather than the window that is open. Conscious intention and choice with non-attachment create a window for spirit. When people use visions and affirmations to seek and ask, they invoke the energy of attraction. Instead of being "anti" (such as anti-war), they become "pro" (such as pro-peace).

Asking is important in order to advocate for something. As a counterweight to the tangible, people use faith to keep going while they are manifesting their dreams. Although they lack the results they desire now, they can see, think, and feel outcomes not yet achieved. Faith frees spirit to create beyond imagination in small and large ways.

THE UNMANAGED EGO

"May my external possissions not be at war with what is within."
SOCRATES

Ego likes to dictate details. If people give their ego free rein, spiritual connection is blocked. Ego has beneficial aspects as well as detrimental ones. On balance, ego creates a sense of selfhood that empowers people externally. Those who know themselves have a healthy sense of ego; they appreciate their own special gifts. Ego provides a distinct identity and personality. Like that of a snowflake buried in a snowdrift, it keeps people from becoming lost in the faceless mass of humanity. A sense of uniqueness and selfhood protects individuals from caving in to selfish others by preserving important boundaries. Those with healthy egos can differentiate between what belongs to them and what belongs to others. They can accept their own worth without measuring themselves against others. Ego awareness is a valuable tool for making choices to establish congruence between the inner and outer selves. It allows people to focus within and open to how things are. Ego in balance means that people welcome information from a flexible worldview. Intact and confident of challenges, they can make personal changes or necessary apologies. They can allow themselves to be of service to others without self-sacrifice. They can serve a high cause without requiring recognition or reward.

People who are threatened and separated from the greater whole have an "easing God out" form of ego. Fragile egos cause people to be inflexible and fearful of what does not fit their fixed worldview or belief system. Separation and judgments of an unmanaged ego create judgments of superiority or inferiority and block spiritual connection. People with unmanaged egos have an insatiable appetite for external status and goods. Unlike spiritual energy, egocentric energy is not sustainable. Ultimately, it destroys, as evidenced by the rapid depletion of the earth's resources and the exploitation of the weak by the powerful for personal gain. The widening gap between the haves and the have-nots through egocentric accumulation without sharing cannot continue as history has shown.

People with unmanaged egos fabricate an external identity, which they attempt to control. The ego of the small self cannot tolerate the conflict between the voice of the inner knower and information from others. The small self meets any challenge to its ego with retaliation, criticism, rationalizations, and resistance. The unmanaged ego, with its tendency to blame and find fault, creates the illusion of victimization and powerlessness over outside circumstances. The tendency to criticize, judge and assume superiority shields a false sense of an inflated or inadequate self. There are always comparisons to be made to reinforce feelings of inferiority or superiority. People with unmanaged egos look to everyone and everything but themselves for reasons why their lives do not work. Those who blame others also blame themselves, so the vicious cycle of I-object relationships continue to increase separation and judgment within the self and with others.

Unmanaged egotism gives rise to materialism and trivialization of life. It takes the focus away from the inner realm, silencing the conscience and the voice of the inner knower. People seeking outer proof of self-worth disconnect from others by passing judgment on them. The more they tilt toward unmanaged, unopposed, and undisciplined ego, the less connection they have with spirit and its life-force energy. As individuals become defiant and fragmented, they increase their need to prove themselves to themselves and to others. The societal cult of personality artificially feeds into the unconnected and superior self, resulting in inner lack despite outer abundance. To compensate for what they are missing, many people seek status and acquisitions. The quest for external gratification spins out of control until the person loses touch with the source of the growing disconnection. Those with the most external goods (if acquired because of the need for external proof of superiority) have difficulty in forming close relationships with self, spirit, and others. If they form relationships, it is because the other is a reflection of their own external orientation and unmanaged ego. Such people require unspoken collusion with one another to maintain a superficial relationship that would fail if the stockpile of things were gone. The trophy wife, the sugar daddy, and the perfect children serve as symbols of status rather than humans to be loved and appreciated. People become objects to possess and show off just like all the other stuff that is accumulated without meaning.

In contrast, people with an internally managed ego seek relationships based on inner traits and values. They are not easily impressed with money and status, because they know that what is external is temporary and in itself ultimately dissatisfying. Self-empowered people manage their egos to maintain a positive perspective, seeking to connect with the external world and others through their positive attributes and inner values. Individuals with inner-outer congruence of the I-One relationship with self enjoy a connection with spirit. They recognize and manage their own egocentric tendencies to separate and evaluate. Their power is real and sustainable because it does not depend on external validation, acquisition or control. When they identify a tendency to project externally what needs to be dealt with internally, they go within for guidance from spirit through the inner knower. No longer stimulus-response beings, they self- reflect to find and bring forward their personal power.

Ego Confrontation

Energetic Coaches must manage their own ego. Through our own discipline and practice, we gain experience to help our coaching clients deal with theirs.

John: I am aware of how my ego gets involved in almost every aspect of my relationships. As a recent example, I have been involved in the personal coach accreditation process through the International Coach Federation. Another Master Certified Coach and I worked together to certify a coach. When we ran into some challenges, I realized that we had to deal with many variables. There was the impact of culture, language, and perception because the applicant was from another country, and there were the differences in perceptions of the ICF competency requirements between the other evaluator and me. In addition, ICF requested that we speed the credentialing process. I doubted that we could meet their deadline. My ego sprang to the surface at the ICF response, "Well, see what you can do." Once I recognized my indignation and stress, I turned to spirit to help me get my ego back in check. As a result, I called on good intention to preside over my ego, and the other coach and I completed the certification process within the requested deadline.

Energetic Coaches mirror for clients how to reflect on the results of their ego's self-protective and self-promoting tendencies. We encourage clients to look at what is working and what is not. When they respond to the world from an unmanaged ego, we have the delicate task to serve as a compassionate witness. External trappings of success do not sway Energetic Coaches. Some clients may find what is reflected by the mirror to be the clear view that they need to see parts of themselves that they had been rejecting or repressing. Those with unmanaged egos often have relationships with others who collude with them to maintain an outer, separate and judgmental orientation. Sometimes they surround themselves with people who do not dare confront them for fear of rebuttal, rejection, or recrimination. Energetic Coaching may be the only relationship to provide nonjudgmental space for individuals to look within, freed from the feared consequences they may have dished out to others.

Energetic Coaches need to recognize and work with ego defense mechanisms. How unformed or unmanaged clients' egos are predicts the amount of opposition clients may pose during initial phases of coaching. We must have a strong sense of self to the extent that clients can challenge and leave their coaching contract, even blaming the coach. We must be willing to take the risk of letting go of clients and anticipated income in order to remain true to our inner selves. It is with extreme caring that we approach clients who have not experienced ego boundaries. The relationship must remain safe and accepting so that the client can take a good look in the mirror. Energetic Coaches commit to continual self-evaluation to balance ego and inner knowing. The knowing of self with acceptance and appreciation helps people to stop wasting energy on defensive and retaliatory thinking and behaving. Those with a strong sense of self-worth free themselves of unfounded assumptions others may have projected onto them because of their own inner conflict and ignorance. With objective and compassionate confrontation, the client's ego stays bounded and balanced, releasing energy trapped by the need to continually self-justify, defend, dominate, or submit (yes, some people are invested in being inferior to others as a form of control). Through learning to explore and confront themselves, clients begin to contain their egos as they learn to manage their thoughts, feelings, and emotions. The ensuing self-discipline and empowerment changes the small i of the unmanaged ego to the large I of the whole person. As individuals come to know and appreciate who they are as loving and lovable, they integrate their ego with spirit. They dispel the resistance and opposition of self-centered intention and undisciplined thinking to release energy in ways that are positive and validating within and with others.

The healthy ego is a friend and protector. It is not a tyrannical controller and defensive embattled guardian against other people and outer situations. With ego intact and fulfilled from within through positive intention, people have no need to expand their territories or take advantage of others. The integrated ego does not need external recognition, reinforcement or material gain for self-gratification. The wholeness of the world within them fulfills them.

Working with exposed egos requires delicacy and skill. Energetic Coaches know balance builds personal congruence. Clients with unmanaged egos may attempt to co-opt coaches in the same way they co-opt others. Once coaches realize that the clients seek control or co-dependence, our inner knower stops the game. We as compassionate witnesses will hold the safe space for the clients to turn within to challenge and confront their own egos. That exercise enables clients to learn how to balance their ego from within, which leads to self-empowerment and self-knowing. Through freedom from the incessant fears and demands of the unmanaged ego, clients find inner peace. Energetic Coaches serve others in confronting and managing their egos because we ourselves have no wish to play the external expert with power over others. We recognize through the inner knower when our own ego is getting in the way. We know we are worthwhile without testing our sense of self through others and outer circumstances. If clients want answers from the outside, Energetic Coaches turn them back within to listen to their own inner knower.

Coaches experience personal freedom by releasing the constant tug of ego demands. We do not maintain a necessity to out-perform due to insecurity. What others think of us does not ensnare us. Our confidence and composure mirror authenticity to clients and motivate them to find theirs. Energetic Coaches maintain balance and congruence so that clients can know the value of the growth and gratification that they can achieve with a managed ego. Because we have managed egos, we do not need or expect accolades or appreciation for our work. We can maintain our independence from others who are seeking external props for their insecure or inflated egos.

The Congruent Energetic Coach

Energetic Coaches do not act as external experts to answer clients' questions. Instead, we prefer holding mental not-knowing and conflicting emotions in an open space. We use clients' lack of clarity and direction as an opportunity to question and listen. In being free of an egocentric agenda, we create space and openness. Eventually, the plot will unfold and the pieces fall together (the work of spirit has been going on all along).

Energetic Coaches find coherence in letting go of intellectual conjugations and projections to focus on what we are experiencing in the moment. Our ability to be in open dialogue is as important as the content and results. When clients allow blocked or hidden information and emotions to surface, the coaching process resolves in a safe and relaxed way. Clients get a deep sense of knowing in answering their own questions. We can model how to hold the uneasy space of questioning, how to let go of expectations, and how to wait outside the comfort zone. We aspire to meet, challenge and question with calm assurance that all things work together for the good.

Energetic Coaches operate at the inner level of relationship with self and an outer level of relationship with clients simultaneously. We maintain congruence in language and actions. Our ability to acknowledge and integrate polar forces and be in the moment without judgment and with positive intention creates the compassionate witness. The compassionate witness provides a safe mirror for reflection and introspection by clients. We know the external world is a reflection of the inner world and that consciously or unconsciously individuals decide their own frequency of interaction. We pick up on multiple paradoxical frequencies within others and ourselves, fine tuning self to the desired frequency and sending the signal for the client to hone into congruence. Congruence from within creates an energizing, expanding spiral of inclusiveness and wholeness in which inner and outer, ego and spirit, dark and light, self and other become one.

Those in congruent relationships (self with self, self with other, and self with community) experience how the energy of spirit compels transcendence to high levels of being. Congruent relationship building is not the easy path, but it is the path of spirit. The whole person perceives difficulty or opposition as beneficial opportunities for growth, self-knowing, and acceptance. To realize individual self-empowerment requires people to seek congruence and inclusiveness. Over time, as they resolve their inner conflicts, individuals choose congruence automatically. They free themselves of attachments and aversions, arriving at inner wholeness that even the insatiable ego recognizes as complete.

The Compassionate Witness of the Energetic Coach

To be the compassionate witness, Energetic Coaches blend with the inner knower to the point of oneness. Through self-knowing and ego management, we align our actions with our intentions. Achieving inner and outer congruence is a spiritual journey that requires receptivity, learning, practice, and action. There are signposts on the path of spirituality to confirm the direction, but there is never a final arrival or destination. There is always learning, growth, awareness, effort, and inner reward along the way.

Through intention we engage our inner knower as an ongoing source of wisdom. As compassionate witnesses, we evoke clients' inner knower. When clients gain congruence with their inner knower, they connect with spirit.

The process of gaining spiritual connection is not a linear path but an in-the-moment decision to invite, be open and let go. There are signs to wholeness that provide reinforcement. People seeking spiritual connection open themselves to seeing the overarching reason for the constant push/pull of egocentric and spirit-centric intentions. Before choosing action, they weigh options with their inner knower to create congruent thoughts, words, and deeds. They develop a relationship with self based on personal integrity, self-respect, and self-love.

SIGNS OF SPIRITUAL GROWTH

Individuals express congruence from within and connection with spirit through the inner- knower in unique ways. Positive, respectful, empowering relationships with self and others demonstrate a sense of inner well-being.

Several people have developed psychometric instruments to document how spirituality contributes to salient life outcomes. One example is the Spiritual Transcendence Scale, (STS) developed by R. L. Piedmont. It appeared in the article "Does Spirituality Represent the Sixth Factor of Personality?" in 1999 in Journal of Personality. The scale consists of three categories: (1) Universality, or a belief in the unity and purpose of life; (2) Prayer Fulfillment, or the experience of the spiritual through prayer, meditation, etc.; and (3) Connectedness, represented by a sense of personal responsibility and close relationship with others and the world. The principles of Energetic Coaching include those three categories. As clients strive for connection and meaning and take personal responsibility for choices, Universality, Prayer Fulfillment, and Connectedness are experienced.

M. Scott Peck discusses four stages of spiritual growth in his book The Different Drum. People can flip among the stages throughout life. The first stage of spiritual growth, according to Peck, is chaotic and antisocial, representing ego-driven people, undisciplined in thoughts, feelings, and perceptions. Stage two is the formal, institutional stage, representing judgmental, legalistic, dogma-bound people who seek answers outside of themselves. The third stage is skeptical. Because of their resistance to institutions and external belief systems, people in stage three may become agnostic and individualistic. If the resulting disconnection results in too much dissatisfaction, people may seek Energetic Coaches for some degree of external support and validation as they search within for answers. People in the third stage seek inner truth and knowing. Any expert or guru who holds and bestows answers from the outside will not empower and satisfy those who want to proceed to the next stage. Stage four is mystical, in which people attain a congruent relationship with self and others and spiritual transcendence. Those in stage four are able to remain with the mystery, let go of the details, and immerse themselves in the whole while maintaining an intact identity. The internal and external become one.

With openness and intention people will recognize the signs of spiritual connection, growth and learning. Energetic Coaches facilitate and empower clients to adopt thoughts, feelings, and perceptions to support their quest. Energetic Coaches as the external other serve as examples of people on the same path, seeking answers from within and validating clients' seeking. Although external validation is not ultimately necessary, clients may ask for reinforcement along the way, especially when their travel is arduous. Some may find it helpful to have a coach to support their stepping outside the comfort zone as they revise their roles and relationships. Clients may ask for assistance to maintain their newfound independence and congruence when others resist the choices they have made to follow their inner knower.

The following examples of signs along the spiritual path are useful to give the client reinforcement to stay the course and continue learning and growing from within. The following examples describe external experiences of congruence, high consciousness; connectedness, balance, self-empowerment, and inner knowing that arise from within and are reflected without. The seven signposts along the spiritual path spell the acronym CHERISH, an excellent word to describe the characteristic of spiritual connection through inner knowing, values, and vision. In Energetic Coaching the active verb cherish means that we put high value on the relationship people have with self, with others, and with community. Cherishing combines the two powerful forces of love and gratitude. Energetic Coaches support clients in their cherishing themselves and others:

1. **C**ongruence: Reflects inner being in outer doing.
2. **H**igher Consciousness: Heightened awareness of the divine nature of life.
3. **E**xperience: Provides learning and validation of spiritual connection.
4. **R**elated Connections: Connects to all of life with a feeling of belonging.
5. **I**nner Knower: Connects with spirit and guides from within for the highest good.
6. **S**elective Choices: Intentionally chooses values and visions based on free will goodwill.
7. **H**oliness (Wholeness): Transcends from duality into oneness with balance and freedom.

Chapter 4 - Appendix 1

Signs of Individual Spiritual Growth

Below are examples of the external outcomes that people may experience as they connect with spirit through inner knowing. The descriptions we give can serve as tangible examples of inner connection, or people can use the scale before and after Energetic Coaching to measure spiritual growth.

Rating Scale: 4 = Experienced often
3 = Experienced periodically
2 = Experienced rarely
1 = Experienced never

Congruence

1. Ability to authentically respond appropriately and spontaneously from within to external events.
2. Personal integrity.
3. Outer actions that consistently reflect inner values and visions.
4. Internal focus on betterment, knowing that the external situation will follow.
5. Compelling desire to keep commitments and expectation that others will do the same.
6. Non-attachment to results and enjoyment of the process of learning with an emphasis on inner being rather than on outer doing.
7. Handling difficult situations with ease and confidence because of faith in self and the universe.

8. Ability to see through flattery and ego strokes from others with no jealousy or envy toward others.
9. Comfort in uncomfortable situations with no need to please or to impress others.
10. Self-confidence through self-knowing and acceptance.
11. Ability to relate with others consistently and authentically.
12. Inner peace and balance free of the push/pull of polarity and inner turmoil.

High Consciousness

1. Increasing energy and vitality through releasing worry and doubt.
2. Detachment to seeming chaos, knowing everything works together for good.
3. Clarity and reasoning to change mental focus; taking responsibility for choosing perceptions, attitudes, and feelings for the inner self.
4. Awareness of negative energy and detachment from it without resistance.
5. Replacing doubt with belief and fear with faith so there is a positive expectancy for the future.
6. Innate knowledge of boundaries between what is personal and what is other. Wisdom regarding sphere of influence and appropriate action to take or refrain from taking in each moment.
7. Distaste for and detachment from exploitive sex and violence, negative media programming, including sensationalist and fear-based news reporting and shows that trivialize the human condition.

8. Detachment from those who want to escalate or exaggerate a situation. No attraction to melodrama and projected fear or worry.
9. Awareness of subtle interactions and the quality of energy exchanges in the moment.
10. Ability to shift depleting energy to fulfilling thoughts, feelings, perceptions, and intentions.
11. Knowing that the small can be as important as the large; awareness that in the hologram of the universe, each is a reflection of the other.
12. Emphasizing the inner state to balance outer doing and achieving.

EXPERIENCE

1. Seeing the good in others and bringing it out in them.
2. Self-nurturing and being one's own best friend because of a desire to take good care of self.
3. Immediate, congruent, automatic, unselfconscious behavior. Ability to change and adapt in the moment while maintaining stable inner identity.
4. Ability to see outside circumstances as inner reflections and to act to change what is not desired, starting from within.
5. Replacing powerless victim thinking and blaming with personal responsibility, self- accountability, and self-motivation.
6. Responding to calls to service on an individual and collective basis in small and large ways to make a positive difference in the world.
7. Contributing without the desire for reward or recognition or an attachment to results and paybacks.

8. Seeing others as equals without judgment or evaluation and desiring fairness and justice in the world without a legalistic stance.
9. Giving and sharing with others reflecting the belief in universal abundance.
10. Laughing heartily and spontaneously, even in solitude and especially at self.
11. Using good manners and civility out of respect for others, despite the way they may behave.
12. Acting based on conscious internal listening and letting go versus external reacting and controlling.

RELATED CONNECTIONS

1. A deep caring, respect, and appreciation for self and others. Nonjudgment and compassion for those who face struggles and challenges.
2. Feelings of peacefulness and oneness with the world.
3. Conviction that there is divine connectedness, so the external is not separate or imperfect with a need to be changed or controlled.
4. Motivation to add positive energy to the world and become the change that is desired.
5. A sense of belonging by seeing, feeling, being, and doing from a perspective of relatedness.
6. Conscious creating in connection with the universe through positive intention and action.
7. Ability to appreciatively receive as well as give without attachment or expectation of a return.
8. Positive relationships with those who appear to be different without judgment or separation.

9. Ability to let go of relationships that create and spread negative energy.
10. Freedom from listening to or spreading gossip or negativity; ability to be around negative people without letting their attitude rub off.
11. Appreciation and acknowledgement that the beliefs and experiences of others are as legitimate, important, and meaningful as one's own.
12. Ability to see the mirror of self in others and avoid projections and perceptions that create false separations and the illusion of superiority or inferiority.

INNER KNOWER

1. Self-control and discipline with ease.
2. Awareness of the underlying divine order of life.
3. No need to win approval from others because guidance and validation is received from within.
4. A sense of infinite personal power that builds faith and diminishes fear.
5. Loss of the need for revenge or apology from others.
6. Understanding of the powerlessness behind negative thinking and negative behavior.
7. Intuition, truthful insights, positive direction from within and sense of going with the flow. Harmony prevails; serendipity abounds.
8. Self-confidence; no desire to influence, control, or justify self to others.
9. Ability to trust and give others the benefit of the doubt, not based on whether the other is trustworthy but because of self-trust.
10. Innate self-knowing and self-love, warts and all.

11. Capable of maintaining close relationships without losing self.
12. Ability to be open in the present moment within questions and without agendas.

SELECTIVE CHOICES

1. Detachment from thoughts, past experiences, relationships, material goods, and emotions that do no good.
2. Positive, diverse relationships that are mutually beneficial and complementary.
3. Ability to decide thoughts, feelings, perceptions, and emotions in the moment. No need to react in stimulus-response ways.
4. A focus on developing an optimistic attitude that provides renewing and sustaining energy from within despite outer circumstances.
5. Prioritizing according to a vision of positive intent and free will to create what is desired.
6. Decision-making based on internal values.
7. Dominion over habits with ability to change and moderate.
8. Satisfaction in getting rid of extraneous material things and letting go of attachments and addictions.
9. Ability to turn pain into joy over time by realizing that appreciation, strength, character, and self-respect come from meeting challenges and difficulties.
10. Eschewing foul language, demeaning nicknames, personal put-downs, sarcasm or dirty jokes.
11. Maintaining patience and serenity in the present moment with no need to react, retaliate, or force things to happen.

12. Seeing strength in humility, weakness in arrogance, and hurt in anger; initiating positive responses in the face of negative experiences.

HOLINESS (WHOLENESS):

1. Seeing that the external is a reflection of the internal with action taken to make the two one: a congruent mirror and reflection.
2. Ease of living based on faith and freedom.
3. Release from need to control, resist, or reject the way things are with ability to see the good in all things.
4. Diffusing differences and boundaries as judgment and attachments disappear.
5. Opening to challenge with an appetite for learning.
6. Sensing mystery, awe, and childlike wonder at the world.
7. Cherishing all life.
8. Awareness of the interconnectedness of life and knowledge that "What goes around, comes around."
9. Knowing that separation and inequality are egocentric illusions.
10. Appreciating nature, beauty, poetry, music, and art.
11. Overwhelmingly and unexpectedly experiencing joy, abundance, love, and well-being.
12. Ability to include all of experience without resistance or rejection. Inclusive and accepting of what is with the ability to vision something better if desired.

CHAPTER 4 - APPENDIX 2

PERSONAL PRACTICE

How can Energetic Coaches help others tap into the energy of spirit unless we do so ourselves? As we balance the external and the internal in oneness, we may notice tangible signs of transcendence. The descriptions for the acronym CHERISH are some ways for people to determine where they are on the continuum of low to high energy vibration. Inner spiritual growth produces external indicators. Do the CHERISH indicators give direction for personal development? Note which items your inner knower flags as opportunities to gain congruence and spiritual connection.

REFLECTION

- What is it that I like or dislike (attach or resist) in myself? Clue: What attracts or repels you about others?
- How can I integrate what I dislike (reject or resist) or let it go?
- How can I nourish what I like in myself without attachment?
- What are some of the conflicting polar forces operating in my life? How can I center on my inner knower?
- How do I connect and disconnect with spirit by hearing or not hearing my inner knower? What do I need to do to achieve congruence between my inner being and outer doing?

INTENTIONAL IMPRINT

Each of our acts makes a statement as to our purpose.
LEO BUSCAGLIA

Note: Each person leaves an invisible yet indelible imprint upon the world. Through relationships with others, people are remembered for who they are and what they do.

Even thoughts make imprints upon the collective consciousness and each individual is responsible for adding to or detracting from the collective whole. The kind of imprint left upon the world is a choice and a lasting legacy of one's life.

Write the eulogy you would like to have delivered at your funeral. Read it to yourself. Recognize any incongruence with what you would like to have said about yourself and what you are now being or doing.

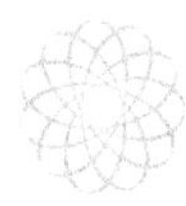

5. THE INDIVIDUAL IN RELATIONSHIP WITH OTHER

Only in relationship can you know yourself, not in abstraction, and certainly not in isolation.
JIDDU KRISHNAMURTI

THE MIRROR OF RELATIONSHIPS

Relationships mirror the inner self and provide outer, tangible evidence of how people regard themselves. Energetic Coaches encourage clients to use the mirror of relationship for self- discovery and growth. And we reflect on our own relationships to develop self-awareness. We know that relationships with others reflect the congruence of the relationship within the self and provide needed lessons and insights. Those in relationship with us look for us to be authentic and integrated. Being congruent with self and forming congruent relationships with others enables us to demonstrate integrity and trustworthiness. Congruent, positive relationships allow the client's inner knower to speak and be heard, opening channels to spiritual energy.

Energetic Coaches use the principle of free will goodwill to choose thoughts, feelings, and perceptions congruent with our highest inner self. Interpersonal relationships reflect our putting ideals into action. Knowing that our coaching relationships mirror ourselves to others, we continually connect with our inner knower to create an authentic coaching process. Holding high standards and values in our relationship with self allows us to hold the same standards and values in relationship with others.

In relationships the mirror is always reflecting. Some may think they are congruent in being and doing from within; whereas, relationships with others may reveal gaps and inconsistencies. Energetic Coaches use the mirror of relationship to reflect to clients what they need to see for inner wholeness to emerge. The physical, mental, and emotional states of coaches and clients are all aspects of the mirror. For instance, we watch for congruence between words and body language to help clients expand their knowledge of self. We reflect what we observe and allow clients to notice incongruence and disconnection in the safe space of the compassionate witness.

Lea: *My coaching client stated that she wanted to connect to her heart. Betty behaved as a rational, reasonable person who greatly relied on her intellect for guidance. Through coaching she realized that she mistrusted her intuition and often missed opportunities to speak her truth. She would sometimes give others more benefit of the doubt than she would give herself. I shared an observation regarding a disconnection between her laughter and her statements. I questioned why Betty would dismiss a difficult subject with a laugh. She realized that was a way to keep others from taking her seriously. She understood spontaneously that she was not behaving in a way to get what she wanted in relationship with others.*

The coaching relationship provides clients with a valuable reflection. They can use coaching to achieve outcomes and inner satisfaction. Through their striving to realize their values and visions, with our holding the ideal of balance and congruence within and without, clients can reflect on what they are attracting. Then they may begin to recognize gaps in their being and doing that they had habitually overlooked or denied. When they say one thing and do another, we can ask questions to increase their awareness of disconnections with self. As they strive for congruence in a safe space, they can self-reflect and choose words and actions that express their true self. Energetic Coaches aim to mirror to clients how to be in relationship authentically. Experiencing congruence in relationship is one of the most valuable benefits to clients of Energetic Coaching.

ENERGETIC COACHING FOR SPIRITUAL CONNECTION

It is preoccupation with possession, more than anything else, that prevents man from living freely and nobly.
BERTRAND RUSSELL

As small children individuals learn how to participate in their society and culture, often at the expense of self-expression and acceptance. Whether reared in wealth or poverty, people tend to relate inner worth to monetary worth. Without recognition and appreciation of others according to their inner being and with orientation toward outer appearance and acquisition, people disconnect from their true self. They feel inadequate because there is never enough outside stuff to compensate for inner lack. They lose trust and connection with their true nature as good and worthy. As people turn their attention to the external realm for answers, validation, and identity, they lose their connection with self and with spirit. The systems of mass media, advertising, socializing, governance, and education emphasize an external orientation so it is easy to disconnect from self and, therefore, from spirit. Outer accomplishments and acquisitions as proof of worthiness seduce many people. Some children are given things and unearned flattery and privileges rather than fundamentals: the time, attention, and love that they need. Others, who lack possessions society labels as "needy" or"lesser than." Adults who feel like wounded, unworthy children have a fear of going within—a fear that keeps them from knowing the truth of inner being as good, wise, worthy, and powerful.

Another reason it is difficult to focus within is because of constant bombardment by external stimuli. Media compete for fleeting attention to entice people to do something, buy something, consume something. Because of their upbringing, socialization, and temperament, many seek external validation and outer acceptance. As a result, they succumb to a persistent need for acquisitions and maintaining appearances to satisfy the small ego. Much of society seems to value external beauty over inner development, youthful vigor over elder wisdom, and fleeting "hookups" over lasting friendships. With such seductions, people risk losing appreciation and meaning for the importance of life. The desire for immediate gratification supplants development of character and lasting values. Without realizing it, people disconnect from their true selves. Disconnected people tend to accumulate things and to isolate and cocoon, further distancing themselves from self and others.

As a result, Energetic Coaches gradually expose the illusion and seductions of the material world in favor of inner knowing. Spirit is constantly calling for consciousness and connection. Outer orientation can distort or block messages from the inner knower. Some people call upon us to help open their inner channels of communication with self and others. Sometimes a sudden change in life causes them to question previous assumptions. Some get a growing awareness that they are missing something, a feeling that "it's" not working, or a sense that there must be more to life than what they are living. Some seek spirituality after a major life event or existential crisis that causes them to turn within. Because answers to life's greatest questions are not found on the outside, people seek something else to find answers, meaning, connection, and wholeness.

When what used to work no longer serves, some begin to question what they have learned through the years. They notice a crack in their worldview and an unknown light beckoning. For them, external assurances have given way to deep questions and not knowing. Their familiar path appears to lead nowhere. To go farther, they have to strike out into the unknown on a solitary journey. Many become stuck on the familiar road or return to their comfort zone, no matter how uncomfortable it has become. Those who dare to learn stare into the abyss that first appears empty and foreboding, the inner world of the self. Few want to venture there alone. To look within means to perceive differently, accepting all of how things are, seeing both sides of the coin, taking the "bad" as well as the "good." Few want to see the "bad" or reveal it to anyone else, so they live one-sided and off balance. It greatly helps to have a nonjudgmental fellow traveler. As a result, some people seek Energetic Coaches, who view clients as ready and able to embark on the inner journey to gain self-realization and self-acceptance.

Lea: *As I began coaching my client Ruth, I noticed her dissatisfied external orientation. Ruth came to coaching because she wanted more out of her career. It did not take long to learn that Ruth wanted more out of life. She had dedicated herself to her children, but as they grew up, they did not need her as much as they had in the past. When Ruth looked into the future, she did not find something to look forward to for herself. As a single mother, Ruth found herself growing jealous of others who had relationships and left out of social circles comprising couples. On the other hand, she feared losing herself in a relationship and being hurt.*

Ruth joined a church and began therapy along with coaching. Throughout her process she faced many challenges. She wanted to take a break from coaching, saying she felt stuck but then continued. In coaching, Ruth realized that she needed something different. She began questioning her past beliefs and making changes. Ruth sought connection and meaning in life. Coaching helped her consider options she would not have entertained otherwise. Ruth faced her fear of commitment and bought a house and started dating. By dealing with other aspects of her life that needed attention, Ruth became more satisfied with her job.

The *Hero's Journey*, depicted by Joseph Campbell, provides a fitting metaphor for what happens when individuals meet their life questions head-on. They separate from the familiar world to deal with their fears of the unknown. When they realize that the external world cannot suffice as complete sustenance for self, they focus on the internal world that at first may appear strange and empty. As their fragile ego faces within, they encounter what they do not want and cannot bear to look at—What if there is nothing there, or worse, what if it is not good?

From early childhood, most people hear more noes in life than yeses. As people judge and condemn themselves (and others, as a result), they disconnect from self, spirit, and wholeness. Increasingly, they try to shield themselves against others with their outer charade (sometimes called the false self) in an attemptto hide whatthey have notintegrated. The outermask they present further separates them from the inner knower, increasing their alienation and separation from self and spirit. The separation creates a sense of inner loneliness, which causes fear and further separation. People with a false front invest their energy in avoiding seeing themselves and hiding a perceived inner lack and emptiness from others. Rejecting a natural urge toward connection and integration, they fear being needy without knowing their wonderful worthiness within.

In such a quandary some turn to Energetic Coaches to walk with them on their path to authenticity. Even though they may feel a strong urge to reach out for help for the inner journey, coaches and clients know that no one can do it for them. Wanting or expecting others to do their inner work would further increase their outer orientation and inner separation. Still afraid to be alone on the journey, they may cling to outdated belief systems, bad habits, and harmful relationships rather than face their perceived inner emptiness. Being separated from within and in relationships with others, they may use addictions and incessant activity to cover the perceived nothingness inside. People can fear humiliation at being exposed as needy and nothing, so the ego takes over to protect them. The inner knower is disconnected from within—all circuits appear to be busy (through constant activity) or dead (through giving up). Having faced such fears in life, often many times, Energetic Coaches know that clients have the answers and the ability to achieve self-knowing, self-acceptance and self-love.

Lea: *Ruth admitted that she was afraid of being alone and did not want to go within by herself. I admired her courage and honesty when she pursued coaching without the mask of complete self- sufficiency. She was ready to take her spiritual journey. Even her therapist told her she was seeking "spiritual connection." Though coaching was coming to an end, Ruth bargained with me to continue meet-*

*ing with her once a month so that I could "see her progress."
This idea appealed to me, but I wanted to make sure that
I could be a compassionate witness to her further growth
and not a crutch or external savior who would hinder her
journey. I trusted that Ruth had everything within to become the fullest expression of her authentic being. My trust
in Ruth helped her to trust herself.*

Energetic Coaching works at the point where the inner self meets the external realm. At a crossroads, people realize that inner being directs outer doing. Although successful in the outer world, they may feel dissatisfied at being discon-nected from inner being. The quest for wholeness calls peo-ple to integrate the internal and to make the external reflect the internal, instead of the reverse. A relationship with an-other person to provide a clear mirror of knowing and accep-tance can help clients stay on the mysterious and sometimes frightening path to authenticity, congruence, and integrity.

The still, small voice wants to be heard. Spirit seeks the seeker. Autonomous, courageous individuals go within for personal truth and wisdom. At the same time, to avoid being absorbed into oneness, the ego resists. Sometimes as people connect with others, their ego defense mechanisms create fears of vulnerability or abandonment. Egotists, who are separated from self, may question and test the love from those who see more in them than they see in themselves. Some who were once driven by ego to satisfy external desires may experience a lack of motivation. Those in relationship with them may resent losing the focus and energy when they decide to take the inner journey. Energetic Coaching pro-vides support, reinforcement, and validation for clients' in-ner knowing to guide the way through external challenges to wholeness.

Lea: *Ruth complained of muscle stiffness in her shoulders and neck and a burning sensation in her throat when she wanted to speak in groups. She could see the connection between her body's cues and what she feared. She began to pay attention to her inner guidance, letting go of the need to speak out in groups. Ruth increasingly stopped giving a lot of energy to relationships that were not serving her. She also began remembering her dreams, which confused and even frightened her at times. I invited her to journal her dreams and to connect them with her emotions. She created a collage that represented who she was and what she wanted. Well on her way to knowing herself, Ruth let go of needing external proof of her importance and worth and became less concerned about the judgment of others.*

Individuals activate a spiral of spiritual energy when they let go of the need for external reinforcement and invite spirit to provide inner direction and guidance. Holographic in nature, the individual lives in the world, and the entire world lives within the individual. People make connections so that they and the world become one. Then, both connected and separate within self and with others, they experience spirit innately and pervasively.

Lea: *Ruth had a difficult time reconciling her idea of God with the fact that she was connected to Source internally through spirit. When I asked her if she felt the same toward "father" God as toward her physical father, Ruth paused to consider. Even though the idea was alien to her, I perceived a connection with her inner knower that allowed new information. With a distant and inaccessible father, Ruth envisioned God the same way, but she sensed that there was more to Source than what she had been inclined and indoctrinated to know. Through coaching, I was able to see what it was like for Ruth to let go of belief systems that did not work and create new ones to serve her high purpose. Through the process of brave questioning, letting go, and re-creation, Ruth was able to revise her beliefs to serve her better.*

LONELINESS

> *The best cure for loneliness is solitude.*
> MARIANE WILLIAMSON

Feelings of loss and loneliness signify a disconnection from within. It is not the presence of others that staves off loneliness. Some of the loneliest times can be in a crowd or with someone distant and inaccessible. Even though loneliness comes from within, some seek its antidote on the outside. Because they fear being alone, they may cling to relationships that do not serve them, often ending up even more isolated and alienated from self and others.

Lea: *During a coaching meeting when I questioned Ruth about why she did not want to go it alone, she looked confused. "No one wants to go it alone," she stated.*

"But what if all of us have to go it alone, but all along, we're not really alone?" I asked. "This may be a true," Ruth admitted, "but it's hard. I don't like it. I need your help."

I told Ruth that although I was willing to help, I could not go within for her. She would have to do her own inner work. I assured her that on the other end of the journey she would know and appreciate herself. I told her that then she could know and rely on herself. Although I agreed to act as a guide on the journey for a little while, I told her that she would need to enter the inner unknown as her own guide, and perhaps even guiding others as they adjust to her inner focus. A change in the relationship people have with them-selves changes their relationships with others. I knew that once Ruth established a knowing, accepting, and loving re-lationship with herself, her inner connection would reveal that she was never alone. When people find wholeness, they may be alone but not lonely because of their connection with self and spirit.

Often people feel lonely until they make an inner con-nection and achieve wholeness. For a time they may try to avoid loneliness by incessant doing, involving themselves in myriad relationships and activities, but they cannot achieve lasting fulfillment until they fill themselves from within. Re-lationships as mirrors will cause people who seek only outer fulfillment to create co-dependency in their relationships. The inner knower senses when another is seeking to com-plete the self through a relationship and resists the pressure to fill gaps for someone else. Those who are complete with-in can be in relationships without setting themselves up for ensuing disappointment by expecting others to compensate for their own inner lack. Complete, connected people can let go of relationships that do not serve their best interests, knowing that they may be alone but never lonely. They will not allow others to live vicariously through them in lieu of pursuing their own growth and congruent self-expression. Ironically, once a person is complete and no longer looks to others to fulfill them, they attract others easily.

SPIRITUAL CONNECTION IS EXPERIENTIAL

Spirit is Cosmic Consciousness. It is omnipresent,
omnipotent, and omniscient.
Everything visible and invisible is the expression of the
same Spirit... Experiencing this truth is the purpose of life.
SRI SWAMI SATCHIDANADA

Energetic Coaches reflect a relationship with spirit. By modeling authenticity and wholeness, we provide an example for others to achieve connection and congruence from within. Close encounters with spirit occur most frequently when people supplant their small ego with the true identity of their inner knower. Aware of the illusion of separation, the inner knower counters the judgment and condemnation of the small i of the undeveloped ego with the truth of the wholeness and oneness of life.

The compassionate witness of Energetic Coaches encourages clients to listen to their inner knower. As they explore the dark and light sides of self in an atmosphere of openness and trust, crucial issues may surface. We hold the space for clients to explore within and align with their inner knower so that they experience the presence of spirit in personal and impersonal ways.

Lea: *Over the two years that John and I worked on this book, we followed the overarching vision of spirit in close relationship, beginning with people's relationships with their selves. We watched spirit operating in the mirror of our one-on-one relationships. We noticed how spirit moved in the community, the natural environment, and the social and cultural organizations and processes. Individually, John and I experienced the reconciliation of our inner and outer selves as we became congruent in thoughts, words, and deeds, according to what we were writing about and what we desired in our separate yet connected lives.*

By having to practice what we preached because of writing about spirit, we connected with each other and with spirit. John and I experienced signs and synchronous experiences that indicated the tangible presence of spirit. Even as I thrived on such experiences, I knew I could not become attached to them. Spirit came in with the intention to be goodness and love and created even more goodness and love in relationship.

Fears and apprehensions spend energy, and I experienced an inner knowing that fear is false expectation appearing real. By connecting with the external world through my internal connection with spirit, I saw that if I experienced negativity in the external world, it was because I charged my experience with my own negativism. Fear, doubt, worry, and judgment lost power as I intentionally gave energy to belief, faith, knowing, and accepting. Spirit manifested through closing the gaps between what I thought and what I said and did. With my growing ability to trust myself, the separation between the other and me diminished as my ability to trust others increased. The more I grew to know and appreciate others as unique and yet very much the same, the more I grew to know and appreciate spirit. My relationship with John was my spiritual radar and compass during this work. Through relationship, we were able to detect and follow our inner knowing. We grew close while holding to our authentic, individual self to keep the spiritual connection going and the energy flowing.

The experience of spiritual connection and growth is individual, forever changing, ever fleeting, infinitely indescribable, uniquely personal, and mysteriously impersonal. There are no external, universal models or depictions of spirit, yet it operates by principles in relationship. People believe spiritual energy exists and readily recognize when they connect with spirit through such experiences as...

- Having warm feelings of the heart.
- Receiving loving looks from another.
- Appreciating the beauty of a sunset.
- Realizing self-satisfaction for a job well done.
- Getting a helping hand from a neighbor.
- Seeing a smile from a passing stranger.
- Belonging to a winning team.
- Laughing heartily from the belly.
- Releasing spontaneous tears of grief.
- Watching a baby.
- Crying on a comforting shoulder.
- Listening to an orchestra play music as one.
- Achieving a goal.
- Going beyond the boundaries of perceived limitations.
- Experiencing the vastness of the present moment.
- Feeling connection and belonging to the world.

People experience spirit when they see beyond the outer illusions to the inner meanings and connect with others through expressing their authentic being. Through connected relationships with self and others, people develop their relationship with spirit as an integral and important part of life.

GOING WITHIN

All search is vain, until we begin to perceive that wisdom is within ourselves...then we may know the sun is rising, that the morning is breaking for us.

VIVEKANANDA

Connecting with spirit neither erases the challenges of the external world nor guarantees continuous bliss. As spiritual beings in a material world, people have to operate in both spheres at once. As inner connection with self arises, validation comes more from the inner knower so that external validation and outer signs of success are not as necessary. As by- products of inner work, self-knowing and self-acceptance prove more valuable than gold. People desiring to express their inner being rather than compensating with outer acquisitions and appearances enjoy greater freedom and power.

The world appears as a duality with apparent opposites such as darkness and light. Many equate spirit with light, but spirit also lives in darkness. Energetic Coaches know that all is not as it seems. We refrain from making judgments of good or bad, desirable or undesirable, dark or light. We know that people often make the biggest advances in connecting with spirit through encountering and experiencing what they call "bad" in life. The harshest learning lessons can lead to the greatest strengths. Difficulties and challenges that are innate in the push/pull polarity of life may cause some to question their spiritual nature and connection with Source. It is during such times that Energetic Coaches can provide support on the spiritual journey, demonstrating faith and confidence that spirit is present even when people experience separation in the "dark night of the soul." Through such knowing, we mirror faith and connection in the face of doubt and separation, integrating light in the darkness.

Lea: *While writing this book, I sometimes felt that I was going into the wilderness. Blocked or disconnected, I felt overwhelmed and inadequate to the task. I thought, "Who am I to be writing about spirit?" My small ego self challenged me with self-criticism and judgment. The more I questioned myself, the more the energy of spirit withdrew. Sooner or later, as I forced myself to write anyway, each time inviting spirit to join the process in faith, my energy returned. The words flowed again, and I felt that I was serving something bigger yet a part of myself. Had I stopped writing, I would not have known the comforting connection that was waiting for me on the other side of the unknown wilderness. Each time I got through the tough spots, I experienced inner knowing, self-validation and courage to continue.*

Energetic Coaches recognize clients' deep questioning, disconnection, and bewilderment as breakthroughs in coaching. Knowing that clients will find their own answers, we hold the space for them to probe their thinking. Many times our presence helps them sit with loneliness and confusion so they can be still and listen to their own inner guidance. By accepting the uncomfortable and difficult, clients can experience simply being without having to do anything.

PARTNERING

No man can live happily who regards himself alone, who turns everything to his own advantage. Thou must live for another if thou wishest to live for thyself.
SENECA

The process of partnering with a coach invites the presence of spirit through equality and respect in relationship. Partnering happens when each person behaves congruently and wholly within and without. When both people seek the best outcome for the relationship without egocentric desires, their intentions foster I-One communication and win-win outcomes. Partnering requires a shift in consciousness from individualism to connectedness at all levels in a dynamic equation of giving and taking. By letting go of ego-based needs to get something from the other, people can fully give in authentic expression of self.

Energetic Coaching is a partnership. At the physical, mental, and emotional levels, clients and coaches coordinate with fluidity. We extend our whole being through permeable boundaries created by trust, reciprocity, humor, and ease. Like the graceful movements of two dancers, we co-create positive energy together in the dance of self-expression. Energetic Coaches feel the rhythm present in a coaching meeting and get in sync with clients to produce balance and flow.

Lea: *My husband Steve and I have experienced a growing relationship in which we accept and appreciate the expression of our individual selves. I have often said that being with Steve is like being by myself. In other words, his inner being complements rather than competes with who I am. We make ourselves happy and share with the other without expectation to be compensated or reciprocated for our giving. Our focus is on the quality of the relationship and not our individual agendas.*

At times, Energetic Coaches take the lead to create a high-level rapport with clients by embracing what they offer and allowing deep discussion through powerful questioning. When we ask questions in an atmosphere of appreciation and acceptance, clients can move to a creative level. Through the positive energy exchange within the relationship, we listen in an open and receptive way that encourages clients to discover inner strengths and insights. We allow ourselves confusion and questioning along with the client, demonstrating faith in the process and outcomes. We model a one-on-one relationship based on equality, respect and reciprocity.

Energetic Coaching encompasses emotion as well as thoughts and perceptions. Emotions play an important role in partnering even though people often downplay, dismiss, or discount them. As mentioned previously, emotions are energy in motion. To harness and direct personal energy, the partners need to tune in to what they want to transmit and what they want to receive. Just as the physical movements of dancers appear mechanical and confined without emotion, partners need to engage emotion with spirit to create energy within a relationship. It is the emotion the dancers put into the physical moves that fuels the excitement of the dance. Comfortable with their emotions of goodness and love that connect them with spirit, Energetic Coaches experience compassion, appreciation and love in partnering with clients. Clients perceive the power of emotions with or without external words or actions by coaches. To withhold feelings in the coaching relationship takes the heart out of the relationship and blocks spiritual energy. We present ourselves to clients as fully present in the emotion of the dance.

Through connecting with the inner self, people are better able to connect with the inner being of others. Each partner combines the experience of self and the other into the experience of connectedness. The mirror and reflection become one. Good intention and practice prepare partners to blend into something new and expansive. Energetic Coaches sense when clients shift in the doing and the being of their work together, and we respond accordingly. We realize that limiting belief systems and negative thinking patterns keep partnering from progressing toward what clients have said they wanted for themselves. Coaching with clarity and congruence provides a safe space to redirect self-limiting beliefs to new ways of thinking and being.

John: *To produce a CD, Tom, a talented young man with a singing career, was partnering with Shelia. She was a promising pianist who supplemented her income by accompanying singers at concerts and in the recording studio. Tom was creating most of the words and music for the CD they were making. He and Sheila were taking a lot longer than Tom had expected, so he was worried about the cost, which included paying Shelia. When Tom hired me as a personal coach to get his singing career on track, he expressed his concern that Shelia didn't seem as committed to the project as he.*

Tom wanted to work things out with Sheila. Having experienced problems with other accompanists, he admitted to being a perfectionist in all aspects of his musical work. I guided Tom into exploring what he wanted in his business partnership with Shelia and questioned him about her expectations. He began to appreciate the process with Shelia because their partnership could produce results more vibrantly than what each had been doing individually. Spirit through equality and good intention replaced ego in the relationship. With insight and connection to a mutual goal, they transformed their partnership into energetically beautiful music.

Synergism

n. the interaction of elements that when combined produce
a total effect that is greater than the sum of the individual
elements, contributions, etc.
–dictionary.com

People create synergism when what they produce together totals more than what they might have created independently. Energetic Coaching promotes synergism through the energy of spirit. The relationship existing between coaches and clients transcends the skills and knowledge exhibited by either. Together they raise individual consciousness, allow authentic expression, and heighten awareness of spiritual connection.

To promote the flow of spiritual energy effortlessly and freely, Energetic Coaching builds a trusting, open relationship with clients. When energy decreases, a block to self-knowing and acceptance is often present. Exploring blocks to spiritual energy can be difficult and frightening for some clients. Energetic Coaches, who continually clear their own inner space, help clients deal confidently with new information and sudden emotions.

When coaches and clients open to the other and the present situation, they connect synergistically. If coaches focus on what might work from their toolkit of "all the things I know about coaching," they cannot focus on clients and be with them. If coaches or clients operate in the past, they are not present in the moment. If either party is disconnected from self, they leave a gap in the coaching-client relationship. Internal disconnection and external attachment to appearances and results block the energy of spirit.

John: *Brian was experiencing conflict between his career in selling and his love for painting. Whereas his educa-*

tion had developed his artistic capabilities, he was unable to make an income to support his family. When the financial situation became too stressful to pursue an artistic career, Brian took a job as a distributor of art supplies for a large manufacturer. His primary customers were companies selling to retail chain stores. Brian's customers liked his creative ideas for expanding their markets for art materials, so they sought his advice frequently. Brian took his ideas back to the manufacturer to make new products to fit the special needs of his customers. However, his sales director was pressuring him to push the existing product line and increase sales with his customer base.

Feeling pulled between providing for his family and his passion to create, Brian sought my services. I guided him to clarify his key values of expressing creativity, providing for family, and participating as a team player. Adding his artistic ability and excellent communications skills to his values, Brian and I began to explore other career options.

Brian found the most helpful part of the coaching—having someone fully present to his needs without judgment—brought results beyond expectation. The trust that he and I developed allowed him the freedom to visualize new opportunities that yielded a match of needs and wants. Neither of us expected me to solve Brian's quest, but together we helped him enlist his inner knower to provide guidance in the situation. Our coaching partnership produced results that exceeded what Brian might have achieved on his own. Brian now uses his artistic ability to express his fullest self while earning a living doing so.

RECIPROCAL NATURE OF THE COACHING RELATIONSHIP

"He who cannot forgive others destroys the bridge ove which he himself must pass."
GEORGE HERBERT

We cannot overstate the importance of the congruent relationship of self with other in Energetic Coaching. While we do not deny the presence of discomfort and disconnection, Energetic Coaches do not entertain judgment, fear, or discomfort. We are vigilant about any bias arising in the coaching relationship. We may not be aware of their beginnings and may not realize immediately the effect on the coaching process. Clients may have innocently hit a nerve by something stated or implied. If we experience any aversion or prejudice, we work with our inner knower to understand the purpose behind what the client presents, which is ultimately for the good. Aware of our own and our clients' projections or biases, we choose to remain present and compassionate. We own our own emotions and expect clients to own theirs. Coaches and clients provide an important mirror for one another, revealing the reciprocal nature of relationships. By accepting one another as we are, we accept ourselves.

As the compassionate witness, Energetic Coaches hold a sacred place for clients who may be wrestling with issues. Through active listening and in-the-moment questioning, we encourage clients to shift from external blaming to internal reflection and learning. The reciprocal nature of the exchange demonstrates partnering, free from judgment or blame, open to the presence of spirit.

John: *In my business experience I found myself a member of a staff of four in the corporate Personnel and Training Department charged with developing a proposal to be submitted to the company Director of Sales & Marketing. He wanted to conduct a series of team building sessions in his regional sales offices. Each in our department was responsible for providing organizational development services to different intra-company clients. Because of the large number of people to attend the team-building sessions, our director asked us to generate ideas for the project.*

One of our team members, Bill, was responsible for Sales & Marketing. Although our director was overseeing our work, he missed many of our planning meetings. After a couple of meetings Bill asked each of us to make recommendations on what we would include in the proposal to be sent to the VP. Having had experience preparing such proposals, I sent my recommendations to Bill. At the next meeting Bill handed out a copy of a proposal saying we had all we needed to proceed. Initially, I was disturbed that there was no discussion about my input. I found out later from one of the other team members that Bill was taken aback by my reaction to what he had done and didn't understand why I was upset. This experience proved valuable to me for owning my own feelings and looking inside for the source of the hurt and resentment. A part of me did not expect to be listened to, which played out in my dealings. Instead of projecting with anger, I might have opened to Bill's explanation for what I considered to be a personal affront.

Energetic Coaches aim to see grievances for what they are and deal with the inner work they require. We recognize a perceived attack as an opportunity to work with the inner knower. Instead of taking the issue personally, we aim to gather data and learn. Because of our own inner knowing, coaches can help clients learn about projection and look within for causes and solutions for negative reactions. We become the objective observer and compassionate witness to our own processes.

THE "GAP" OF RELATIONSHIPS

We carry within us the wonders we seek without us.
SIR THOMAS BROWNE

Spirit lives in the connection of relationships. To the degree that people maintain positive relationships, they experience spirit. When they struggle within themselves and with others, they create gaps in spiritual connection. Then they feel separate, alienated, and lonely. Even though spirit abides in everything always, personal alienation blocks its energy. Energetic Coaching seeks to use the mirror of relationship to resolve incongruence and bridge gaps between self and spirit. Outer relationships mirror the relationship with self. People cannot trust others unless they first trust themselves. Self-love is the basis of love for others. Self-respect is the basis of mutual respect. Energetic Coaches provide the mirror to reflect the highest being of clients within. We also reflect gaps or incongruence between what clients do and what they say they want. As clients close gaps between being and doing and achieve congruence from within, they come to hear their inner knower and experience a spiritual connection. Within the relationship of Energetic Coaching, clients have the experience of creating greater energy through a congruent relationship.

Lea: *Several experienced coaches met on a conference call to learn from each other. One of them, Donna, presented a recent difficult coaching situation. Although initially she had discussed with her client the boundaries of the coaching relationship, he appeared to be seeking a friend rather than a coach. The coach as mirror reflected the underlying dynamics of a relationship that might keep her client from seeing his hidden agenda. She pointed out to him that she thought the coaching relationship had stalled. When the coaches on the call questioned how Donna had relayed her assessment of the situation, she replied, "With love."*

Even though there was no further questioning by the group, I wished for a better answer. I sensed a deflection of the real issue. Intentionally creating friendships and connecting with others is vital to personal growth. I thought the situation presented an important coaching opportunity. I wondered if Donna had been clear on her intentions so that she understood her client without projection or defense. I questioned whether this particular client could have benefited from coaching about how to create and maintain friendships. A situation that appears stuck or stalled may hold a wonderful opportunity to explore different directions.

Both coaches and clients must know their coaching intentions and personal triggers. To clarify the relationship means that there is openness and questioning, allowing the agenda to surface for examination with acceptance. Coaches need to open to clients' wishes, then reflect them back for the highest good, starting with the relationship clients have with self. The coach becomes a mirror of positive possibilities.

Ego, when used for self-centered intent and desires, disconnects relationship. Ego rises early in life to provide a distinct sense of self with which to achieve individual identity and goals. But people can let their egos overshadow their inner self with defense mechanisms. As they learn to connect with their inner knower, mature individuals begin to release self-protection and self- serving ploys. Ego serves to separate and differentiate from others—to be superior or special. People fill their egocentric agendas by acquiring goods and manipulating and controlling others as objects. To create material abundance, they can bankrupt their internal worth by using others to further self-centered objectives.

A close connection with spirit through the inner knower allows people to appreciate themselves as unique and equal without relying on external appearances that may indicate otherwise. A congruent relationship between inner being and outer doing lays the groundwork for congruent relationships with others. People who are whole and complete within do not need to possess, manipulate, or exploit others for personal gain. They do not need to co-opt others to support their identity because they rely on internal guidance rather than external validation. They rely less on what others think than on what they themselves think. They tend to attract those who also reflect congruent identity. Those who know and accept self recognize and let go of relationships with others who need to use or seduce them to feed their own egos.

Energetic Coaches provide good examples of ego management. We do not seek to impress nor are we impressed by the external possessions or appearance of others. We know how to relate without trying to impress. Our balanced internal state creates the space for connection on meaningful levels because we do not need defenses or projections. Energetic Coaches possess the attributes of openness, allowing, and releasing to invite spirit into relationship. In the presence of clients who are conflicted and attached to egocentric desires and agendas, we can observe and remain neutral, knowing that what clients over-compensate for externally probably reflects what they lack internally. By seeing the client in the essence of being without giving energy to ego, we invite spirit into the relationship. Of course, our having to be aware of our own ego ensures that we continually accept clients as they are. Energetic Coaches model for our clients how to function in the moment without judgment or expectation. By relegating ego to its proper place, clients can choose to go in the direction that is most beneficial—within.

EGO IN RELATIONSHIP

We need in love to practice only this: letting each other go.
For holding on comes easily – we do not need to learn it.
RAINER MARIA RILKE

It is no wonder "Ego" has been used as an acronym for "Easing God Out." By orienting outward and allowing ego to dominate, people silence their inner knower and lose their center of balance. Connecting with spirit completes self-identity. When people are missing connections with self and others, they try to compensate with ego. Without beneficial relationships as mirrors, they use ego to justify their actions, blame others for inner failings, and feel superior or inferior. It takes a great deal of energy to keep up pretenses. Without the connection with the inner knower, people tend to perceive themselves and others differently from how they are. People who lack self-awareness even question positive relationships. Projections abound, and relationships become difficult and distant as the small self of the little i tries to fill the space that would otherwise allow spirit to enter.

When people do not realize the orchestrations of their unmanaged ego, they disconnect from their inner knower. A one-on-one coaching relationship can be beneficial to close the gap. Relationships provide people with information about what they are missing within themselves. Because of the external orientation of the little i, egocentric people may gather information from a skewed perspective. The inner knower of the other resists such projections. Self-knowing provides a beacon of light for the egocentric other to recognize how ego separates and attempts to dominate and control.

It takes practice for people to confront their own ego. Inner practice leads to outer results. Energetic Coaches monitor our own ego and its justifications, judgments, and generalizations so that we can respond in the moment to what clients present. We know when someone is stroking our ego. At the same time, we accept that having an ego is a human trait. There is usually a humorous component to recognizing the unmanaged ego, so we often find reasons to laugh at ourselves. Because we can examine our own egoistic motives and manipulations with inner acceptance, humility, and humor, we can reflect to others how to do the same.

People with healthy, managed egos avoid the hidden agendas of others. Egocentric people perceive challenges and questions as threats. They avoid inner scrutiny because they fear allowing their true self to emerge. Being dominated by ego, they mistrust themselves and their co-creative power. In the space where spirit might dwell, they fill the gap with ego. Others may find it difficult to get to know egotists, who keep a constant guard against scrutiny by others as well as by the self. Through their inner knower Energetic Coaches can put the egocentric other at ease, knowing that the ego is compensating for a perceived inner lack. We open to spirit by emphasizing the values within clients and accepting them as they are. Empowered by being able to accept ourselves, we can do this with others. Coaches and clients alike always have to manage ego so that spiritual energy can flow. Energetic Coaches seek to give spirit-strokes and not ego-strokes. Ego- strokes are based on external accomplishments and appearances; spirit-strokes are based on inner values and character strengths.

Energetic Coaches focus on the positive while tracking the negative in relationship. After all, clients hire us to work with what is not working for them. Exposing their lack may seem risky. There is a natural tendency in relationships to collude to avoid what each does not accept within. Often people resist changing their ways of relating because they fear that changing will cause them to lose relationships. What if the significant other refuses to accommodate reasonable requests? Fear and denial inhibit change and growth toward spirit. The risk appears immense until clients realize that what they are avoiding will eventually be confronted and what they deny will become apparent to others even if not to them. People let go of relationships based on fear and denial because egocentric others shun growth and sever connections with others. To bloom and grow, relationships need positive intention, free will goodwill, truth and appreciation for the authentic self.

Joining and separating, compressing and expanding, pushing and pulling are two sides of the relationship coin. Instead of shying away from examining an issue for fear of losing a relationship, Energetic Coaches see the connecting force of engaging the other person at the inner core. Through the compassionate witness, we support clients to look within themselves and share what they find. We encourage them to use the mirror in relationship to find answers within. Clients gain a sense of their essence and inner knower through the coaching relationship by learning how to be authentic and open with another person and therefore, with themselves. Energetic Coaching requires ego management so that both coaches and clients open to their inner knower. Managing the ego in relationship with self and other requires a process of self- reflection, self-realization, and self-respect. Energetic Coaches provide the support and mirror to reflect goodness of the inner self despite the badness that may appear. We address games, false projections, and misperceptions in the context of knowing that if clients are willing to grow, the process is all good.

There are coaches and clients who want ego strokes and not ego management. They will attract one another into relationships that satisfy on an external level. Some part of each person's inner knower recognizes collusion and manipulation by the other. Each may feel like an object and treat the other as an object. Some may find the strokes satisfying for a short time, but the energy of connection is not sustainable because it is ego/externally-based rather than spirit/internally created.

Managing the ego takes practice. The ego of clients can trigger the ego of the coach. We must consciously overcome the natural, automatic, internal urge to separate in judgment or self- protection. Instead, we choose openness and connectedness as a way of life, knowing that at some level clients have the answers that will allow them to let go of false projections and self- protections. Recognizing ego triggers such as fears of inadequacy, worthlessness, confusion, and exposure, we remove our ego and our issues from those of our clients. Such recognition and removal is an ongoing practice of Energetic Coaching. Even though it may appear that inner results and positive changes require time and effort, people can sustain in the long run what comes from within when it is an authentic expression of who they are.

By knowing ourselves, Energetic Coaches honor the client's ego and bring it to the forefront for examination. At first, clients may feel a need to deny, justify, or ignore their egocentricity. We let go of denial and hold the space for them to safely face all aspects of self. We ask clients questions out of curiosity, without innuendo, suggestion or judgment in the pure attempt to help them achieve congruence. Our compassionate witness fosters an I-One relationship, which allows a safe space for clients to examine their agendas, intentions, and blind spots.

Though difficult and demanding work, examining ego for integration leads to wholeness. As people manage their ego, they lighten up and laugh at themselves, allow others to be different and equal, let go of self-justification and blame, release draining relationships, and live free of the need for eternal youth and external acquisitions. Energetic Coaches provide a safe space to release defense mechanisms so clients can listen to their inner knower and connect with spirit. Instead of straining to attain superiority or hide inferiority and insecurity, clients learn that they no longer need to fill emptiness as spirit flows in.

If Energetic Coaches fear confronting the unmanaged ego of clients, we receive a message from our inner knower to let go of our ego's insecurities so we can act as compassionate witness to our clients. Then concurrently, we can let go of our own ego defense mechanisms.

Energetic Coaches know that avoiding work with ego can undermine the coaching relationship. It may be tempting to bypass examining the ego, but that lapse only allows clients to continue separation, incongruence, and superficiality. We serve them when we draw attention to the outcomes of an unchecked ego. The inner knower of clients cannot help but acknowledge that authentic coaches care enough to venture where clients have found it difficult and risky to go alone. Even though examining ego may evoke uncomfortable feelings, we know clients have a rich opportunity to grow. When they present the opportunity to expose their ego to scrutiny, we can respond with objective openness as a compassionate witness. Each time clients do this and let go of fears and pretensions, they find greater self-knowing and self-acceptance. They begin to bear the fruits of their endeavor. People in relationship with them begin to perceive them as less superficial and more real.

BOUNDARIES IN RELATIONSHIP

No one outside ourselves can rule us inwardly. When we know this, we become free.
BUDDHA

Boundaries are essential in relationship. People need boundaries for unique self-knowing and expression. Even though the bliss of a dissolved boundary feels wonderful, such as in meditation or when falling in love, people eventually have to return to the world as separate yet connected individuals. If they can form and define boundaries in organic ways, they can allow others to share the same space without threat or seduction, that is, with respect and acceptance. People must manage their ego to maintain healthy relationships with others. When they practice the Golden Rule as an internal value, the connected I-One relationship creates reciprocating positive energy that honors individuals in relationship as equal and separate yet connected.

When they feel chemistry between them, two people thrive on the sudden jolt of recognition and collapsing boundaries. Many mistake such attraction as oneness and love, but there must be a "snap back" sooner or later to reestablish boundaries. Collapsing ego boundaries produces the euphoria of erotic love. Paradoxically, for a relationship to grow into a whole, sooner or later, lovers will want to return to their own personhood. Even though they risk feeling alone once again, only through dispelling the illusion of boundless oneness can they achieve lasting, dynamic oneness. Only individuals, loved and loving for each other's uniqueness, achieve the highest form of love—recognizing and appreciating others in the full essence of their being themselves.

Rather than perceiving the positive energy in the restoration of boundaries, "love junkies" experience a great loss. Some people translate their loss as a lack in the other rather than a reflection of their own disconnection within. A healthy relationship serves as a clear mirror for people to look at their inner relationship. Those on the path of spiritual growth look within to work on what is missing in them rather than expecting others to compensate or placing blame for what they want but do not have. To the extent that people become whole on the inside, they free themselves to find love with a unique other without the need to change, manipulate, play games or test the other.

John: *Energetic Coaching is a love relationship. I have not experienced many coaching relationships in which there is not a snap back by the other at some point in the process. Often clients become disappointed in the coach because they have not yet learned that what they seek outside themselves can only be found within. For a while they may project their disappointment on the coach, whom they may view as inferior, especially if they had originally projected a superior illusion. Whenever this snap back happens to me, I am always glad that I did not set myself up as an outside expert. Even though clients may think they want me to fill their gaps, I hold the space to empower them to do so for themselves. I may be able to help people learn to fish, but I will not fish for them.*

Clients may express or act out resistance and disappointment, but when they own what inner work they want to do, they often return to the coaching process with a high-level perspective eager to learn. With inner motivation they can achieve wholeness. Knowing the dip to be a part of the coaching dynamic, I find it easy to hold a space for clients to return without projecting my own ego and self-judgment of inferiority. By accepting myself, I accept clients where they are.

Those with intact boundaries can maintain close relationships without fear of losing themselves for another person. Individuals can accommodate intimacy and allow vulnerability in a space of acceptance and appreciation for the way things are in the present. Because of the safety in acceptance, people can look at themselves directly in the mirror of relationship to find truths they had avoided in the past. The fear of loss or judgment from another diminishes as people develop a closer relationship with self.

People need boundaries to know themselves in relationship, but they must be permeable to allow others and spirit to connect. With known boundaries, people can separate and connect with equality in relationships. They are doing the sacred work of maintaining a close one-on-one relationship as they experience spirit within and manifest it without in positive and fulfilling relationships of two wholes coming together into one.

PROJECTION

All relationships exist to validate the perfect being of the other. So why don't all relationships work? People tend to project their incompleteness onto the other. If one reacts from stimulus response, the other may internalize the reaction of the other. It is important to know what belongs to self to solve and what belongs to the other. Knowing self is essential to maintaining healthy relationships and growing spirituality.

Sometimes clients project something onto coaches that they want or do not want within themselves. Without realizing it, they resort to a way of being that avoids self-examination. Aware of such dynamics, Energetic Coaches can deflect what clients project. Our mirror in a relationship reflects from our inner knower, so clients see something different from what they have projected. Our intact boundary through self-knowing helps them self-reflect instead of allowing them to project falsely onto someone else. If clients do not self-reflect or if they continue acting on erroneous assumptions, they may need therapeutic help. It is beyond the scope of coaching to help those who deny or disconnect from reality through projection or transference. Coaching aims to establish a relationship of equals that brings out the best in each other. If clients do not want to see themselves clearly in relationship with coaches, we need to end the relationship. Coaches facilitate process so clients can gain what they want and let go of what they do not want in life. We help them to understand that energy and knowing comes from within. We can mentor and guide them, but we cannot and will not do the work they need to do for themselves. Knowing that clients have their own answers within, Energetic Coaches stay within the bounds of helping clients help themselves. It is important to distinguish between when we are doing the work of coaching and when we step too far and go into the work of the client. Even though it may be seductive to our ego to act as an external expert, giving advice, suggesting actions to take, and imposing preconceived models weaken rather than strengthen clients in the process of knowing themselves and becoming whole.

Energetic Coaches seek to bring out clients' inner knower. The coaching agenda and desired outcomes serve that process. By acting as the objective mirror in the relationship, we operate on the micro and macro levels simultaneously, keeping clients' best interests in the forefront and maintaining the boundaries of our coaching-client relationship. By operating primarily from within in connection with spirit, we reflect clearly for clients because we do not distort the reflection ourselves. Instead, we deflect projection or transference back to clients for safe examination. The open, objective, nonjudgmental nature of the compassionate witness allows us to remain connected and separate in relationship with others.

POLARITY

I have learned silence from the talkative; tolerance from the intolerant; and kindness from the unkind. I should not be ungrateful to those teachers.
KAHLIL GIBRAN

The attracting energy of polarity can bring people into relationship because they often seek in others what they need to learn or what they desire for themselves. As long as clients use the relationship with coaches and others to learn what they need to fulfill from within, they can use polarity to contribute to balance and wholeness. However, polarity can throw a relationship out of balance. Compensating polarity separates; balancing polarity connects.

Relationships based on compensating opposites we call "co-dependent." Breaching boundaries and denying individual sacred identity results in co-dependency. Relying on the external other blocks people's connection with their inner knower and with spirit. Depending on someone else might seem to provide what is missing within, but such relationships are certain to disappoint. Dependent partners operate from fragile worldviews such as, "It's you and me against the world," or "I need to stick it out with this person, because no one else would put up with me." Such relationships are based on weakness rather than strength.

Energetic Coaches stay alert when clients seek to co-opt us into providing an external crutch rather than connecting with their own inner knower for their own answers. We turn clients within again and again. We continually empower them, which is why they seek coaching and why it can serve them profoundly.

Relationships provide clues to people's inner world. Likes or dislikes in others reflect likes or dislikes within. What people reject or embrace may reveal a polarity, showing what they themselves lack and desire. Humans value individual differences for the full inclusiveness that such diversity can engender. Also, they can learn by example in a relationship with another who possesses the desired qualities. Qualities people reject can serve as good examples of what to work on within. Relationships are vital for self-awareness as long as people do not use them to compensate for their own incongruence.

When Energetic Coaches recognize polarity in coaching relationships with clients, we focus deeper into the issue and present it to clients for learning about themselves. We explore together the reasons for resistance or attraction. Clients may at first feel disappointed that we do not provide the antidote or magic pill to fix their problems. But our inner redirection rather than external expert stance helps them find their own answers through their inner knower. In our not knowing, we empower clients to seek, discover and know for themselves.

THE CONNECTED RELATIONSHIP – A METAPHOR

All happiness comes from the desire for others to be happy.
All misery comes from the desire for oneself to be happy.
SHANTIDEVA

There is enormous energy in splitting the nucleus of an atom, which is held together through the binding energy of polarity. Fission creates nuclear energy. There is even greater energy released by fusion, the sun's energy. Fusion is the process of combining the nuclei of atoms of lightweight elements such as hydrogen. Relationships contain immense energy, either in splitting apart or in coming together. There is tremendous energy in both fission and fusion, but the greater is in coming together. Splitting apart is what happens when people use a common enemy to unite against rather than a common vision to unite for. Resisting a common enemy means that people unite in blame, victimhood, fear or scapegoating. They decrease their energy and cause destructive consequences. Sharing a common vision means that people agree on wanting something. Even if those who split apart eradicate one enemy, another will take its place. Without a common vision, people do perish.

The sun provides a metaphor for the energy of spirit. As it produces tremendous life-giving energy through fusion, the internal light of spirit nourishes, grows, and enlightens the inner knower. As the sun shines equally on all, providing light and giving life, spirit nourishes those who choose to connect with its energy. Even though religions and philosophies draw broad generalizations and artificial distinctions among people of different beliefs, spiritual energy comes from the one Source. In the illusion of the external world of the five senses, people experience self as separate; but the light of life within connects to the light of life of Source with everyone equally. Each is like a lens, closing down the aperture or opening wide to allow light to flow in. Individuals decide how much to open to spirit through removing barriers to receive its energy.

Different But Equal

The more we let each voice sing out with its own true tone,
the richer will be the diversity of the chant in unison.
Angelus Silesius

Treat all men alike. Give them all the same laws. Give them
all an even chance to live and grow.
Chief Joseph

There is energy in separation and polarity, but it is not as great as the energy of connection and integration. The energy of no is not as great or sustainable as the energy of yes. When people come together by identifying or creating a common enemy, they give in to fear and separation. It is much better, but perhaps not as immediately compelling, to create energy through identifying a common vision. There is not the energy-depleting effect of rejection, resistance, and opposition to others. In order to come together, people must deal with what separates and alienates them or continually lose energy by spending resources to resist, deny, or repress.

The common enemy approach that enlarges differences rather than commonalities creates fear and separation. By choosing to focus on small separations rather than large connections, people differentiate and separate from one another.

The collective consciousness, which reflects individual consciousness, reveals the state of the world at large. As people become congruent internally, they naturally become congruent in their relationships with others. Their congruence expands to the world. One-on-one relationships provide the direct experience of the inner self. Challenging and difficult relationships offer opportunities to decide boundaries and to let go. Through building and maintaining positive relationships, people bear responsibility for contributing to the energy of the collective consciousness. Rather than focus on negativity and separation, they invest their energy in common visions. Transformation of relationships is the important opportunity for individual and world betterment that Energetic Coaches facilitate through our one-on-one relationships. It is easy for people to maintain relationships with those they like. It is not so easy with those whose beliefs diverge. When clients differentiate from, judge, or decide to dislike others, Energetic Coaches work to dispel the illusion of separation. Energetic Coaching contributes to the betterment of the world by channeling positive and visionary energy rather than allowing depleting and separating judgments. By seeing the unity behind superficial disconnection and duality, people connect. They naturally practice the Golden

Rule, which recognizes the reciprocal nature of relationships with others. Sometimes people need to let go of relationships without judgment. We help facilitate what it takes to achieve personal congruence and create positive relationships.

Energetic Coaching seeks the connecting energy of common values and vision by maintaining equality in relationships without judgment. Seeing differences as building blocks to a greater understanding instead of superficial separations of "not that" brings forth acceptance that would not otherwise occur. Relationships that are different and challenging present opportunities for individual and collective growth.

UNIQUE—NOT BETTER THAN OR LESS THAN

Your love for God is only as great as the love you have for the person you love the least.
DOROTHY DAY

Love is the only force capable of transforming an enemy into a friend.
MARTIN LUTHER KING JR.

Like snowflakes, no two people are alike. The natural world evidences wonderful diversity. Species are connected through the web of life in dynamic balance. In their relationships to each other, people can be different yet the same. The differences among people are superficial; commonality is at the core. By letting go of judgments of others, people can allow and appreciate superficial differences by seeing the much greater commonality.

As related beings in the world of duality, people naturally compare themselves with one another. Through spiritual connection, they can come to appreciate the unique qualities that make every person an irreplaceable treasure. Individuals experience spirit by being like spirit— inclusive and appreciative of diversity. Energetic Coaches work with clients to value the uniqueness of each other. The mirror of one-on-one relationships helps them discover and appreciate the different qualities in both self and other. Often they experience that spiritual connection and energy create feelings of love and goodness within and without. Through intentional practice in relationships using metaphors and principles such as in Energetic Coaching, people can learn to accept and appreciate themselves and others more. The mirror of the relationship with other reveals congruence between the inner free will goodwill for self reflecting the same for other.

Chapter 5 Appendix

Reflection

- In what relationships with others do I experience an equal and reciprocal I-One relationship? What characteristics in that relationship do I want more of with others?
- What can I be and do to have it?
- What relationships challenge me by holding the mirror to what I may not want to see in myself?
- How do I experience signs, synchronicity, and serendipity with others that connect me with my spiritual self?
- How can I be vulnerable and open to greater connection with others?

- What do I want more of from others that mirrors what I am seeking in myself?
- What relationship do I have with others that has disconnected me in judgment and negativity? What insight does my judgment and negativity provide into the part(s) of myself I need to integrate for wholeness?
- How can I include the difficulties and diversity presented by others into my being and doing for wholeness?
- What do I need to let go of to have a good relationship with others and myself?

CONTEMPLATE THE FOLLOWING

When you hold resentment toward another, you are bound to that person or condition by an emotional link that is stronger than steel. Forgiveness is the only way to dissolve that link and get free.
CATHERINE PONDER

Today, see if you can stretch your heart and expand your love so that it touches not only those to whom you can give it easily, but also those who need it so much.
DAPHNE ROSE KINGMAN

INTENTIONAL IMPRINT

- What will those in one-on-one relationships with me remember and value about me?
- What can I do now to create the remembrance of me I would want others to hold?

6. THE INDIVIDUAL IN RELATIONSHIP WITH COMMUNITY

I say to you all, once again—in the light of Lord Voldemort's return, we are only as strong as we are united, as weak as we are divided.
Harry Potter and the Order of the Phoenix

The higher you go, the more you see the perfection, and therefore the less you see problems. The more one sees problems, the lower one is.
LESTER LEVENSON, *Happiness Is Free*

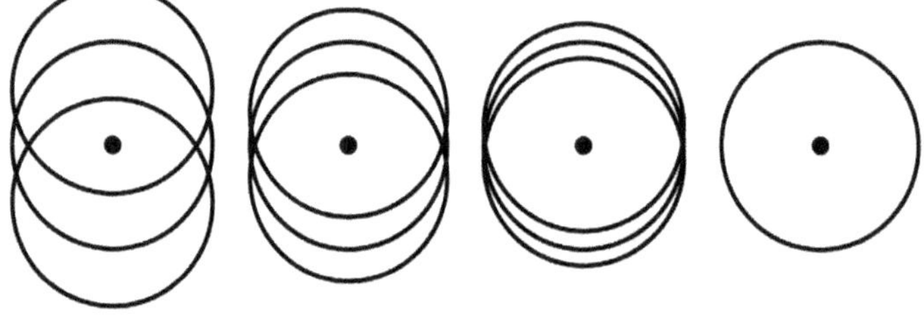

The illustration above provides a framework for thinking about how people achieve oneness through interconnections. Individuals first establish congruence within and without themselves and then connect with others in one-on-one relationships. As connections grow, they overlap with the sphere of community around the centerpoint. As relationships blossom, the spheres merge. The centerpoint provides the locus for the overlapping relationships to align with one another. It represents common vision and values. Spirit provides the connecting and aligning energy at the centerpoint when individuals choose to be in relationships based on spiritual qualities such as love and appreciation.

Relationships come into congruence through the quality of the internal and external relationships each person has with self and others. Energetic Coaches work to build community from within, one person at a time, starting within themselves. As the energy of the alignment around the centerpoint grows, outer actions connected through community produce benefits and significant results more than one person could achieve alone.

TRANSFORMATION OF THE INDIVIDUAL THROUGH COMMUNITY

Transformation of the self does not occur in isolation. The context of community provides people with the greatest mirror for reflecting their values and visions. The collective force of community affects individual experience and influences each person within it in positive or negative ways. The collective force becomes a spiral of energy in which individuals in relationship in community affect the community as well. Every individual intention and outward expression influences the community. People may complain about taxes, for instance, and feel like victims of the system, but there is always something that they can do, individually and collectively, to influence the community they are in for better or worse.

People connect and influence one another through community; however they tend to disconnect from community when it does not suit their values. The illusion of separation allows some to deny responsibility for creating the outer experience. The larger the community, the greater the opportunity people have to disconnect without self-reflection and self-accountability. Individuals wield great power when they as members connect and take personal responsibility for their relationships within the community at large. A community of self-responsible individuals in alignment with a common goal has a great impact. Community improvement initiatives almost always need to begin at the grassroots level because those at the top are more invested in the status quo and insulated from the effects of their actions on others at the ground level.

Medical studies show that having a positive support system enhances personal well-being. Those who have participated in support groups feel the energy of the group when members share their personal stories. As if something within awakes to a high consciousness, they connect beyond what any individual experiences alone. When people extend themselves to the possibilities offered in community, their self-imposed isolation transcends to much larger and more powerful identity of belonging and connecting. In Energetic Coaching, clients examine and take responsibility for the quality of their community. As people replace artificial separations with spiritual values and vision, they connect to community for the common good. What is held in common becomes much larger than superficial differences. The more people connect, the less they need to be the lone hero of their own isolated story. As they reach the centerpoint of congruent inner-outer balance, people realize common ground motivated by the common good.

John: *I recall attending a conference jointly sponsored by the Robert K. Greenleaf Center for Servant-Leadership and an association of leaders representing community de-*

velopment programs. The meeting was the first joining of the two groups to share ideas. As I listened to the impassioned speakers from both, I was struck with the similarities in their purpose and philosophy. Their words differed, yet both spoke of compassion and service to their fellow men and women. As I discussed ideas with various people, I found it hard to tell who belonged to which group. They shared common ground not specifically mentioned by either group. What was the unspoken quality? I read it as the blending of individual intentions into oneness of purpose, which was the expression of goodness and love through service. I hoped they would see the power of their combined intention and form a larger, even more powerful community.

Each person operates as an important part of a whole, and no one part can be missing or changed without altering the whole. Community provides the greatest opportunity for personal transformation because it calls the individual to service for the sake of the greater good. In times of disaster or despair people exhibit innate human desire to help others. They know that "There but for the grace of God go I." Compassion connects people each time there is a call to aid others who suffer. Once they have dealt with the disaster, however, people often go back to business as usual. With the ebbing of empathy and compassion, many return to their artificial separations and self-imposed isolation once again.

Energetic Coaches seek to build community around common humanity without the need for disaster. In Energetic Coaching, clients reflect on being and doing. The community encompasses family, friends, co-workers, country, and other groups to which they belong. In each group we encourage clients to contribute through caring connections. As a rule, as they serve the community, so the community reciprocates by serving them. If a community does not serve clients, we help them to influence the community to do so or to find another that provides opportunities for self-expression and positive relationships.

John: *As a member of a group called A Center of Transformation, I sometimes wonder what is unique about my experience in it compared to others to which I belong. I know I feel a vibrant and vital connection among the members of that group.*

The mission of the group is "We are a healing, teaching and learning community dedicated to creating a sacred space for transformational practices that balance and align the mind, body and spirit to achieve peace, harmony and enlightened evolution." When I tell my friends and family about my experiences in the group, I feel excited about upholding and demonstrating my alignment with our values. The group calls me to be in harmony with spirit within and with others. The energy of the common carries over into my coaching because the same energy that connects me with community is present in my individual relationships moment to moment.

A community reflects each member's state of consciousness. When people do not take personal responsibility for contributing, then they need to examine their connection to the group to ensure that they participate in a way that allows expression of their being. If not, they have work to do, which may include letting go. In the same way that the greatest power for change and growth comes from within the individual, improving the community from within provides the greatest potential for transformation. Once again, no outside, external expert or change agent can provide the insight and lasting contribution for improvement that is possible through the committed members of the community.

If members cannot bring about positive transformation, they need to make a choice that serves their own best interests and those of the community. Sometimes the best they can do is to connect with a different community instead. Energetic Coaches help clients examine such situations for choices that provide the best outcomes. We encourage examination of community relations to ensure that they connect with groups that support individual enhancement and growth. We listen to the words in clients' stories and dramas for how they find meaning within community experience. Community serves as a powerful catalyst for self-knowledge and authentic power. Participation challenges people to be and do more than they as individuals might in isolation. They can use community relationships as opportunities to challenge and expand their isolated and separated views of the world.

Of course, there are those who feel unconnected to their community. They may experience isolation or alienation from other group members or from the group's agenda. Rather than blaming the group, a beneficial question might be: "What part of me chose to have this life experience for what reason?" Instead of playing the role of victim in the group, they might use the negative experience to self-reflect. What was the purpose for joining the group? What contribution did the group expect? Their inner knower may then reveal what role they and others could play successfully. Asking and answering the right questions can turn group relationships into learning experiences.

Lea: *For two years I belonged to a volunteer organization in which I had invested a great deal of time and energy. Through coaching I realized that I was not getting the satisfaction from membership that I had sought when I joined and that I was not producing the results I had in-*

tended. I began focusing on my personal mission statement and sought membership in a community that would provide what I sought. I realized that I was not giving up but letting go of something that did not serve me because of my inability to have a positive influence on the group. The group labeled and marginalized me because I did not agree with their active agenda (which was different from the expressed agenda). I realized that even volunteer groups have systemic problems beyond one person's ability to influence. Because I have limited time to volunteer and there are many volunteer opportunities from which to choose, now I choose carefully the communities to which I give time, money and energy.

Sometimes people find it difficult to change or let go of a community such as a family tribe or a job that provides income. It can take a change in employment or a change in attitude to adjust, but something has to give to maintain personal integrity and congruence.

John: *At one stage of my career my position changed because the organization was merging different areas into new departments. The stated purpose of downsizing, commonly referred to as "reorganization," was greater effectiveness and efficiency along with cost savings. As I viewed my new department like the odd man out, I felt excluded from the activities of the other group members. I knew I had to create a purpose for being there or leave altogether. My efforts to gain clarification from my boss on my new role and responsibilities fell on deaf ears. I even reached the point where I thought there was a move to force me out.*

Seeking the advice of a co-worker in another department, I participated in a series of discussions with him and a third person on how best to handle my situation. We decided on a dramatic move to bring in an outside training program to open communications within and between departments. Starting small, we offered the training to employees on a voluntary basis after work hours. Funding came from a manager after she had experienced reorganization problems in her own department. In two years the program grew into a major undertaking with voluntary participation of people from all levels of the organization. Spirit worked through me and in conjunction with others to change a negative situation into a benefit for the whole community.

THE CONNECTED INDIVIDUAL

Communities create spiritual energy through people: (1) trusting inner wisdom to listen to and work with spirit; (2) reaching out to others in relationship through spirit, influencing them, and being influenced by them for the collective best; and (3) combining talents, skills, and interests with guidance from spirit to do the work of community that will have positive results for all involved. Being a part of a community provides opportunities for individual transformation. It may not be easy to assume responsibility, but the effort to express, participate, and grow within a group satisfies the human need to connect and contribute to the world.

When the energy of congruent internal being manifests in the energy of external doing, people accomplish more with better results through community than if they worked alone. Community provides the opportunity to individually experience the energy of spirit as well as (and because of) the larger results that can be had through groups. Aligning as a group with a positive common vision engages and enhances the energy of spirit. Even if the results are not readily apparent externally, group members provide individual enhancement and empowerment by connecting, belonging, and advocating for each other.

Abraham Maslow, in his book Toward a Psychology of Being studied the hierarchy of human needs, which culminated in self-actualization. Energetic Coaching equates self-actualization with individual oneness. Maslow identified the need to connect as a necessary part of human growth. According to him, fulfillment of social needs is a vital step to achieve the ultimate state of self- actualization. A cohesive, congruent community satisfies esteem, belonging, and connectedness needs for its members.

Energetic Coaches listen to the words in client stories and worldviews for meaning relating to community experience. We hold that community serves humans as a powerful catalyst to increase self-knowledge and authentic power. Through participating in a community, clients can lower their defenses against interacting and relating. They can use the group experience as a mirror to look beyond individual isolated or separated views of the world.

Throughout human history the delicate balance of individualism versus collectivism has sent the pendulum swinging to and fro. To find the point of balance between the seemingly opposing forces of individual and group interests, Energetic Coaches take the macro perspective. Knowing that we are all connected, we challenge clients to give and receive in community as a positive, personal investment. Even though individuals may feel overwhelmed and insignificant in relationship to the whole, through coaching clients come to appreciate their contribution. Each person's thoughts, attributions, projections, rationalizations, and attitudes create the community collectively. The inner being or culture of a community reflects the inner being of its members. In the dynamic organism of a community, individuals are like cells within the body. A virus that invades one cell can spread to many others. The immune system, however, knows how to identify and immobilize a virus to avert a serious illness. Because of the connectedness of those in community, each person's effect on others has a cumulative effect on the community. Every member is responsible for its health whether they want to own responsibility or not. No one can stand outside the community to which they belong. Each person is either part of the problem or part of the solution.

To achieve personal wholeness and integrity, individuals take personal responsibility for the role that they play. The inner knower senses incongruence in those who abdicate their responsibility for being and doing in their community. Sins of omission are just as bad as sins of commission to the inner knower. To achieve congruence between their inner and outer selves, people must look to see what projection comes back from the community to them. If they find the reflection acceptable, they can enhance the good qualities (and there is always something good). If unacceptable, they risk losing congruence within self and with community unless something is done about it.

Lea: *Even though the following happened almost 30 years ago, I still think about it. I was talking to someone who was in the League of Women Voters. She told me about her work in the organization, but I was not interested. In my youthful arrogance I stated that I did not trust most politicians and that I did not vote because there was no one to vote for, and I did not want to risk voting for the wrong person. The League member expressed shock and dismay. She told me that I was not fulfilling my obligation as a US citizen, and that if I weren't so lazy and self-centered, I would delve into the issues and find candidates to support. Even though I suffered a harsh chastisement, a part of me understood and accepted what she said. I was living in a free country, so it was my duty to exercise my freedoms and rights instead of taking them for granted. I could not stand outside and criticize without doing something positive to maintain my personal integrity.*

There is no community that is flawless because people are imperfect. The community reflection magnifies human faults and foibles. It takes many individuals working cohesively to make the world a better place. Societies depend on money and politics to influence individual constituents and build strong coalitions. Equal voting rights give citizens without money or political clout the same power as a rich or influential person. Even though there may be a slow, cumbersome, corrupt, and bureaucratic system in communities, when isolated individuals refuse to participate, they withhold their influence for improvement. Unless all take part, the needed changes in social responsiveness and responsibility continue to diminish. People become mere critics, who blame and play victim. It is easy to complain and blame and remain an outsider. Individuals of power build communities for impact. Those with the most resources may have the most influence, but many individuals do not exercise their resources through community to balance the polarity of external power based on external resources versus internal power based on values. When people connect for a compelling cause, they instigate incremental change out of shared vision. Even though some feel like underdogs, collectively the community appreciates those who overcome the odds. People like to root for the underdog.

John: *I swim in the Senior Olympics. When I was participating in a regional swim meet doing the 200-yard butterfly, I needed a couple of seconds to rest at the 150-yard mark. While I held on to the wall, the timer motioned for me to keep going. When the spectators saw me start moving again as the last, lone swimmer, they stood up, cheering me on. In all honesty, it was the spirit of the crowd that kept me going those final 50 yards. I finished last, but the crowd cheered more for me than for the person who finished first.*

Those who feel overwhelmed or ineffective might take strength from what has happened in the last hundred years. There have been great advances in human rights spearheaded by brave individuals willing to take a stand. Women won the right to vote and the people mandated civil rights in the US. The Berlin Wall came down. Ghandi initiated the Salt March in India and overturned British rule through peaceful resistance. Individuals coming together to support what in their hearts they know to be right plants seeds to create far-reaching changes. Each one, acting true to self and to community, worked to make the outer world congruent with the inner self through common values and vision.

Those who do not connect with their community tend to blame, second-guess, and criticize rather than do what can be done to make improvements. If people judge or criticize their community without becoming the agent of change they want to see, they have taken no responsibility or self-accountability to improve the situation. Individuals who judge and criticize separate from the community, becoming isolated and alienated. Energetic Coaches help clients to influence their community for the better or make a decision to join a different one in which a positive contribution can be made.

Lea: *Joel works in a federal prison. With 20 years in, Joel is counting the days to retirement. Each time I talk with him, he complains about his work in the system. I remember him as a young man, determined to make positive changes everywhere he went. He worked hard to contribute. Now he feels beaten by the job. He has developed a pervasive cynicism toward others and himself, yet he wants something out of life. Joel hesitates to leave his employer because he wants the guaranteed retirement. He values the macro-level benefit of security but operates on a micro level of criticizing and rejecting his employer, some coworkers, and the overall system. He has tried to make macro-level changes, but on an individual level without building coalitions. On a micro-level Joel could change his attitude toward his job to eliminate the negative impact it has on his life. He loses personal power by disconnecting psychically from his work community while remaining physically connected to it. This separation between Joel's internal being and external doing causes conflict that erodes his energy and passion for life.*

To connect with spirit and derive personal power, people need to develop a drive, a purpose, a passion, a life mission. Energetic Coaches play a significant role for those who act in a stimulus- response mode through external orientation and who separate themselves through blame and criticism. We challenge clients to find positive ways to tap into their inner knowing and create self-empowerment. Some people consciously empower themselves and create their purpose through self-expression in work and community. We help clients translate what energizes them internally into authentic action in community. The more dysfunctional the community appears to be, the more opportunity for improvement.

Lea: *Even though I left the volunteer organization I spoke about earlier, I could not let go of the experience and the part I played within it to make the outcome less than satisfactory. Knowing that changes needed to be made in the system as a whole, I acted outside the volunteer organization but within the larger community to make improve-*

ments. I helped build coalitions and worked methodically with an overall vision to connect. Now the organization has undertaken a survey- feedback project as a first step in helping the agencies communicate and cooperate with one another. A strategic mission can sustain energy of good intention to create incremental improvements. I had to let go, but I didn't give up.

Even though they are acting authentically, many people encounter constraints that make their choices, intentions, and objectives challenging to achieve. The difference between those who "go for it" and those who don't is a matter of internal attitude—wherein lies the greatest individual power—to choose. For whatever excuse some use to avoid pursuing what they desire in life, there are others, facing even harsher circumstances, who achieve despite greater odds. Success depends on where individuals decide to focus. They may view their locus of control in the seemingly larger outer world or within the seemingly smaller internal world. The external world does have the ability to overwhelm and weaken if people view it as large. A congruent person seeks within for the immense power to balance and offset outer circumstances. People have the personal power to choose their internal state to align thoughts, feelings, and perceptions with spirit. Spirit aids to "put the endeavor over the top" in ways an alienated unaided person could not do.

Energetic Coaches create connections with community by working with individuals to expand their internal sphere of influence and find ways to act and behave that are congruent from within.

We know that wherever there is something that can be criticized and rejected, there is something that can be supported and joined. We help the externally oriented, blaming, or separated individuals in a group find what they can do to improve a situation and follow up on their choices. Energetic Coaches hold individuals accountable and challenge them whenever the self-serving and superior attitude focuses on what is wrong rather than on opportunities for improvement. Even within very negative situations we help people find the challenge and opportunity within them to transcend obvious external dilemmas. Energetic Coaches know that overcoming difficult situations creates self-esteem, courage, and power for the future. People benefit when they connect as responsible members of community despite difficulties and challenges confronting the group. The transcendence over adverse situations through an internal positive attitude and self- empowerment provides a direct connection with spirit, individually and collectively. It's not those who achieve the most, but those who overcome the most who gain the rewards of inner peace, self-satisfaction and power. Through personal integrity and spiritual connection, members and their community benefit as a result of commitment to common vision and values.

It often happens that those who seek recognition are not the ones who get it. The group knows when someone is doing something for self-edification rather than for the greater good. Some people seek recognition, reward, and responsibility to fulfill their ego needs. Others, practicing servant leadership, work for the good of the community rather than for their own singular promotion. Such individuals know that what is done for others benefit them in the connected world of community. They experience spirit and sustainable inner energy in contrast to those who act from the self-serving, ego-based need for external recognition and power.

THE ASPECT OF HERO IN COMMUNITY

*It is not the critic who counts, not the man who points out
how the strong man stumbled, or where the doer of deeds
could have done them better. The credit belongs to the
man who is actually in the arena; whose face is marred
by dust and sweat and blood; who strives valiantly; who
errs and comes short again and again; who knows the
great enthusiasms, the great devotions, and spends himself
in a worthy cause; who, at the best, knows in the end the
triumph of high achievement, and who at the worst, if
he fails, fails while daring greatly, so that his place shall
never be with those cold and timid souls who know neither
victory nor defeat.*

THEODORE ROOSEVELT

Each person has a hero within. In times of tragedy, danger,
or threat, the hero rises to the challenge. On a daily basis,
the mundane aspects of life conceal the hero aspect. Even
though people may sense who they are as powerful creators
of reality, they may have no idea how to express their spiritual nature as the hero within. The external world portrays
the hero as a special individual who performs superhuman
feats in impossible situations. In reality, the hero is what people tap into when they choose to act authentically by expressing inner congruence and connection. Once people no longer
need to impress others, their hero can emerge. Small acts of
kindness are heroic, although they may go unnoticed. Heroic
acts happen every day. Speaking the truth rather than going
along with the crowd is an act of heroism. There may be no
outer recognition or reward, but the inner knower knows. By
acting when and where called, individuals become heroes to
themselves. By caring and acting on behalf of others without

thought of individual advancement or reward, they demonstrate to themselves and community what it means to be whole and complete. By finding the hero within, people discover and express the unique aspect of self that provides a meaningful connection with the world.

Energetic Coaches help clients realize their inner hero despite lack of recognition (or even active resistance) by the community. An external hero is not necessary because nothing external can match the power of the hero within. Those who play for external validation never feel good enough, and the inner knowers of others recognize those who may be acting for hero worship. They are not trusted. Like imposters trying too hard to be seen and acknowledged as special, showoffs compete with others and drain the resources of the group.

Energetic Coaches focus inside so clients can develop the qualities within that they admire in others. We assist people in cultivating a sense of inner greatness and finding ways to express it without depending on external acknowledgement or reinforcement. We celebrate internal satisfaction and appreciation in lieu of hero worship, which is based on temporary superficial attributes such as fame, money and physical prowess. Energetic Coaches foster self-knowing and self-appreciation so that clients can let go of any need to prove to themselves and others how valuable, lovable, perfect, and wonderful they are. Clients come to appreciate their inner hero, who replaces riches, rewards, and recognition with heroic inner values.

By knowing that there is a hero within each person, communities can cease trying to create external heroes to save them. Instead, they can foster relationships based on common vision and values. Members can share contributions and accountability so no one needs to take all the responsibility or credit for the results of the group effort. Because the guiding force of group effort is the common good, members can function effectively without a coercive or charismatic external leader or savior.

Everyone is equal and each person is special and unique. Each individual has an important role to fill within the community. Even the existence of a top-down hierarchy does not mean that one person is more valuable than another. Once people in community know and acknowledge individual equality, they can appreciate one another's unique self and contributions equally. Those with a special gift or talent in one area complement others with different talents and gifts. Community energy and impact is exponentially greater than the sum of the parts.

Communities reflect the state of consciousness of the individuals within them. If a community allows group think through external judgments, it isolates itself just as individual egos judge and separate from others they perceive to be inferior. Communities that focus on external status reflect the need to judge and be inferior or superior to others. Such groups seek to evict or marginalize those who differ from them. One such group would be the good ole boy network. Isolated communities consist of isolated individuals with superficial bonds based on you scratch my back, I'll scratch yours.

Membership in a community that values only external expressions of separateness and superiority such as wealth, elitism, religious zeal, or physical beauty fails to satisfy people. Based on transitory outward appearances, such a community lacks sustaining inner values and vision. The hero within each person can come forward in communities in which results and rewards are recognized as a result of everyone's contribution.

THE CONNECTED COMMUNITY

Only those beneath me can envy or hate me. I have never been envied nor hated; I am above no one. Only those above me can praise or belittle me. I have never been praised or belittled; I am below no one.

KAHIL GIBRAN

Members who value the equal uniqueness in one another create the living, dynamic organism of the connected community. Everyone respects each other's role and contribution equally. People in a connected community balance inner values with external goals. Their group mission or vision statement keeps them aligned. Matching an active vision (doing) with inner values (being) connects through the group spirit to form a cohesive community.

Lea: *I asked a professor in one of my classes for my Organization Development degree what might work to bring people together. I wondered how to dispense with individual agendas for the sake of the whole. His answer disappointed me. "Create a common enemy," he told me. Certainly his approach does work, but is it sustainable? I thought there were enough external enemies, so no need to create more. I was seeking to learn about ways to use creative, proactive, visionary approaches to build healthy, sustainable organizations. The positive aspect of coaching attracted me to the field. Coaching supports creating the external from the positive, internal vision of what people want. Organizations can do the same by focusing on what is wanted rather than reacting to external threats.*

Energetic Coaches know that working against something is not as powerful and sustainable as working for something. We want to support individuals coming together to address the large problems facing humanity. The need for clean water and renewable energy, health and social problems, the burgeoning world population, and the economic disparity between the have and have-nots will create either disaster or the greatest opportunity in human history for people to work together. Energetic Coaching has a role in bringing together people with diverse needs and backgrounds united for the common good. If we envision and strategize solutions collectively, we can address and overcome the serious problems of today.

The I-One community of connected people consists of individuals committed from the inside out to create relationships based on mutual respect, equality, and goodwill. Everyone joins—no outsiders are left behind. No one has more worth than anyone else. All are invited to contribute. Combined spiritual energy creates a compelling force to work together to overcome challenges the community faces.

A community is made up of individuals in relationship. If people respond to the connection within that calls them to congruence, then their outer relationships mirror integrity and equality. Envision what it would be like in the world if individuals treated one another with respect because of self-respect. Think of what it would be like if the customers and the constituents of an organization treated each other as valued parts of the whole. What would it feel like if all family members intended the best for one another? What if friends and acquaintances were able to be in the present moment with one another in authenticity and acceptance, no matter what the past or prejudice? How do people create such an ideal community? Begin with individuals' being who they want to be within themselves and in relationship with others, living the Golden Rule.

Energetic Coaches examine the community and the support systems of our clients to see if their relationships manifest the energy of spirit for the common good. Then we help clients envision and create the community that they want. Focusing on their life purpose, they participate in the community in ways that lead to personal integration. The community acts as a mirror of individual vision and values. Because individuals in the I-One community contribute to making their outer world reflect their inner selves, congruent clients serve as catalysts for improved community relations. Balanced and connected with spirit through positive intention, free will goodwill, and—yes, love—they create community relationships as mirrors of who they are.

COMMUNITY IN THE WORKPLACE: THE ENERGETIC COACH, THE ENERGETIC ORGANIZATION, THE COURAGEOUS EXECUTIVE

Maslow said that introspection full time in a cave all by one's self someplace was an approach to self actualization which he had never seen work for anybody; that the quality all of his self-actualizing subjects shared was that they were motivated by some great and important job.
Excerpt from, "Communication, Language and Meaning,"
by George A. Miller

Because of the importance of work and the impact of organizations on the individual and society, the organization as a connected entity holds great energetic potential. The organization that people create mirrors each individual's reflection. How each connects with the work of the community and one another produces the spirit of the organization. Because individuals create workplace communities out of their own free will, we refer to them as "members" rather than employers or employees. As Jane Galloway Seiling observes in her book, The Membership Organization, to achieve individual empowerment and organizational enrollment, employees must be connected to their workplace as a community.

The scientific method and scientific management have served their purpose; however, we are left with an entrenched paradigm that keeps us short of potential. Energetic Coaching holds that something intrinsic and qualitative, although difficult to measure, is as important as what is extrinsic and quantifiable. Valuing objectivity over subjectivity has left us with a lopsided way of looking at the world. Especially in organizations, the quality of relationships and opportunity for congruent self-expression in the workplace must be valued along with short-term, tangible goals. Some organizations state that people are an important asset but still see them as a liability on the balance sheet. When companies reduce payroll as a short-term way to increase profits they lose trust and erode relationships.

This does not mean that all members are guaranteed lifetime employment. In an organization everyone is accountable for doing the work. Unfortunately, some people seem to care only about self- promotion. There are those who don't do their job, and some who make it difficult for others to do theirs. Detractors undermine community and create work and difficulty for others. As people in the organization compare their values with their outcomes, they will see gaps. Members must address the gaps to resolve incongruence in how they speak, act, and treat one another in the organization. Some members will not fit or refuse to contribute so must be reassigned or let go for the sake of the whole.

Lea: *Judy was a particular challenge at work because she behaved erratically. Depending on her mood, she might be pleasant and talkative or surly and uncommunicative. Sometimes, she would cheerily greet people she passed in the hallway; other times, she would allow the door to close on the person following her. There were days when she seemed intently interested in visiting with her co- workers. There were other days when she would stay in her office and shun contact with others. If people interrupted her, she would glare as they walked through the door. Sometimes she would extend herself to help others, and there were other times when she would refuse extra work. Judy listened to gossip and spread it widely. Her incongruent and inconsistent behavior kept co-workers out-of- balance, which was how she maintained power over them. For some reason, her supervisor allowed such behaviors at the expense of morale and productivity.*

Situations in which people have to work with moody, unpredictable colleagues hamper productivity and workplace satisfaction. Even though most organizations suffer many Judys, few address their behavior. There are no written standards for such irregular acts, and the irregular person keeps slightly beyond reproach by doing the job. Such people have probably been at the organization for a long time because new employees like Judy would not have lasted.

Organizations must address behavior, not only in terms of productivity but also in terms of values and relationships. Only by clearly defining the parameters for how individuals treat one another can organizations address negative behavior in a positive way. Energetic Coaches can assist by sleuthing out the reasons for the disconnection with the individual, with co-workers, and with organizational values. Not everyone needs to be happy in an organization, however, we work to uncover and resolve the reasons for poor behavior to diminish the impact of continual negativity. Our aim is to promote free will goodwill and connection within the individual, the organization, and the community at large.

THE CHALLENGE AND OPPORTUNITY IN THE WORKPLACE

The work of organizations is not only to make a product or to employ people; it is to create belonging, meaning, and opportunities for individual growth. Given the diverse relationships among members, achieving integrity, balance, and congruence of inner values and outer actions becomes exponentially complex in community. The unique qualities of each relationship make balancing conflicting goals with limited resources challenging. Between stimulus and response lies the center-point where the values of an organization guide each member in the moment. By requiring diverse individuals to work together on common goals, organizations sponsor connections to achieve large results. The opportunities for connectedness, common goals, rewards for effort, satisfaction, and individual self-actualization invite spirit into the organization.

Some find it difficult to work closely with others who are different. Organizations offer wonderful opportunities to do so. Producing an outcome that is not necessarily meaningful in itself (like making widgets on an assembly line) can demand a stretch in human creativity and inner purposefulness. Energetic Coaches see that the organization is often a challenge that, if addressed, can provide even greater connection within, with others, and with spirit. Energetic Coaching provides a relationship perspective that connects individuals with one another and to common goals. Individual employees set the example to promote equality and wholeness, especially those at the top, who have greater power and visibility in their words and actions. Working as a live organism with inner and outer congruence, the organization can convey spiritual qualities. Members benefit, no matter what their job or status. Does this vision of organizations as an equal, unified whole sound idealistic? Even though relatively rare, organizations do exist that strive for congruence, integrity, and equality. Individuals can change and align with common values in an instant when sincerely invited. With continued focus and effort, the organization reaches a tipping point as it accumulates energy around a vision that creates congruent relationships from within and without. The vision of an energetic and spirited workplace becomes reality.

What Would an Energetic Organization Look Like?

Visualize this. Before an energetic organization hires anyone, the employer reviews the handbook with the prospective member to outline the organization's values and vision. In the handbook there are the usual guidelines for conduct—the doing part of the job. There is equal emphasis on the values of the organization, regarding how people treat one another and how they care about their work—the being part of the job. Such a handbook might contain the following language:

Company X employees are known for their kindness, respect, and appreciation for one another. Gossip, backbiting, and negativity are not part of the company culture. We address issues with one another directly, one-on-one, with respect for differences.

Company X always welcomes member suggestions for improvements. Instead of talking about problems, members at Company X speak about solutions and take ownership for results.

Members trust the company, their supervisors, their coworkers, and the Human Resources Department to express their concerns and suggestions regarding how they are treated in the company. Management will follow thorough on each concern to its satisfactory resolution, with members providing guidance in the process.

Members of Company X take pride in their work and assume responsibility for their contributions. Blaming others or second-guessing their decisions is not a part of our company's culture. Instead, before we make decisions, we encourage people to speak up and to receive answers. We will address any apprehensions. Those who will be affected by decisions have opportunities to give their ideas to shape policy in advance of action. Members will ask questions and provide justification for decisions so we can achieve understanding and collective accountability for outcomes.

Even as Company X continually improves, members will make mistakes. We view mistakes as opportunities to learn. We encourage research and open discussion to make necessary corrections, additions, or changes to standard operating procedures so we can lessen avoidable errors. Company X members take responsibility for their contributions, including the valuable lessons that accompany "mistakes."

At Company X individuals receive rewards commensurate with their contributions. Teams, departments and the overall organization will be rewarded according to profitability and performance. Many factors are involved in the reward structure, including the market value of a cer-

tain job position and wages of others in the industry and the area. To keep Company X profitable and healthy, we distribute rewards fairly and review them continually. We do not give automatic rewards. We do award meritorious contributions with merit increases. We increase salaries in accordance with increases in contribution to the organization and to one another. Members may initiate salary reviews and present their reasons for requesting an increase at any time. The organization provides avenues for advancement for those who want to make the necessary investment of effort and learning.

People tell the truth to one another, to customers, and to constituents. By free, open, honest communication, members collaboratively cooperate for the best solutions—discussing problems openly without judgment of persons, ideas, opinions, or perspectives. By contributing to the continuing effort to find improvements and common ground, members bridge the gaps that may exist in individual perspectives. Trust is intentionally promoted and gaps in trustworthiness are addressed. The organization is based upon authentic action—we do what we say we will do.

Company X encourages members to examine their intent for working here. The company dedicates its energy and vision to high standards, growth, and continuous improvement through all members assuming individual responsibility for living values that contribute to the common good.

Value statements expressed coherently by an organization at the outset of employment communicate expectations in a realistic job preview. An Energetic Organization holds all members throughout the organization accountable for expressing such values individually. Of course, there are going to be bad days for everyone, but it is not acceptable that a person uses the bad-day excuse for poor behavior. There must be coherent consensus about how people treat one another at work so that the group extinguishes negative behavior and celebrates and rewards positive behavior.

Because there are many different people and situations in an organization, all individuals— especially those at the top of a company—need to speak and practice values such as equality, kindness, respect, appreciation, truth, authenticity, and trust. The spirit of the organization expressed by a living value system provides energy for human relations at work creating phenomenal results.

Lea: As president, Mark would often remark to his colleagues that he could give the company's strategic plan to the competition and it wouldn't matter. It was the caliber of the people who carried out the plan that achieved the significant outcomes and not the plan itself.

THE POWER OF EMOTIONS

Lea: *Brad was unhappy with his job in the accounting department. Because he was good at it, his manager gave him more and more work. When there was a special assignment, he dropped it on Brad's desk because he knew Brad would complete it in his usual prompt, accurate manner. Brad grew resentful and sullen. Naturally his behavior reflected on his work. When his boss asked him what was bothering him, Brad exploded in frustration and anger. Brad's boss listened as Brad vented. Then, as he calmed, his boss asked him for suggestions on how to improve his situation at work. Together, they outlined some parameters regarding special assignments. His boss agreed to delegate some jobs to another department so that Brad would be available for the additional work when needed. In return for his intervention, Brad's supervisor solicited Brad's agreement that he would be kinder and more cooperative with others.*

Brad's boss acted as an Energetic Coach by listening to him and allowing him to express frustration without negative ramifications. Instead of being intimidated by Brad's outburst, he relied on his inner knowing that Brad was a competent and caring employee. In fact, if Brad had not cared about his job, he would not have reacted so emotionally. Through the positive receptivity and openness demonstrated by his supervisor, Brad discovered that his employer cared about him as a person. Because Brad felt empowered by telling what was bothering him, he came up with solutions and took ownership for implementing them. Brad's boss encouraged him to care about his job and strengthened his emotional connections with the community.

When members in an organization feel that the organization cares about them, they are likely to reciprocate. Emotions are a powerful bond between people and the community to which they belong. No one works diligently and productively in an organization without forming an emotional bond. Often the members who care the most in an organization are the most frustrated. Energetic Coaching helps people find ways to emotionally bond in a positive way with their work or helps them find different work that suits them better.

The Stimulus-Response Organization

Lack of planning on your part does not constitute an
emergency on mine.
Sign posted in many organizations

Many workplaces are not value-driven even though they have crafted a mission statement that every member is expected to memorize. Without relationships within the organization that reflect the published value statements, organizations are incongruent; they operate like stimulus-response individuals. Without the connection and unification of a living vision and value system, the people within organizations have no overriding guidance for behavior, standards and outcomes.

In a stimulus-response organization with low self-esteem, members practice avoidance tactics and behave like puppets, automatically responding to external events. They generate a great amount of activity with little progress. Each crisis—much like the crisis of the day before—is met with pseudo, unsustainable energy. Without a fire to fight, members wait at their desk, facing piles of work they have avoided because they lack the energy of purpose and commitment. It takes an emergency to get a reaction, and problems are addressed only when they can no longer be ignored. What might have been a minor problem if addressed proactively flares into a major attention-getter. People tend to lay aside work until they have to finish their projects for fear of exposure and retribution. Even if someone gives a direction, most ignore it. Strategic planning goes out the window, and people wait for any new initiative to go away just like the last flavor of the month. Members wait like children to be rewarded or punished. Good employees leave, and no one knows why or bothers to ask. The organization lacks spirit because it lacks teamwork, respect, and authenticity. Without the connecting energy of spirit embodied by a community congruent with its stated values, members put in time like indentured servants. They dread their workplace, which resorts to command/control tactics to get the job done.

Many organizations play out this scenario to a greater or lesser degree. How do people change such a situation? First of all, they must live their values-based vision. Those at the top must emulate core values, especially in their actions (doing) and their personhood (being). They can transform managing a stimulus-response, fire-fighting organization into leading a values-driven, visionary organism. Difficult as change may be, leaders must be and do differently if they are to attract and keep members who are individually congruent with desired values and vision.

Lea: *My husband, Steve, was the sixth hot mill superintendent in seven years. When he was promoted from his position in research, he knew he had to accept, even though the job was a revolving door. The mill had been the bottleneck of the steel-making operation. Steve knew he would be reassigned if he did not increase efficiency.*

Steve began by letting everyone know that he could not succeed alone. He relied on his integrity and intelligence, rather than status, to work for improvement. Steve studied the operation, spending many hours getting his "arms around" the facts. He knew who he was (internally) and what was going on (externally). The changes he made did not work right away, and at first things got even worse in the mill, but Steve's supervisor continued to support him.

Steve risked judgment and dislike by holding each person accountable. He worked with those who did not perform and let go of those who blocked improvement. Even though he was very unpopular at first, he told the truth and ex-

pected the same from others. Enlisting the support of those members who cared, he began to take the pulse of the operation by listening to the people who were doing the job and asking for their suggestions.

After a year and a half with some major downturns, the mill turned around. Steve succeeded where five superintendents had not. Many resisted his initial efforts for improvement and tested his personal integrity. However, in the long run, Steve won the respect of his most ardent critics. He shared the credit for the turnaround with his co-workers, who had taken ownership as they saw the benefit of working together and followed Steve's example for authentic action.

Most individuals want to change a firefighting, stimulus-response, parent-child organization into a mature, effective, pro-active entity. At first, however, some may resist the drive toward excellence. They may wait on the sidelines to decide if they want to connect with the whole. As the organization becomes congruent through individuals' acting in accordance with a stated vision and values (starting with those at the top), the energy of spirit is palpable in an excellent organization. Spirit adds energy, aiding those who align with it to stay the course. It takes courageous, risk-taking individuals who know themselves to slowly turn the ship around to sail with the wind of spirit, even as it appears to be heading into uncharted territory.

THE CULTURE OF NOT KNOWING

Those who hold high places must be the first to start, to
mold a new reality, closer to the heart.
Song by RUSH

As individuals become incongruent through ignoring their inner knower, so do organizations. Many communities ignore the truth that holds the seed of excellence. To achieve congruence and balance, the inner knowers of individuals must connect with the inner knower of the community. There are organizations in which members implicitly agree to ignore the truth and uphold sacred cows. The book Driving Fear out of the Workplace by Kathleen Ryan and Daniel Oestreich revealed how individual and systemic incongruence creates situations and issues called "undiscussables." Although it is sometimes made to appear that the taboo subjects are insignificant or useless, avoiding difficult truths blocks the energy and inner knowing to achieve individual and organizational congruence. To the extent that the truth cannot be stated openly and freely, energy is depleted. The organization is deadened as individuals within it are shut down.

Whenever people in an organization act against the stated value system, they cause the organization to lose connection and energy. People mistrust and separate from one another and the organization to the extent that they feel they have to criticize or remain outside to maintain personal congruence. But the inner knower keeps reminding people that working for a disconnected, inauthentic organization wastes energy. Incongruence, which permeates the place, eats away productivity and job satisfaction from the inside out, much like a voracious virus that eventually kills its host.

Leaders of organizations hold great responsibility. If they do not seek truth, they shirk their responsibility. Those in leadership positions are especially accountable if the organization is out of alignment with stated values. Members of an organization are co-opted easily if they fear ramifications from higher-ups. Those who care and want to tell the truth give up because management does not want to know. Sins of omission become prevalent in a "don't ask-don't tell" environment. It is vital to talk about undiscussables and speak the truth. Even if leaders lack the resources to address a shortcoming, it is still important to acknowledge the concerns of the community. Despite inherent challenges that keep organizations from operating continuously at peak performance, leaders need to address constraints directly and openly.

Lea: *Steve's boss, the COO of a major steel maker, also served on the Steel Import Committee in Washington, DC. The COO asked Steve to purchase steel from a foreign supplier to save money. Steve asked his boss what would happen if someone on the import committee found out. Without receiving a reply, Steve realized that his boss would have acted as if he had nothing to do with the deal. If anyone in the industry found out, Steve would be the scapegoat.*

Some ways to make money are quicker and easier than others, so profitability cannot be the sole goal of an Energetic Organization. The path of least resistance leads nowhere. Just as congruent individuals know that they must do difficult inner work, the Energetic Organization knows that profit is the result of upholding values with authentic action. The practice of not knowing by those at the top of organizations needs to be addressed. Truth telling is difficult work but pays great dividends for the community and its members.

It has been said that employees treat customers in the same way that the organization treats its members. Top management must walk the talk or they cannot expect anyone else to do so. Leaders must live the value statements in order to expect that others will follow suit.

THE ENERGETIC ORGANIZATIONAL COACH

Energetic Coaches operate in the realm of relationships, examining gaps in internal values and external expressions of them. Starting at the top of an organization, we aim to achieve executive- level congruence between values and behaviors. Only when executives embrace congruence can individual members be coached to achieve high standards in relationships and performance. Energetic Coaches identify and communicate gaps between layers of the organization so that not knowing becomes knowing. Even if nothing can be done about a situation, at least the lid is off the pressure cooker, and members feel connected with one another as they face their common constraints and challenges honestly.

Energetic Coaches become messengers to management on behalf of the members so that the organization can address barriers to trust and respect. We mine for the truth and place tough issues before management. We challenge the leadership to hold itself accountable and set the example for others. As individuals at all levels of the organization follow the examples set by leadership, everyone increases ownership and self-accountability. Positive sustainable energy— that of spirit—lifts the organization to high standards of personal integrity and performance.

Energetic Coaches may need to help others identify and weigh risks. As the objective and compassionate witness to organizations, we can communicate in ways that allow members to speak the truth and act authentically. When we challenge members to do their personal best, we tap into the inner hero in all members. We help leaders face their challenges with courage. Energetic Coaches become the mirror for the courageous executives to align within and operate according to high-level values of truth, integrity, and authenticity, creating congruence throughout the organization.

John: *In my previous career as an internal OD consultant, I was given the opportunity to work with Joe, who was in charge of Retail Sales with many direct-reports. Joe was given new goals each year by his boss, the Corporate VP of Sales. Joe was very jaded because the new goals had nothing to do with past performance or any other metric that was relevant. He was upset that corporate could be so far removed from the day-to-day reality of the division's problems and constraints. Instead, headquarters issued sales quota's that were outside the reach of his staff. I consulted with Joe regarding how to deal with the upper-up's in a way that would be factual and professional without allowing his resentment to show through. Looking back as an Energetic Coach, I would have dealt more at the gut level of the emotion, helping Joe to work through maintaining his integrity with his staff while juggling the unreasonable demands of corporate. Joe and I would have been equals in our quest to determine how best to present the new quota's to his staff in a manner that would be congruent and authentic. In that way Joe could coach his staff through the same reactions that he had already experienced in a more positive, proactive way to avoid the stimulus-response reaction to the unreasonable demands, and the loss of motivation that would ensue. I would have encouraged Joe to relay the truth back to corporate in a way they could hear while conveying the goals to his staff in a way they could receive. If we could not come up with a way of doing both with integrity, I would have worked with Joe to deal with what it means to be caught in the middle with the loss of integrity that happens when he is expected to please both sides.*

Energetic Coaches, like courageous executives, realize that the greater the risk, the greater the reward. Through non-attachment to any particular client or income level, we can personally set an example for truth and integrity. We mirror the organization's standard so that executives can operate in congruence with their stated values. With a willingness to risk income and ostracism to expose and confront delicate issues within an organization, Energetic Coaches engage the energy of spirit. By eliminating double-speak and double standards, we foster connected relationships and real communication. By demonstrating risk-taking for the sake of truth, we exemplify to the courageous executives the commitment required to behave congruently. Truthfulness invites spirit, a powerful catalyst to sustain energy for positive change in organizations. As organizations become cohesive, growing entities, they reflect the characteristics of spirit, which permeates the culture and creates the drive toward excellence. Courageous executives mirror the values of the organization, and Energetic Coaches challenge them to reflect high standards and provide support for tough choices. Courageous executives demonstrate congruence so that the outer organization mirrors the inner values of its members.

THE ROLE OF THE SPIRITED INDIVIDUAL IN ORGANIZATIONS

Sustainable improvement in organizations cannot take place without all individuals taking personal responsibility for their part. Top management support comes first, but it is but one ingredient in the mix. Each member of an organization must intend good. Just as a small amount of salt can drastically alter the taste of a recipe, so every single person in a community affects it.

To approach large, complex organizations from an individual perspective can appear impractical. But, like a hologram, the whole mirrors its parts: Each individual reflects the organization. When the organization achieves congruence, everyone profits from the spiritual energy. Spirit is what makes the sum greater than the parts. It assists in doing the work that could not possibly be achieved individually. We have no explanation for how spirit works, but if people and organizations consistently align with their vision and values, they form the critical mass to

create a congruent culture that calls individuals to their personal best.

To create, sustain, and build energy, all individuals must exercise free will choice. People create organizations for people. True power is the ability to have options and choose from them. When empowering choice comes from individuals linking themselves to the organization's vision and values, their synergistic alignment opens to spirit. As teams operate cohesively, their work flows, and they solve their problems without external demands or threats.

According to Michael Abrashoff, in an article in Fast Company magazine: *"You cannot order people to become cohesive. You cannot order great performance. You have to create the culture and climate that makes it possible. You have to build the bonds of trust...I found that the only way to do that was one member at a time."*

Powerful Relationships

In organizations, real power and energy is generated through relationships. The patterns of relationships and the capacities to form them are more important than tasks, functions, roles, and positions.
Margaret Wheatley

Lea: *During our weekly lunch my friend Herb and I were brainstorming how we could improve our workplace. We both have backgrounds in human resources and organization development, so we usually engaged in stimulating discussions about how we would run the company. We had a saying that sounds simplistic, so we always laughed when we said it to one another: "It's the relationship, Stupid!" "Stupid" meant that it was obvious what was going on in organizational dynamics, but that management was overlooking, downplaying, or ignoring the relationship dimension. Herb and I would often notice how some people would work together to put a project "over the top" whereas others would work against one another or avoid work whenever possible. The difference showed in the results. To us, it was obvious how important human relationships were, yet we seemed to be the only ones who paid attention to that aspect of the organization.*

Organizations today are talking about "powerful conversations." A powerful conversation is one in which the individual in relationship connects at a deep level. Everyone knows the difference between "How are you?" and "How are YOU?" Eye contact, focus in the moment, and true caring characterize real conversations. Each individual in an organization has the power to engage and create relationships of respect and trust in which spirit flourishes. People light the spark of connection with intention in the moment, creating connected relationships, which makes going to work a lot more fun!

Abrashoff goes on to point out, *"More than anything else, your people want authentic leadership... They need to believe in you as the living exemplar of a clear purpose that you communicate to them every day in ways large and small."*

Abrashoff's points seem obvious, but that does not mean his recommendations are easy or commonplace. To the extent that an organization's management has inner-outer congruence, members throughout the system can be challenged to exhibit the same. Many organizations are lacking spirit because they are missing spiritual values. Energetic Coaches have the opportunity with organizational leadership to help courageous executives develop a far-reaching, positive impact on entire organizations through being and doing good.

In all relationships no one is better or worth more than anyone else. Organizations operate under the illusion of greater and lesser worth through hierarchical pay structures and command/control systems. If leaders expect people to uphold the organization values, they have to treat them with equality and respect. Because the true work is that of expressing personal authenticity, people's rank in the organization is not important—their values are. When an organization engages its inner knower, it attracts spirit through sustained values and vision. The CEO may retire, but the organization's spirit will survive and thrive.

A VISION FOR THE FUTURE

Individuals and communities are evolving beyond the objective, linear mindset using just scientific method, measurement, and management. People are looking for more than the medical model in which clients rely on an external expert rather than their own inner wisdom. When people express their authentic being, they have done their greatest work. Spirit assists them to realize their greatest potential.

Organization Development works from the macro perspective of the overall system. Energetic Coaching works from the micro perspective of the individual in relationship with others, holding the ideal of oneness from the macro perspective. The two fields can blend to help individuals and organizations reach and sustain wholistic equilibrium for the good of all. The following is a brief comparison of some distinguishing features of Energetic Coaches and OD Professionals.

ENERGETIC COACHES	OD PROFESSIONALS
Deliberately enlist spirit to aid growth and discovery	Focus on dynamics of organization as a system
Encourage developing options from which individuals can choose collectively	Complete assessments and make recommendations
Work with members at the level of their highest selves	Work with the culture of the organization with top-level support
Ask questions of executives and members to cause introspection	Ask questions of members to understand the system

ENERGETIC COACHES	OD PROFESSIONALS
Guide members in presence of creative energy of spirit	Create strategic plans and direct energy toward system change
Focus on relationships of the member with self, with others, and with community	Focus on systems of control, influence, and diplomacy
Guide members to resolve individual incongruence	Identify strength and weaknesses of the overall organization

Organizations sometimes need external experts to introduce new paradigms, lessons, and technology essential to meeting the fast-paced demands of the environment. Energetic Coaches help individuals and organizations apply their innate knowing and the power of exercising free will goodwill to connect with one another for evolutionary change. OD professionals import external expertise, whereas we promote inner knowing to find truth, develop new ideas, and put them into practice. This may take more time, but the results are lasting and worthwhile.

Because Energetic Coaching is an inside-out endeavor, it may meet with resistance or skepticism in the business setting. Many individuals and communities believe that what is inside is hidden and perhaps unimportant. In actuality, what people think is revealed in the relationship mirror. It takes time with great effort to achieve inner-outer congruence, but the powerful effects last. Oftentimes, individuals and organizations tolerate working under the cloud of incongruence and inconsistency rather than address the gaps between ideals and actions. They may find it difficult to admit to ways in which the part has created what the whole experiences. Necessary change builds momentum to overcome the inertia of the status quo. The energy of alignment with high-level values requires expression. Energetic Coaches hold the vision and mirror inconsistencies that need to be resolved. We embody the courage and consistency to which we subscribe as individuals, and we risk resistance and resentment for the prolonged and even painful process as clients change.

THE POWER OF THE WORKPLACE COMMUNITY

Some people think that work is a four-letter word. They live for the weekend and dread Mondays. They work for retirement, but afterward, they look for work. They can't tolerate the people they work with, but when they are unemployed, they most miss their relationships with others. They ricochet in their dichotomy, unwilling to look within for the source of dissatisfaction that they project onto their community.

The community of the workplace challenges people to stretch in relationship with others, who may be people they would not choose to be with otherwise. And they may be asked to accomplish what they do not wish to do. The undesirability of both associates and jobs can be the impetus for some to search out spirit. Spiritual connection through inner knowing compels them to examine their being and make it congruent with their doing. Individuals increase in power and effectiveness through community, which challenges members to be and do for the common good.

Community is the means to impact the world to a greater degree than one person can do alone. When individuals in relationships make a caring, congruent community, spirit emerges. People manifest spirit in forming gratifying relationships based on equality and deserved respect from doing work well. They find meaning and purpose in whatever they do because it reflects who they are through the outer expression of inner values. The centerpoint of individual values provides the focus to achieve the outer expression of individual wholeness through community.

ENERGETIC COACHING IN COMMUNITY

Energetic Coaches know that individuals want to work for organizations not only for money but also for meaning. Energetic Coaches help people find connections with one another, their work, and the values and vision of the community to which they belong. We know that through one-on-one relationships embodying respect and inner-outer congruence, the organization becomes whole because each of the individuals within it is congruent and connected.

Energetic Organizations are led by courageous executives who focus on long-term qualitative criteria rather than short-term financial goals. They function in the immediate moment, person- to-person, with mutual respect. The triple bottom line is a guiding principle as members are encouraged to take responsibility for their unique contribution. Command and control tactics disappear as courageous executives mentor and set the example. Because people want to contribute and feel free to do so, individuals empower themselves and each other. The Energetic Organization evolves in which...

- Passive, aggressive and resistive behavior morphs into cohesive team spirit.
- Incoherent, unpredictable and negative behavior is addressed.

- Respectful relationships replace social subordination and marginalization.
- Individual connection and contribution to the real work replace micro-management and "busy-ness."
- People discuss "undiscussables."
- Honest, authentic communications replace politics.
- Individual empowerment replaces autocratic leadership and parent-child dependency.
- The exercised expertise of many supplants the expert role of few.
- Individuals aligning with a common vision replace the pseudo power of the hierarchy.
- Individual initiative and accountability render control tactics unnecessary.
- The common good trumps egocentric and self-centered motives.
- Open, honest communication replaces repressed individual expression.
- An atmosphere of authenticity creates congruence between what people say and what they do.
- Instead of using policies and procedures to compensate for a lack of common sense and caring, leaders provide examples and guidelines.
- Truthfulness and risk-taking reap rewards.
- People want to work for the organization rather than have to work for it.
- Individuals connect through vision, values, and long-term objectives so that the organization becomes one.
- Individuals realize their unique, complementary, and equal roles in maintaining the health and viability of the organization.

In the evolution of sustainable improvement in community, true power replaces the pseudo power of the ego-based culture existing in many organizations today. Just as you are the individual reading this book, weighing its words and deciding for yourself what may work for you, individuals within organizations do the same. The Energetic Organization calls members to their highest selves and seeks to connect everyone so that each and all can realize spiritual energy. Organizations become the conduit of the energy of spirit, connecting people in positive relationships to achieve greater outcomes than could be realized individually. Members connect and identify with the vision of their organizations, knowing that they will benefit from the reciprocal nature of free will goodwill. Organizations function as live, dynamic organisms. They operate as cohesive entities with members contributing according to ability. Everyone reaps the rewards of the connection and the energy of spirit, which benefits individuals and the organization as a cohesive and congruent whole.

CHAPTER 6 APPENDIX

WAYS ENERGETIC COACHING SUPPORTS THE ENERGETIC ORGANIZATION

1. Helps disconnected and dissatisfied members of an organization make decisions to connect with their job, co-workers, and the values of the organization.
2. Aids in preparing individual members to advance to roles of organizational responsibility.
3. Aids in preparing individual members for transfer or out-placement if they do not connect with the values and vision of the organization.

4. Listens to individual members to communicate with top management the concerns, issues, complaints, "undiscussables," and opportunities for improvement.

5. Coaches executives for inner congruence with the stated values of the organization in words and actions.

6. Collaborates throughout the organization to provide opportunities for connection with the stated vision or assists in revising the language of the mission of the organization to make it congruent.

7. Helps members and organizations achieve inner-outer congruence by pointing out when their walk is different from their talk.

8. Models personal inner-outer congruence and the power of authenticity, connectedness, and free will goodwill.

9. Provides examples and training for individuals within the organization to energetically coach one another.

10. Coaches executives to make the tough calls that move organizations to excellence with vision and spirit.

11. Coaches individuals to develop discernment, intuition, and inner guidance to make decisions and take action with congruence and confidence.

12. Provides a sounding board and space for inner knowing to emerge for unbiased, confidential, positive support of courageous executives to make difficult and complex decisions.

13. Operates as the compassionate witness of the overall organizational culture to observe and communicate ways in which the organization can become congruent and conducive to spiritual energy and connection.

14. Engages the inner knower of the organization by promoting individual truth-telling and reconciling gaps between what is wanted and what is done.

REFLECTION

- How do I provide a personal example and advocate for inner-outer congruence for my community?
- How does my community reflect the person I am?
- Does my community support my integrity and authenticity? If not, how can I influence my community for greater congruence?
- Are changes needed, or do I have to leave a community I am in to maintain personal integrity?
- What would my ideal community look like?

INTENTIONAL IMPRINT

- What would the community be like without me?
- What can I contribute through community powerfully to make positive change in the world?
- How am I the truest expression of my authentic being in each community to which I belong?

7. SHADOW AND ENERGETIC COACHING

One does not become enlightened by imagining figures of light, but by making the darkness conscious.
CARL JUNG

Flight usually intensifies the very thing one flees, and establishes a special intimacy with it.
THOMAS MOORE

THE INNER SHADOW

As a part of the inner work to achieve wholeness, Energetic Coaching deals with the shadow side of individuals. All people have a shadow side, which most deny. The shadow is an unknown aspect of self that holds important information needed for integration and wholeness. Even though the shadow is often repressed and unknown, people release tremendous energy through self-knowing and self-acceptance of all aspects of self. Because shadow is usually a blind spot, individuals often perceive shadow first in characteristics they project on others. The work of relationship is often the work of recognizing and integrating the shadow aspect of self. What people like or dislike in others is the mirror of shadow showing what they like or dislike about themselves. They also project the light aspect of their inner being through hero worship. If people are to know themselves, they must do shadow work to achieve wholeness and recognize their inner hero. Otherwise, they lose energy and resist and deny important aspects of the self.

Groups and organizations as a whole also have a shadow that exists in the hidden side of the members collectively. The shadow work that needs to be done to accomplish wholeness in organizations is a collection of the shadow work that needs to be done by the individuals within the group. It is especially important that the leaders of organizations have an understanding and acceptance of their shadow selves. If the individuals in an organization repress shadow work, they cannot recognize it to address it in order to release blocked energy in their relationships.

Even though some community members know that something is missing or incongruent, they may operate in work relationships with a fake quality and superficial compliance to policies and procedures that keep people in line. Those who are willing to reveal shadow may be marginalized, labeled, or ostracized—or fired. Organizations that deny the shadow work often punish truth tellers. Repressing shadow keeps members in the dark, operating from the shadow side without knowing the potential for positive energy that truth telling and shadow work can create.

Cultural norms, social caste systems, and mass media reflect the shadow work that needs to be collectively done. People are exposed to shadow every day. The dark and negative that dominates the media reflects the shadow of the collective consciousness. Those who are attracted to media violence, exploitation, fear, and suffering have personal shadow work to do.

The frightening and exploitive aspects of shadow pervade society. Society reflects shadow and presents opportunities for shadow work for individuals. In dealing with the shadow self within and in relationships with others, the light of consciousness illuminates. Instead of being morbidly and sordidly attracted to violence and exploitation of others in the media, people can work with their shadow teacher. When they become aware of their attraction to the negative aspects of their shadow without resisting or judging, they dispel the polarity of a denied shadow. People find wholeness by acknowledging all parts of themselves especially those that lie hidden in shadow. A reflection cast by what individuals like or dislike in others, in society, and in the media give them hints to what shadow work they need to do. As people collectively acknowledge what they reject, resist, envy or condemn in others, individuals and organizations will reflect integration and wholeness also.

Because spirit is wholeness, there cannot be a relationship with spirit that does not include shadow. Shadow exists in every person and in every organization. By denying their shadow side, people erect a barrier to their inner knower and to spirit. Energetic Coaches learn from the shadow teacher. We know that we must do our own shadow work before we can help clients work with their shadow aspects.

C. J. Jung, the preeminent Swiss psychologist of the early 1900s, extensively investigated the concept of shadow. Jung saw shadow work as vitally important to integrate the unconscious with the conscious. To Jung what appeared to cause conflict within the psyche was exactly the energy that could lead to wholeness, or what Jung called "individuation." Jung purported that the lessons and wisdom of shadow provide the means and challenge to grow and enlarge consciousness.

Denying or repressing shadow causes fragmentation. People disconnect from their inner knower when they judge others without seeing aspects of self. Being human is a dynamic, imperfect state. There is always room for improvement. Self-knowing people integrate shadow with spirit by making conscious choices. To deal with shadow means acknowledging and integrating foibles and flaws. It also involves acknowledging internal greatness, innate goodness, and infinite power. Enormous potential can be just as difficult to acknowledge as what people don't like about themselves and others.

Studying shadow requires an open, compassionate stance toward self and others along with a great sense of humor. Coaches who are most aware of their shadow side do not go into judgment of good or bad or right or wrong. We know that shadow will be cast each time spiritual light shines. By aligning the self through inner and outer congruence, we help clients assimilate shadow into the whole. Our job is never done. Managing the dynamic interplay of spirit and shadow is a constant challenge of consciousness. Those who see themselves completely—good, bad, and ugly—and continue to consciously choose free will goodwill achieve balance, growth, and wholeness.

THE SHADOW AS TEACHER

Unfortunately there can be no doubt that man is, on the whole, less good than he imagines himself or wants to be. Everyone carries a shadow, and the less it is embodied in the individual's conscious life, the blacker and denser it is. If inferiority is conscious, one always has a chance to correct it. Furthermore, it is constantly in contact with other interests, so that it is continually subjected to modifications. But if it is repressed and isolated from consciousness, it never gets corrected.
CARL JUNG, *Psychology and Religion*

Energetic Coaches use shadow as a teacher. When we are open to the never-ending stream of lessons that shadow presents, we expand our awareness. It is easier to acknowledge only the "good" without the "bad," but there are pros and cons to everything. Good can be made into bad and bad can be made into good. The perception of good or bad is a subjective evaluation creating judgmental, dualistic illusions of either/or thinking. People balancing at the centerpoint allow shadow into consciousness to reflect on their choices and outcomes, neither attaching nor resisting—but allowing shadow and spirit both.

Consciousness creates awareness of the shadow teacher. When people react strongly and emotionally, they have an important clue that the shadow teacher is presenting a lesson. A troubling encounter offers an opportunity to discover the part of the self that would rather judge and separate from what is happening than take personal responsibility and deal with it. Energetic Coaches value our most challenging clients for the lessons that they trigger. The capacity to hold a receptive space for those who are dealing with their own shadow teacher (or especially for those who are unwilling to deal with it) reflects our ability to learn from our own shadow. People who learn from shadow can remain as an objective observer when someone pushes a hot button. Rather than responding negatively or disliking certain clients or circumstances, Energetic Coaches exercise discernment without judgment and evaluation without condemnation. We help others accept all aspects of self, especially those aspects they would rather not admit.

John: *Each time that I deal with shadow, I feel out of sorts. Often when I am learning from the shadow teacher, dreams join in to help with the lesson. Sometimes they terrify me; more often they disquiet. I know that I feel uneasy about what is going on because something in my situation has triggered my shadow.*

Lea: *Shadow can sometimes come to me as a feeling of crushing loneliness. I know I am missing something within me because nothing external seems to satisfy. I can run from the feeling through incessant activity, but it's always there. Until I investigate, it haunts me. When I do study myself, I realize that there is something within that I need to work on to become the fullest expression of my authentic being. I often have to admit what I had denied the part I played to create what I did not like in my life. Shadow reveals itself to me when I refuse to admit my shortcomings or submit to my inner guidance and try to play the victim rather than the powerful creator of my life.*

Pain and suffering reveal the shadow teacher. No one escapes from the inevitable hardships of life. Shadow is not in the pain of a tragic loss or a terrible ordeal, although it does feel dark and frightening during such times. Shadow is in people's attachment to the suffering. Until they choose to let go of suffering and cast light on shadow, they will maintain their initial pain of loss, rejection, disappointment, or disillusionment. The shadow does not cause suffering unless people refuse to accept and deal with all parts of themselves in relationship with what is happening. The shadow teacher holds secrets about how to transcend pain and suffering to become whole. Without learning from the shadow teacher, the ego creates alienation and separation when people most need connection with others and integration within.

Old grief separates people from themselves and others. It may be hard to imagine why anyone would want to hold onto suffering. But some, after their natural feelings have run their course, cling to grief like a badge of honor. Instead of transcending to a learning state, releasing pain, and going on with their lives, they sometimes prolong their pain by blaming themselves or others for what happened. Caroline Myss uses the term "woundology" for an attachment to suffering that arrests growth and erects a barrier to close relationships with others and with spirit. Tragedies that stop people in their growth can eventually propel them to higher consciousness. Those who have risen above their suffering attest that there is no greater inner strength and self-respect than that gained from getting through the unfair, disappointing or tragic experiences of their lives.

The Shadow of the Past

Praise and blame, pain and loss, pleasure and sorrow come and go like the wind. To be happy, rest like a great tree in the midst of them all.
ACHAAN CHAA

Coaches usually deal with clients in the present and future. Because Energetic Coaching means that clients must bring their whole selves to the process, they may have to deal with unresolved grief or attachments to suffering carried over from the past. If a client's worldview or belief system is not working, they may be clinging to childhood loss, disappointment, and grief. They may be compensating for incompleteness through incessant activity or accumulating material possessions. When the present is not working, the shadow may be operating below the surface. Without engaging in psychotherapy, we encourage clients to exchange a negative experience of their past for a positive one of present learning. The past is irrevocable, but we can choose to look back on it flexibly. People can reframe their perception of past events to discover strengths and lessons they achieved that contribute to the present and future. As grownups, they can learn to exercise conscious decision-making. Despite how terrible or wonderful life once was people have the power to choose how to experience the present. Growing up with the silver spoon can present just as many adult challenges as growing up impoverished, depending on how people perceive their lives. Sometimes people punish themselves for having it too good as a strategy to keep others from resenting them or as an excuse to be less than their potential. Wholeness requires an ongoing practice of releasing thought patterns that perpetuate suffering to move fully present into the best possible future.

John: *Jack was 40 years old and painted houses when he felt like it. Steeped in poverty and blame,*

he made sure that he had no hard assets, responsibilities, or commitments. He came from a wealthy family; both parents were physicians. Because as a child Jack felt they cared about their careers and wealth more than they did about him, he created his adult life in rejection of them.

Jack was not dealing with his shadow teacher. As a young boy he played the parental rejection tape, which he had been rerunning ever since. Because Jack had felt rejected, he justified rejecting his parents, even though he continued his negative behavior with them much longer than they had with him. Jack had more self-awareness than his parents, but still acted out at their level, playing off their greatest fears. He reasoned that hurting his parents was fair because they had hurt him. In coaching, Jack came to realize that by hanging onto the past and perpetuating the hurt, he was continuing to live a life less than what he wanted.

To be the mirror for clients, Energetic Coaches acknowledge our own attachments to the past so that we clear childhood experiences and ensuing scripts from our coaching. Presence and inner clarity ensure that we will not be co-opted by clients stuck in the past with excuses and feelings of guilt, blame, regret, or self-pity that keep them from learning from the shadow teacher. While acknowledging the past, we serve as the compassionate witness, maintaining the focus on the present and not giving any energy to what is not present. Compassionate and curious questioning of the client may go like this:

- What keeps you from being happy now?
- What is the attachment that you have to carrying this past hurt?
- I'm curious how you benefit from focusing on something that happened 20 years ago.
- What do you need to do now to finish the grief process and let go of what happened?

Children do not know better, but mature grownups have the ability to look at the reasons for beliefs and actions to see what the shadow teacher presents. Whenever people think they can justify a hurtful, deceitful, or vengeful act to self or to others, the shadow teacher waits with a lesson. Shadow lessons make for difficult work, because such introspection and self-reflection compels change. Some people invest in keeping things the same and use the justification of past hurts to resist seeing things differently. Energetic Coaches portray shadow in a positive way so that fear and resistance do not keep it below consciousness. Negative attitudes, distorted perceptions, resistance to forgiveness, and condemning judgments keep the shadow teacher in the dark. By acting as the compassionate witness and by posing thoughtful questions, Energetic Coaches offer opportunities for clients to observe shadow objectively. We help clients see how they can update childhood scripts to new attitudes and beliefs that serve them better.

By encouraging clients to identify ways in which they continue their hurt, Energetic Coaches support clients' realizing how they contribute to what they say they don't want. Then they can see how to change their present. Dealing with their shadow can reveal how they create powerlessness and negativity by entertaining egocentric thoughts, feelings, and perceptions. Even though some find it hard to admit, if their past is affecting their present, they have made choices that they can shift. Energetic Coaches focus on the choices that are often unconscious and help clients to intentionally choose something better. The more clients deny their power to change, the greater the shadow work that they need to do. They do not have to be who they don't want to be. Clients can choose to be whom they really are to get what they really want.

When reframing internal thoughts, feelings, and perceptions, coaches do not belittle, obfuscate, or trivialize clients' issues. We compassionately witness through acceptance. We help clients make different choices and manage the ensuing loss of the ways they had. Because Energetic Coaches have dealt with our own losses, guilt, disappointments, excuses, and disparaging self-judgments, we have garnered wisdom and courage to be with clients without getting hooked on the awfulness of their difficulties.

The open space that coaches and clients create out of goodwill and positive intention is the still centerpoint in which clients can meet their shadow. In the connected relationship of coaching, clients pay attention to experience as what is without exaggerating or diminishing it. As they release judgment and melodrama, clients can integrate their shadow into consciousness. Integration may feel like an initiation into a club to which no one wants to belong. Coaches tutored by the shadow teacher can sponsor clients as initiates. With consummate compassion we remain present at the centerpoint while the client turns and faces the shadow self using the mirror of the coach. Facing shadow alone can be intimidating and result in self-recrimination, which often causes people to reject shadow even more forcefully. For Energetic Coaches, the opportunity to look at and learn from shadow offers a great challenge with a commensurate reward.

Coaches are not ready for shadow work with others unless they can learn from their own shadow teacher. The ego tends to compensate through false bravado and superficial superiority toward others. Because attaining wholeness diminishes the ego's role, that part of the personality does not want to learn from the shadow. While clients are doing shadow work, it is important for Energetic Coaches to realize when the clients' ego gets in the way. Clients may project their personal issues onto the coach or end the coaching relationship. Their choice to not deal with shadow or hide behind ego remains their choice. If clients persist in attempting to co-opt the coach, we can release the coaching relationship. But shadow work, once begun, is compelling, and clients who leave may return later to continue self-exploration.

SURFACING THE SHADOW IN COACHING

Nature teaches us a principle in the body that is also true in the soul—that pain is a teacher, protector, and definer of one's self.
BERNIE SIEGEL

Shadow has many more positive aspects than negative. It presents a difficult but important opportunity to help willing clients see things differently. This releases energy because it is exhausting to continually deny or run from self-knowing. The path to wholeness is through integration (integrity) of whatever is present now.

Light and shadow play balancing roles in self-realization. We can't have one without the other. It feels good to work with light, but shadow teaches the defining lessons. As people accept their shadow side, they serve as examples to others. Some refuse to deal with shadow, focusing solely on light—positive and attractive attributes—so that they leave shadow in the dark. To connect with spirit through the inner knower, people must acknowledge and integrate shadow for the learning and wholeness it brings.

The work of shadow includes personal lessons we learn while coaching. Such shadow lessons lead to increasing self-awareness so that we can help clients learn from their own shadow teacher. Light and shadow play out in a dynamic balance between coaches and clients.

John: *I received a call from Vernon to coach him in his relationship with money. Vernon had heard about my work from a friend who had attended a course on life purpose I had taught at the community college. We set up a time for an introductory meeting so he could experience my approach to life success coaching and so I could assess whether my approach would match his needs.*

In our first meeting I learned that Vernon had already sought help from many other sources without success. As I listened to him, my solar plexus tightened. I have learned from years of consulting and coaching to pay attention to my physical reactions, as they generally signal important information. I found Vernon to be open and willing to share his story, and he presented a challenge that interested me. His words, "I have made a lot of money for other people and haven't made much for myself," suggested to me opportunities for effective work. Vernon found our initial meeting beneficial, so we began to cover the coaching agreement. Predictably, he raised concerns about the cost, so we explored options for paying for my services. The meeting closed with Vernon's taking a copy of the coaching contract and saying that he would decide within three days.

In spite of my initial reaction, I believed that I had a lot to offer Vernon. I hoped we could look into how his expressed desire to work through the money issue might help him succeed in other areas of his life. I had enjoyed his engaging manner, and Vernon had told me that our time together had already been helpful to him. I felt optimistic and excited about moving ahead with our work.

The shadow in my coaching was in the subtext that I initially chose to overlook. The first was that I had an uncomfortable feeling in my gut that all was not well in our discussion. The second was the message my internal voice was giving me after the meeting that said Vernon's issues around money are a smokescreen for some deeper issue. The third was that I envisioned being caught in a downward spiral as I sought to break through Vernon's repeated stories about not being able to generate income. I noted a lack of congruence between my desire to go ahead with our work and my internal signals. Vernon called on the third day and requested to meet again to discuss arrangements for coaching.

This time I consciously paid attention to my feelings, inner thoughts, and vision of our working together. I began to see clearly the pitfalls that lay ahead. When the conversation finally got around to the subject of payment for our work together, Vernon kept dodging the issue with stories. I decid-

ed that I was feeling uncomfortable with our discussion and that it was unlikely that I would be the person to help him resolve the money issues. I offered that Vernon might want to seek other professional help and that I could recommend a person if he liked. Our meeting ended on a congenial note, and Vernon thanked me for my time.

This example demonstrates the interaction between light and shadow in coaching work. If coaches ignore the value subtle incongruence and deep insights that the shadow provides, we risk becoming unbalanced and offering less than our best. We hold that clients must be willing to look at their shadow and that we cannot be seduced along with the client into dodging shadow work. Clients usually interpret the shadow side as unpleasant and even distasteful to the point it must be hidden or ignored to avoid internal discomfort, disagreement or outright fear. Clients may make strong assertions, excuses, or denials to justify why their life is not working for them. Aware of the benefits of doing shadow work, Energetic Coaches focus on work that would benefit clients in the long run. Through doing our own shadow work, we know that the denied shadow grows and undermines clients' ability to discover and achieve their fullest expression of authentic being.

John: *The parents of another client asked me to coach their daughter because she was unable to maintain an adequate income level. June agreed to contract with me for four meetings to determine her life purpose. Even with intelligence and skill, June had become a financial drain on her parents. During coaching she stated that she did not want to be a burden. She was convincing in her assertions, but her actions spoke otherwise. The mirror of the coaching relationship displayed shadow immediately. Even though our coaching was to be brief, June could not tolerate even a glimpse at what she was creating that she said she did not want. She contacted me indirectly by email to end the meetings without completion, even stating that she was "not well" as an excuse to refrain from doing her necessary self-reflection and shadow work.*

People reveal shadow in language and behavior. Very often they bury the most difficult emotions in their subconscious to quell hurts, disappointments, shortcomings, or inadequacies. To capitalize on the squelched shadow energy, the ego separates the individual from others who exhibit the same tendencies or challenge them. Because people learn in relationships with others as mirrors, what they project and reject in others often reveals what they need to look at within themselves. The shadow teacher appears during discomfort and denial.

Lea: *In a former career in sales, I was having a particularly difficult time with the shipping department. I saw my job as serving the customer. Shipping perceived people in sales to be impatient, demanding, and unreasonable; salespeople perceived shipping to be unreliable and resistant. Each department blamed the other for poor performance. Everyone undermined corrective policies or marginally complied by not going all the way to do the job. Each conflict widened the gap.*

On one particular day when shipping did not answer my calls, emails, or voice mail, I jumped to the conclusion that they were ignoring me. With an air of superiority and downright indignation (on behalf of the customer, I believed), I barged into the shipping department to find the supervisor ignoring the blinking voice mail light, just as I had suspected. I was so exasperated that I could barely speak. When I finally did begin sputtering out my demands, I burst into tears. I told the shipping supervisor about how unrea-

sonably the customer had treated me during my weeklong attempt to expedite his order. I explained how I was only trying to do my job, and I apologized for how I was coming across in my single-minded effort to get the sale. Suddenly I realized that I had been trying to use the shipping department (I-object relationship) behind a smokescreen of customer service. I also realized through my strong emotions that the problems I had with the shipping department were magnified by a childhood hurt of being ignored.

As tension fell, the shipping supervisor sat down next to me and shared his frustrations with his role in shipping for 23 years. He admitted that he was tired of making sales look good when everyone assumed that his monumental efforts to serve the customer were part of a day's work, nothing more. No one rewarded shipping for service. The monthly on-time shipping report was used more as a punishment than a reward. What happened next, no one in sales or shipping would have believed—he and I hugged each other and promised that we would do our best to help make each other's job easier. Hearing the shadow fears and frustrations of the other allowed us to respect and appreciate each other.

There are very negative situations involving shadow that are not so easily resolved. If people react to shadow without knowing what is going on in a fear-based, stimulus-response approach, they can repress lessons even deeper. It takes courage and change in habitual response patterns to invite shadow to become a mirror for continuous learning.

Lea: *In an introductory meeting with a potential client, Melissa, I sensed her separation as she spoke about her need for coaching. I perceived she doubted coaching would be worth the investment. Toward the end of the meeting, I felt she was questioning my coaching abilities, and I doubted that she would sign up. As Melissa left, she emphatically told* me that she would call me. I realized that any follow-up on my part would seem as if I were trying to drum up business.

I turned to my shadow teacher to tutor me. It took a few days until my lesson came as a dream. In the dream I had learned to drive a semi truck, a repeating symbol warning me that something would run me over if I were not careful. I was gratified in this dream to know how to drive the truck but tentative about taking a new assignment (which represented coaching to me). I agreed that my first job would be to help another person who had just obtained his license. This person happened to be Mike, my ex-husband, who represented a very self-centered person to me. Because Mike asked for my help, I made my first job one I did for him and not for myself. He said that he would pay me in advance (which being paid represented another apprehension I had about coaching).

Mike paid me, but when he gave me the purchase order and the route, I saw that it encompassed the entire western half of the United States. I would have had to stop at numerous places along the way to pick up Looney Tunes characters (isn't shadow funny?). I wanted to help Mike in his new career, but I knew the job was too much for me.

In my dream I gave Mike back the purchase order (coaching contract) and told him that the job would take too long. I felt bad about reneging until I asked him why he didn't do the driving himself. He told me that he could make more money in the month while I was driving for him. I then realized that he wanted to use me to advance his agenda but that he did not respect or appreciate my offer as a gift to him.

This dream represented to me that, as a coach, I needed to sort out whose responsibility was whose. I had allowed my client's focus on money to trigger my apprehension *about being a cost- effective coach. When I realized her concern about money had mirrored my own, I knew I needed to deal with my fears of being worth what I charged for services.*

At the onset of coaching, clients often perceive themselves as an object of the coach's moneymaking desires. Before they can profit from coaching, they have to work through such a notion to trust their coach. Clients who project a concern (such as money in this case) can trigger a similar concern in the coach. In fact, we often attract just the right client with the right issues at the right time to help us with our own shadow work. If we reject or project back to clients rather than look within, we may miss the shadow work we need to do.

Money often presents the opportunity to do shadow work because many tend to determine worth or value in monetary terms. There are those who see others as objects, seeking to use them to achieve egocentric agendas. Clients who view others as an "it" or a separate and unconnected "you" think that others have the same attitude toward them. While coaches are professionals who do expect to earn a living, we must be motivated by a higher calling to coach effectively. Money itself is not a sustainable motivational energy, and if that is all we seek, clients become objects rather than whole people. As coaches we need to know our attitudes and motives to ensure that we are operating in the best interest of our clients. We coach for the sake of coaching, because it is a calling to serve others, and the money follows.

Lea: *Melissa did become my client, conscientiously paying for every meeting. She immediately began dealing with her feelings about finances. Even though she first saw me as an object, I did not take on her projection. Our work grew congruently and energetically. Melissa initially wanted to depend on my input but quickly realized she had her own answers. Remembering the lesson of my dream, I resisted taking on her work, even though I felt I could have given her direction. As Melissa assumed personal power through finding her own way, she expanded her support system and made significant progress toward her goals of valuing and connecting with others. As Melissa's self-worth increased, her finances improved. Because I did not take on her projections, Melissa learned to value and connect with herself. Melissa became her own best coach. This was gratifying to me, even though my ego liked the idea of being needed and admired.*

People's relationships with others reflect their inner relationship with self. In the mirror of the other, they witness what issues they need to address and integrate. They tend to take for granted easy relationships and comfortable situations, where they learn little except perhaps to appreciate a relationship after it's gone. But complex and difficult relationships with others cause people to grow in ways that they could not have accomplished alone. The shadow teacher uses the mirror of the other for lessons, and if people are able to look into it with openness, it bypasses ego's defense mechanisms of projection and false perception of self and other as good or bad.

Ego avoids the opportunity to learn from the shadow teacher by separating and judging. The ego does not want to take responsibility for difficult relationships or situations. Energetic Coaches know that we are all connected. The illusion of separation allows us to treat others as we would NOT want to be treated without feeling remorse. By blaming something outside of themselves ("the devil made me do it"), people can avoid responsibility but become less powerful. Energetic Coaches treat others as they want to be treated, knowing that somehow positive energy spirals back to the sender. We observe our own egocentric attempts to separate from something that we have judged as superior or inferior. Energetic Coaches help clients look into the mirror, because we know that when clients become congruent within, they will recognize the outer reflection as none other than themselves.

THE CHALLENGE OF THE MIRROR

Everything that irritates us about others can lead us to an understanding of ourselves.
CARL JUNG

It is easy to identify with complementary people or situations; they share beliefs and a compatible worldview. In the external materialistic paradigm of success, people's ability to accumulate money and goods demonstrates personal worth. But an externally oriented person seeks relationships with others who share the same need to prop up their ego. The inner knower seeks lasting values. When people orient outside, they leave a gap between themselves and spirit. Unspoken collusion takes place with others to maintain an outer orientation without challenge. But those who only seek external achievement and validation lose balance and neglect developing inner capacities. They need masks to be in relationships with others so that no one discovers their inner lack. The shadow teacher provides a mirror to reveal masks for what they are and to dispel illusions of lack. Shadow work reveals the ego's contrivances, putting outer achievements into perspective and motivating people to look within to create congruent relationships with self and with others.

The Chinese saying, "talk does not cook rice," express-es the truth that it is much easier to talk the talk than walk the talk. Without putting action into words, people's inner self becomes incongruent with their outer expression, taking them away from the centerpoint. Whenever they do or don't do what they declare, people increasingly avoid their shadow teacher's lessons. When people deceive self or others, shad-ow is present. It is better to move into the lesson because it will be impossible to avoid it or ignore it for long. The shad-ow teacher increases consciousness with its lessons. When ignored or avoided, it tends to escalate the degree of difficul-ty to get people's attention ("pay now, or pay later with inter-est"). The inner knower uses the shadow teacher to promote congruence and achieve balance and wholeness, connecting with spirit. People who heed their shadow teacher cannot lie to themselves or others. As much as they might like to avoid inner work, they know learning is required to be authentic and whole.

Energetic Coaching and Shadow Work

The shadow teacher works within the coaching relationship for the benefit of both clients and coaches. Shadow work produces benefits, but people do not learn difficult lessons without effort. Energetic Coaches make shadow work easier, encouraging clients that the effort is worth it. We know that the lessons don't go away until we face them. The work nev-er ends. Energetic Coaches welcome stimulating challenges, knowing they are necessary for growth. End results satisfy a short time before other opportunities are presented. Tutoring is always available through the close connection with spirit that shadow work offers. Human nature avoids shadow work, but Energetic Coaches know the outcomes are well worth the work.

When people resist and reject what they don't want to admit, they activate the energy of shadow and its potential to connect with spirit. Spirit responds to what people want. It does not know the negative qualifiers of no, don't, not, or never, so overcoming resistance to shadow allows clients to turn what they don't want into what is wanted. The dance of shadow and spirit balance dark and light energy, transforming the weak Law of Polarity into the strong Law of Attraction. Wanting something and going for a goal has more power and sustainable energy than avoiding something. Once people have transcended resistance to learn from their shadow, they can freely visualize and value what they want. With spirit, they become visionary creators of their own reality. Of course, some might rather live totally in spirit and not have to deal with shadow at all, but learning life's lessons is imperative to growth. Shadow work is necessary for Energetic Coaches, and the more we recognize and embrace our shadow teacher's lessons, the better we can support our clients in doing the same.

Lea: *My two-year old granddaughter Ava is a great teacher of shadow lessons. In her straightforward approach she lives spontaneously and behaves unapologetically. Her freedom of expression and strong wants and demanding needs challenge her parents. Attempts to manipulate or control Ava into becoming the perfect child do not work, and she rapidly dispelled their illusion of perfect parenting. Like my daughter and son-in-law, I started out grandparenting by trying to be perfect. Being the perfect grandparent was only slightly easier than being the perfect parent (still impossible). I recognized my striving in the mirror of my daughter's exasperated efforts. So I decided to accept my imperfections and let go of how I wished I could be. As I became the compassionate witness to my granddaughter's growth and self-expression, I addressed my shadow work to be perfect or in control. My granddaughter and I have a special relationship now that she is four years old. I continue to give her guidance and consequences when needed but let go more easily. Through my consistency and demonstrated good intention, Ava respects me when I speak...I see Ava as a unique person and I do not have anything to prove through her, such as, seeking to vindicate myself as an inferior parent in the past. I am enjoying my granddaughter as she is. I observe her emerging ego with humor and hold the space for her to test her boundaries. With wonderment I accept Ava in her childhood spontaneity without the parental worry I once had that kept me from being accepting and present in the moment.*

SHADOW WORK

When we must deal with problems, we instinctively resist trying the way that leads through obscurity and darkness. We wish to hear only of unequivocal results and completely forget that these results can only be brought about when we have ventured into and emerged again from the darkness. But to penetrate the darkness we must summon all the powers of enlightenment that consciousness can offer.
C. J. Jung, *The Stages of Life*

Shadow work may discomfit people because it eludes description or capture—just like spirit. Some, such as the renowned monk Thomas Moore, separate spirit from shadow. Energetic Coaches see the shadow as a mirror that reflects gaps in

288

wholeness and disconnection with spirit. As with the shadow cast by sunlight, the longer it appears, the greater the angle to the sun. Conversely, when aligned with the sun directly overhead, people cast no shadow at all. Shadow lives in the parts of people not aligned with light.

Shadow presents many opportunities for growth. As people learn from it, they draw close to spirit. Shadow is an important part of oneness as it reflects what they may not want to see but still know is there. By shifting position (perspective), people integrate shadow with spirit

Carl Jung sought to know shadow work in dream symbols because shadow, like spirit, is not subject to description in words or language. The more open people are to shadow, the more the shadow teacher comes into awareness with the lessons they need to learn. According to their willingness to self-reflect and go deep, shadow responds, often with challenging dreams.

Lea: *My client Joy began having disturbing dreams, which she correlated with the work she was doing in coaching. As she related one after another of them to me, we both began to realize that her shadow was at work. Even though her dreams were unpleasant, she made sense of them to reveal beneficial insights. The disturbing dreams lessened as Joy talked about them and learned from them.*

The shadow teacher appears when people deal directly with their hidden or unacceptable thoughts, feelings, and perceptions. By exploring their motivations and intentions with honesty, individuals come face-to-face with their shadow. At first, they may find seeing and accepting such aspects of the personality difficult, but those who look objectively within usually discover the missing pieces that lead to self-knowing and wholeness.

THE RISK OF SHADOW WORK

Lift up your heart to God with humble love; and mean God Himself and not what you get out of Him. When you first begin, you find only darkness, and as it were a cloud of unknowing—but still go on longing after Him in this life, it must always be in this cloud, in this darkness.

JULIAN OF NORWICH

People avoid looking into the darkness where the shadow lives for fear that this hidden part is inherently bad. Society may exert pressures to do or be something in order to be acceptable. There is even the concept of original sin, which means that people must repent and strive to overcome an inherent flaw. Once recognized that people are innately good and that no one who sincerely tries can fail, they can understand the concept of shadow as teacher rather than adversary. Resistance subsides. People can look at themselves objectively—even humorously. Viewing the shadow aspects curiously and bravely helps them gain inner and outer congruence.

The more realization and integration, the more people grow. The light shines in the darkness, and they become beacons to others. As a result, some relationships become congruent and complementary, whereas others fall away as the light shines on the shadow of the other. Those who have integrated shadow operate at a high frequency, likely to tune into others on the same frequency. They tend to reflect the clear mirror for others, but there will be some who don't want to look into the mirror. They may try to distort the mirror rather than deal with their own reflection. Others may find self-knowing and acceptance threatening because it comes at the price of subordinating ego and integrating shadow. Energetic Coaches give support and encouragement to clients as they shift. They may face family, friends, or co-workers who, refusing to do their own shadow work, challenge our clients' willingness to look within for truth and self-empowerment.

As people grow, they may not want to sustain some relationships. Endings can be sad and painful. Some may question the spiritual path clients have chosen; however, as clients take responsibility for their intentions, motivations, and identity, they find themselves strong enough to meet challenges, questions, and confrontations. Because they recognize shadow, they can react authentically and objectively. Individuals with internal congruence and wholeness know how to let go of relationships that are not working. As people make choices from their inner being, which is much more powerful than anything external, they can better make their unique and beneficial contributions to healthy relationships with others.

Lea: *There was a time in life when I could not tolerate being alone, particularly as I contemplated divorce, even though my ex-husband and I had ended our marriage years before. I would wake up afraid of the dark with terrible nightmares. Once I finally mustered the courage to move out, my nightmares ceased. Even though I left my home and those closest to me questioned and challenged my decision, I experienced inner peace. Even though I did not know how I would pay my bills, faith and self-confidence to start over came to my aid. Once alone, I no longer felt lonely. Because of my improved relationship with myself, I found I actually liked being alone. Being in a disconnected relationship disconnected me from myself. When I had been married, I could not walk into my house without turning on the TV for background noise. In my small, inexpensive apartment, I discovered inner quiet. I connected with a part of myself that I had left when I had compromised who I was and what I wanted to be for a relationship that did not serve my highest good.*

Depending on the willingness of each person to learn from the shadow teacher, relationships can grow close or fall away. Some find using a coach or therapist as their mirror for the shadow teacher helps them learn to connect and let go according to what is best.

RECOGNIZING SHADOW

Coaches recognize shadow when clients try to co-opt them into a game or melodrama. We observe it when clients make positive or negative projections or judgments about others. We see the shadow teacher in clients' rebuttal or excuses for inconsistencies between what they say and how they behave. When they are afraid or defensive, some aspect of shadow is there. When they resist introspecting, shadow teacher is usually waiting with a lesson.

Most clients will want to ignore their inner knowing when they begin to deal with incongruence and shadow. It takes courage and receptivity to open to shadow lessons. Energetic Coaches demonstrate inner knowing and compassionate witnessing to make it safe for clients to look within objectively. Initially, the ego tries to deny or defend. The inner knower of the coach, connecting with the inner knower of the client, allows shadow work to progress with respect for the ego. People connect spiritually through becoming whole, providing the motive and reward for the outcomes of their shadow work.

As clients experience coaching and the example to openly, lovingly, even lightheartedly address and accept shadow side, they learn to do the same for themselves. Those who face their shadow heighten their awareness; whereas, those who do not choose to work with shadow may leave the coaching relationship. If we coaches release them with good intention for their best outcomes, we maintain a clear, unbiased, and nonjudgmental mirror for them to see themselves clearly. Of course, some people will never look, which we need to recognize as soon as possible in a coaching relationship. Later, clients may return to coaching in a receptive state, or not. Some may perceive Energetic Coaches as catalysts for self-knowing and acceptance, others as perpetuators of yet another unsatisfying relationship that challenges their limiting beliefs and egocentric tendencies. We release relationships with clients (as we do with any other relationship) with acceptance and love.

The more clients are disconnected from their shadow teacher, the greater their potential for learning. The most important shadow work often occurs in family groups, who have the greatest potential for judgment and separation as well as the greatest potential for acceptance and close connection.

Lea: *Carson disapproved of his son's life choices. At 30 Jason, who had yet to hold a "good job" and lived with three other men in a dingy apartment. Even though Jason had writing talent, he continually asked his father for money, which his father continually refused. Instead, Carson told Jason to find a real job. The more he failed to live up to his father's expectations, the greater the gulf between them. The relationship became so judgmental and disconnected that both father and son disliked being in the same room with the other. Neither recognized that they were mirrors for each to recognize individual paths to wholeness. The son rejected that he was worthy and that his father loved him. Carson refused to acknowledge that his son had reason to be critical of his absentee father and over-indulgent upbringing. Carson's way of compensating his son for being gone a great deal in his childhood had been to lavish him with presents.*

When Carson received a terminal diagnosis, he confessed how much he had missed out on his Jason's young years. Jason was surprised to realize how much his father's apology meant to him. When Carson stopped criticizing Jason about money, he realized that material things were not a part of his son's value system and that, perhaps, they had played too large a part in his own. Jason stopped condemning his father because he realized that he had tried to hurt his father for neglecting his childhood. Both recognized that love, not money, was the issue. Months before Carson died, father and son cleared the way to love each other in time to share close, respectful moments. It was difficult and very troubling for both of them to know the part that they had played in the negative dynamics between them for so many years. When they saw that they had nothing to gain by egotistic posturing, they opened to each other. Despite their difficulties, they confronted their shadows and reconciled. After his father's death, Jason began earning his living as a writer. Reconciliation had freed Jason to accept his father's wishes for him to succeed as his own and he was able to make a living doing his chosen work.

People establish relationships with others that reflect their relationship with themselves and the degree to which shadow work needs to be done. Those who know a person best are the best mirrors for reflection. A gap in a relationship is often wider between family members or close friends than between acquaintances. Parents tend to project their shadow on same-sex children, and shadow work between newlyweds arises soon after the honeymoon. People who do not want to deal with their inner selves are likely to widen the gap in relationships with those who have the greatest potential for closeness. Those who do not want to look within bar others from looking within them too.

Shadow lessons repeat until people learn them. When individuals encounter challenging relationships, they can choose to stop blaming others and reframe the lessons as opportunities to bring shadow to consciousness. Shadow is present whenever there is a negative feeling toward another person or situation. Any perception of being separate, superior, or inferior to another contains hidden aspects of self that need to be known.

Ego always comes to crash the shadow teacher's party. As shadow reveals what people do not want to see in themselves, their ego deflects the reflection. Ego makes it look as if people are not responsible for their unwanted thoughts, feelings, and perceptions, even though they have dominion over them through choice. If people choose to keep negative thoughts, feelings, and perceptions, they cannot achieve congruent and energetic relationships with self and others. Whether they allow negativity and separation consciously or unconsciously, people's perceptions define their relationships. It is healthier to let go of relationships than to continue hurting others with lessons never learned.

When lessons present themselves, some people do anything to avoid them. They deny their own power to change. Through placing the focus on the inner being, clients realize their great power to see and do things differently. Energetic Coaching offers practice and insights for those who want to know and accept all parts of themselves and others in relationship—the good, the bad, and the ugly. In fact, the ugly, like the ugly duckling of the children's story, has the greatest opportunity for transformation. The most troubling relationships present the greatest opportunity for self-reflection and growth. Once people learn their shadow lessons, they can let go of a detrimental relationship because it has no further beneficial purpose. What cannot be changed needs to be released. Once individuals learn the shadow lessons and release the outgrown relationship, people free themselves to stop allowing harmful relationships and self- defeating situations to detract them from inner knowing and growth.

Rather than labeling others as difficult, Energetic Coaches look to relationships for opportunities to learn. We do not buy into the illusion of separation and superiority or inferiority. Instead, we model to clients how to learn from shadow. Modeling requires that we know, accept, and love ourselves despite our awareness of our own shadow and shortcomings. Energetic Coaches are the first to admit that no one is perfect. We laugh at ourselves when ego tries to get its strokes through power or influence over others. We know we serve as the channel or instrument for clients to do their work. We serve something much larger than ourselves. We commit to learning our own lessons in order to create the space for others to choose and learn theirs.

SHADOW AND SPIRIT

The following are examples of coaching situations in which shadow work needs to be done:

- When coaches realize after a meeting that they stepped into their clients' role.
- When coaches fear being ineffective.
- When coaches revel in their coaching skills and outcomes rather than appreciating the work the client has done.
- When coaches need to demonstrate expertise and knowledge to clients.

- When coaches feel defensive or need to prove something to someone else.
- When coaches view clients as objects of their money-making desires.
- When coaches spend time and effort thinking about themselves rather than being fully present during client meetings.
- When clients attempt to co-opt the coach into a game, blame, or melodrama to avoid looking at themselves.
- When clients try to convince the coach to buy into something that is not true.
- When clients focus on the past or cling to limiting beliefs.
- When clients attempt to control or influence coaches.
- When clients resist or refuse to look at inner-outer incongruence.
- When clients allow relationships that reflect less than what they say they want.
- When clients perceive the coach as superior or inferior.
- When clients break their word repeatedly or resist taking action on the goals they have set.

In the above situations Energetic Coaches are able to put their automatic ego response aside so that spirit can provide guidance through the inner knower. As the compassionate witness we mirror in an open and curious way what clients present. Experiencing fear, separation, or anxiety in a coaching meeting signals an opportunity to return to the compassionate witness—observant, present, engaged, and accepting. By keeping ego out of the interaction with clients and connecting with the inner knower, coaches empty themselves to allow what is present to be okay. We want to keep any self-reference or egocentric need from interfering with clients' work. If we lose the compassionate witness stance and separate, or worse, pass judgment, we lose our connection with spirit and give the client the message that part of them is not okay. Such judgment would damage any relationship and drive shadow deeper into the dark.

When we encounter shadow work, we remain open to spirit in relationship by:

1. Recognizing body sensations and relaxing tensions to become open.
2. Observing critical, negative, judgmental, or condemning thoughts and releasing them.
3. Knowing when our ego creates defensiveness and the need to justify or prove something.
4. Consciously creating feelings of goodwill toward clients.
5. Becoming the compassionate witness and reflecting what is without distortions of the ego or taking on the clients' projections.
6. Remaining at the still centerpoint between polarities of judgment of good/bad, want/don't want, like/dislike, etc.
7. Seeking connection with clients where they are and expecting growth to occur.
8. Allowing the inner knower to guide words and actions.
9. Releasing expectations of outcomes.
10. Staying present with the client despite the urge to avoid discomfort or uneasiness about what is happening.

Our coaching stance requires effort and consciousness in the immediate moment. Through practice and self-awareness, we can remain as open conduits if we are doing our shadow work for personal wholeness. We are no longer susceptible to personal agendas or ego-driven motives. The present moment becomes expansive, and the process of opening to spirit and receiving guidance from the inner knower happens.

ENLISTING SPIRIT TO INTEGRATE SHADOW

Even though the night darkens your spirit, its purpose is to impart light. Even though it humbles you, revealing the depth of your wretchedness, its purpose is to exalt and uplift you. Even though it empties you of all feeling and detaches you from all natural pleasures, its purpose is to fill you with spiritual joy and attach you to the source of that joy.

St. John of the Cross

The less the experience of the polarity of "not this" and the weaker the attachment to something different from the way things are, the closer people can get to their centerpoint. They receive spiritual energy by doing shadow work. Here are some ways to move out of polarity toward the centerpoint of balance:

- Hold the space during first impressions so others can show up as they are.
- Know that all people are unique, equal and important.
- Recognize when separated, withdrawn, or alienated, and act to reconnect with life and others.

- Work on personal issues at every opportunity by practicing relaxed neutrality about self and others.
- Add positive energy to the collective consciousness, taking responsibility for negativity and changing it from within self.
- Recognize when caught up in melodrama, and exercise compassion, discernment, detachment, and observation.
- Keep things in perspective. Ask what will matter in 20 years (or two years, for that matter).
- Practice courage and self-discipline through addressing fears.
- Continually invite and open to spirit.
- Practice releasing minor daily annoyances and work up to the hot buttons that trigger strong negative thoughts and emotions.
- Decide to deal with shadow from a positive perspective, exercising free will choice for the greatest positive outcome in small and large ways.
- In a difficult relationship or situation, create outcomes that include the highest good for all involved.
- Cultivate connections with all living beings, including plants and animals that provide opportunities for practice in every moment.
- Practice love, starting with those easiest to love and moving toward those who require the most.
- Recognize perceived positive or negative experiences as being teachers presenting necessary lessons.
- Remember and record dreams and journal thoughts, feelings, and perceptions to reveal shadow, objectively looking at what is revealed with acceptance rather than aversion.

- Ask close others to provide insights about possible shadow work that needs to be done.

Growth and wholeness require integration of shadow—an ongoing, never-ending process that includes recognizing shadow and dealing with troubling thoughts, uneasy feelings, and uncomfortable physical sensations. By going within to ask shadow what is needed to integrate, people can move with grace from self-reflection to self-acceptance. By assimilating new information, they consciously choose how to apply shadow's lessons to increase their energy. By finding positive and beneficial reasons for difficulties and personal foibles, people maintain awareness of habitual triggers that kept shadow in the dark. People can look into the mirror of their relationships with others to monitor their progress in letting go of judgments of self and others to integrate shadow.

THE SHADOW SIDE OF COMMUNITY: LEADERSHIP INCONGRUENCE

Many organizations represent themselves, for a multitude of reasons, as being member focused. They make statements such as, "we are a family," "teamwork works here," "employer of choice," and the like. Yet in some of these same organizations, if one talks to an employee, his or her "yeah, right" scoff says it all. There are gaps between what is claimed and what is experienced on the job. The goal is to align the stated or hoped for with the experience of the members inside the organization.

Excerpt from The Meaning and Role of Organizational Advocacy: Responsibility and Accountability in the Workplace, by Jane Galloway Seiling

For a bankrupt company that is doling out millions in golden parachutes to top executives to say that it must cut off the health care benefits of people who worked a lifetime in the mills is a disgrace.
Leo Gerard, President, United Steel Workers of America

Now as never before, the actions and lack of accountability by the leadership of organizations, small and large, profit and not-for-profit, are coming to light. When heads of organizations do not have higher consciousness, personal responsibility and integrity, they have a far-reaching negative impact on other individuals, economies, and markets. Energetic Coaching is important to support pursuit of accountability, authenticity, and congruence for those who have the most responsibility and impact. Organizations multiply the effects of individual incongruence exponentially.

As people move into positions of influence, they have increased responsibility because of their greater impact on others. Energetic Coaching for executives deals with incongruence directly by exposing egocentric justifications for avoiding shadow work. Just as executives have greater responsibility to their organizations because of their impact on them, Energetic Coaches engaged in executive coaching have increased responsibility in our role with executives. Leaders mirror the state of consciousness of their communities and vice-versa. Communities need their leaders to elevate consciousness, integrate shadow, and increase spiritual connection through practicing individual integrity and authenticity.

Insincere, inconsistent, and duplicitous behavior at the top of organizations is obvious to everyone if they choose to look rather than overlook. Politics and collusion in the leadership ranks underwrite incongruence throughout the organization. People do not have to do what they promise or hold themselves to high standards if their leaders do not. There can be no expectation that others will be truthful or trustworthy if leadership is not. Shadow permeates the organization in a culture of avoidance and defensiveness or worse—actively hiding, blaming and gaming by those at the top to keep position power without challenge.

If shadow work is to be done, there needs to be safety in exposing and addressing incongruent words and actions no matter who exhibits the behavior. Laws, controls, policies, procedures, and punishment do not create safety and compliance. As exhibited in recent examples of corporate malfeasance, by the time the SEC lawyers and judges brought corrupt individuals to justice, the perpetrators had already irreparably damaged the organization. In most organizations there are few internal mechanisms to speak openly and halt the negative effects of poor ethics by those with rank. In big or small ways daily incongruence blocks spiritual connection and the energy that could heal and bind the community into an effective collective. Individuals know when they are not speaking or acting from their highest potential. Energetic Coaching for executives address the gap between what leaders say they want for their organizations and what they do to achieve goals while setting the example for others.

It takes a courageous executive to do shadow work, especially for an organization that has been damaged by a culture that allows less than what people are capable of being and doing. As courageous executives struggle to right the system, they may call on Energetic Coaches to support their continuing inner work. As leaders climb the company ladder, they see the big picture and are able to make a larger contribution. At some point courageous executives may realize that they must decide to support the existing system or to challenge it by acting congruently and holding values and vision for something better. Those at the top set the example for excellent standards in decisions and behaviors for others to emulate.

There may come a time when courageous executives realize they are not upholding their internal values because of what the system requires to succeed. Those executives face a conflict of inner values and outer constraints. They recognize when getting along or climbing the ladder means ignoring their inner knower. How they decide to act affects them personally and all those associated with their organization. Courageous executives who do not risk making changes toward personal congruence lose confidence and self-respect by allowing and advancing the system's status quo. If they dare to maintain higher standards, they risk being targeted or labeled by others who feel threatened by exposure in the mirror of relationship. By speaking and acting congruently and expecting others to do the same, courageous executives may even lose status and income. For them to remain true to themselves in an incongruent culture, they must make difficult choices.

Energetic Coaches help the courageous executives listen to their inner knower to address fears and do shadow work to create spiritual connection from within. If the culture supports incongruence, members will be aware of unpleasant consequences for speaking the truth. Energetic Coaches support the courageous executive in making necessary changes to gain organizational congruence or to let go of the relationship to maintain personal integrity.

Lea: *Dave was the president of a midsize manufacturing firm. He was promoted to his position by the parent company, which had bought the firm as a customer for their product. It did not take long for Dave to realize the parent company wanted to use the downstream subsidiary as a consumer of their off-quality products. As scrap at the division increased, company morale decreased. Then the parent company initiated a company wide initiative for Total Quality Management. The employees challenged Dave to procure quality material from the parent company in accordance with the "talk" of TQM. Maintaining his personal integrity but challenging corporate, Dave responded by rejecting defective shipments, as he would have from any other supplier. Dave's direct supervisor, the COO of the company, responded angrily when Dave told him he held the parent company to the same standards as all other suppliers. He told his boss that the parent company could not have it both ways; it either needed to supply better material or shelve the TQM program.*

Dave knew that he could not please corporate and maintain personal integrity in his relationship with others, so he chose to be true to himself. While he earned the respect of his fellow employees, he was branded as a troublemaker. After 22 successful years with the company, Dave was fired before he was able to find another job. Two years later the one billion dollar organization filed for bankruptcy because of numerous bad decisions made at the top. Because he had been fired, Dave had exercised his stock options before they became worthless and had a new job working for a better company.

Energetic Coaches are allies for courageous executives to improve the system and retain membership in the community or leave the organization. Knowing that spirit will aid such efforts we assist our clients' assessment of their organizations from a meta-cognitive perspective. We help clients review their sphere of influence, possible choices, and opportunities within the organization so they can maintain personal integrity and inner/outer congruence. Together coaches and clients compare stated values and actions. At times, courageous executives admit that they have no good solutions to a particular challenge, but admitting limitations, allowing the truth, and doing shadow work brings consciousness and coherence to the person and the community.

Energetic Coaches help clients face apprehension and doubt when dealing with the organization's shadow. It is inherently lonely at the top of an organization. A witness is helpful for self-reflection without risk of being judged or doubted for revealing vulnerability. Everyone has private worries, apprehensions, and fear from time to time. Even the best, most experienced executives question themselves. The ability to do so is a sign of strength. Those who cannot question themselves are dangerous, especially at the top of an organization. Engaging Energetic Coaches to pursue personal congruence with internal values and external means to express them provides a safe sounding board. Courageous executives can evaluate themselves and their actions so they can make important decisions. They examine the shadow side of the organization evidenced by collusion, denial, "undiscussables," defense mechanisms, power plays, and subtle political forces and make necessary changes starting at the personal level.

Today more than ever, organizations need self-questioning and truth telling. If people are to deal with the increasingly complex challenges of the future, they need the engagement of everyone's heart—not just their heads and hands. When leaders of organizations behave congruently and authentically, they have far-reaching effects. Their personal journey to integrity establishes trust in relationships. Organizations can risk change when they increase trust. As respect is built, risk is diminished. As the organization exhibits authentic behavior by its leaders, others respond in recognition of high-level values and vision. Those leave who do not want to enlist. Along the way, courageous executives withstand the criticism of others because they have already scrutinized their own motives, decisions, and actions. They do not need defense mechanisms, insulating layers of yes-men, closed accounting, politics as usual, gatekeepers, and superficial communications to prop up a dysfunctional system. They replace threatening control tactics and rigid policies and procedures with living values and vision. Courageous executives embody and expect the truth no matter how difficult.

Transparent organizations, visible at all levels, engage everyone in high standards for performance and results. Lasting positive change takes place because those at the top seek to improve the community by first improving themselves. The expressed values in the mission statement of an organization come alive as executives emulate and demonstrate the values in word and action. Courageous executives actively seek out the truth. They view sins of omission as sins of commission and do not turn a blind eye to what needs to be revealed and discussed. Courageous executives deal with shadow as an opportunity to learn and as a prerequisite for wholeness. The dead zone created by turning a deaf ear and a blind eye to unacceptable behavior and dysfunctional relationships transforms as energy (spirit) pervades the organization.

Just as people must take responsibility for the quality of one-on-one relationships with others to achieve an I-One dynamic, executives must examine their relationships with others, especially friends and family, to see what reflections they observe in their close relationships. Courageous executives must also examine their congruence with the values and vision of the organization to achieve personal congruence with the organization's culture. If individuals decide the organization does not emulate their personal standards, they must next assess if they can effect a change that supports excellence. Throughout the process of becoming congruent with self, others, and the community, coaches and clients turn to the shadow teacher to expose gaps in integrity and how each person within the organization has contributed to the situation. As they expose individual incongruence throughout the organization, they expose the collective shadow. It takes courage to learn from the shadow teacher, but it provides the means to achieve a healthy community of individuals operating in unified wholeness for the long term. Functioning as Energetic Coaches, themselves, courageous executives hold the light for the organization to illuminate and integrate its collective shadow.

Just as individuals may have to withdraw from tribal belief patterns, courageous executives, who value individual wholeness and integrity, may have to leave organizations that systemically practice incongruent and unethical behavior. Individuals who take an authentic path sometimes commit to difficult and frightening choices. Without allowing speculation or attachment to specific outcomes that can block spiritual connection, Energetic Coaches support their clients' decision-making process and assist them in embarking on positive, energetic paths in or out of the organization. They expose shadow to deal with doubts and fears about the future. The courageous executive may not know the details of how things will work out, but he or she does know that by being true to self, that special energy that causes all things to work together for good joins to create something better.

Chapter 7 Appendix

Reflection

- What lessons is my shadow teacher trying to teach me through people and situations I do not like?
- In what areas do I experience incongruence between my inner being and outer doing?
- What are my dreams, conscience or intuition telling me about aspects of myself that I am not consciously dealing with?
- How can I develop a relationship with shadow as a friend and teacher in order to integrate all of myself for wholeness?
- How do the relationships and organizations I am in display my shadow teacher? What do I need to learn from shadow?
- What is rejected within is projected without. What do I project on others that I need to work on within myself?
- Does the community I am in deal with shadow? If not, what can I do about it?

Intentional Imprint

- What lessons are repeatedly presented by shadow teacher that I need to learn?

- How can I let go of blame, resentment, fear, or powerlessness to become the fullest expression of my authentic being?
- What can I do now to change the past to create a positive future?
- How does my ego keep shadow in the dark?
- How can I integrate shadow for personal wholeness?
- Have I experienced any recurring, uncomfortable feelings while reading this book? What may that indicate?

8. PRACTICE FOR SPIRITUAL CONNECTION

*Vision is not enough. It must be combined with venture.
It is not enough to stare up the steps, we must step up the
stairs.*
VACLAV HAVEL

*If people knew how hard I work to gain my mastery, it
would not seem so wonderful at all.*
MICHELANGELO

So far, we have discussed ways to increase spiritual connection and energy as well as what blocks the process. It is a personal choice to bring spirit into relationship, starting with relationship with self and branching out to relationship with others. Spirit awaits invitation through intentional goodness. We have talked about respect for others and equality as well as the interplay of ego and shadow and the importance of integrating all aspects of the human experience to move toward wholeness and oneness. For the most part, it is just talk—using words to convey esoteric dynamics between coaching and spirit. Now we are going to challenge you, the reader, to create your own spiritual connection if you have not yet already.

People need awareness, congruence and intentional choice to realize spiritual energy and connection. Practice demonstrates the will to experience a spiritual relationship. What to do and how to practice is an individual choice that can take many forms. The personal and unique ways people create a spiritual practice may change over time. Energetic

Coaches tailor our spiritual practices to what works for us and encourage our clients to do the same. This chapter suggests some of the spiritual practices we and our clients can use. Some have arisen out of today's lifestyles and some out of ancient times. As with any other endeavor, practice hones skills. Everyone has the innate ability to connect with spirit. Practice with pure intention to have a congruent relationship with self and with spirit provides the fertile ground for the seed of spiritual energy to grow. People who want to connect with spirit use regular practice to remove blocks and open to something beyond the five senses. Regular practice forges a strong, long- term, sustainable inner connection with spirit.

Humans bridge the spiritual and the material worlds. Much has been written about people who have experienced a spontaneous, transcendent, loving connection with spirit. Those who have had such close encounters have reported desiring to stay in the state of oneness. However, that experience cannot be maintained continuously in the everydayness of life. Spiritual connection may be transient, but it reminds people of their perfection in oneness and wholeness. What people cherish as a memory of direct spiritual experience may be difficult to relate to others and to duplicate. Remembrance of it creates the awareness of essential being. Such awareness dispels the illusions of the secular and separate world or of superiority or inferiority of self. It recalls a state of being that reflects the wholeness of humanity and the importance and power of the person.

Just as people work out at the gym to develop the physical body, they can deliberately use physical, mental, and emotional practices to develop the spiritual body. Practice invites an in-the- moment connection with spirit. Spiritual contact may not always be dramatic, but the development of a close relationship with spirit opens the inner knower to provide insight and guidance through the still, small voice within. Whether people directly experience spirit through practice is not the point. They demonstrate intention that invites spirit to come. It's a process. The ongoing relationship with spirit is like the joyful melting into oneness of two lovers, but it is more sustainable over time. Love involves the collapsing of ego boundaries and the vulnerable submission to something greater than self. The acknowledgment of something greater opens to spirit, but the human fear and vulnerability to submit and let go erects barriers. Spirit will not abandon or assert a separate will. Individual free will is inviolate. Connection with spirit empowers people. They may be physically alone but are not lonely. Invitation and practice allow lasting realization of separate identity and connected oneness.

John: *A key to practice is having a reason. I recently participated in a spiritual retreat to open my being to spirit. There was a one-year preparation leading up to the experience of opening to spirit in the present. One phase involved fasting. Up until that point I had felt I was busily getting ready to do this thing I called a spiritual retreat. Once into the practice of going without food and water, I realized I was doing on-the-job training or real-time practice for how I wanted to live my life. I am not talking about becoming a religious ascetic. Rather, when I incorporated fasting into all the other practices of my spiritual retreat, I could concentrate on the moment. Fasting showed me how I could change my reality to better support my longing to be at one with the One-in-All.*

In the process of learning through being and doing with intention to grow spiritually, people experience "aha's" that lead to new ways to balance the stresses of daily living. Through practice they learn about the vast, inner spiritual self. Practice is not often easy or convenient. At first people may be diligent and then over time drift away. They may wonder why they have returned to feeling out of sync and disconnected. They may feel guilty about quitting the practices that worked before. Ebbing and flowing in practice is characteristic of human nature. The process is one of maintaining a dynamic equilibrium, giving and taking, being and doing, holding on and letting go. Spiritual practice requires wanting to do rather than having to. Practice is a gift people give themselves. It requires choice and commitment and time and effort, but it makes spiritual awareness and connection real so that the relationship remains even when the practice wanes.

Many begin a spiritual practice when they feel that they are missing something. Ironically, addressing the missing something through personal growth opens the door to another missing something. The learning process continually evolves. Life presents infinite opportunities to seek truth and experience spirit to become the fullest expression of authentic self. The process reveals a state of oneness that is separate and distinct yet united and whole. Practicing to connect with spirit is a moment-by-moment choice. It invites guidance and energy to have new experiences that provide further opportunities for growth. People show by doing with conscious intention that they desire to maintain a close personal relationship with spirit. Their intention sustains the openness and invitation to spirit. Practice puts the "walk" in the "talk" and demonstrates good faith, intention and invitation.

This chapter lists a brief description of some spiritual practices. We do not attempt to present an exhaustive accounting of the myriad methods to invite spirit into relationship. There are thousands of texts and teachings that describe practices that open channels to spirit. The essence of the "work that works" across all practices is intentional willingness on a practical level and on an ongoing basis to invite spiritual connection. People send energy where they focus. The laser- like energy of attention to spirit with intention to connect creates many different opportunities and experiences to do so.

Because individuals are unique, different practices work better for different people at different times. The key to what works is what uplifts over time. Far from short-term, quick fix solutions, spiritual attunement requires renewing good intentions on a daily basis. By doing, people demonstrate what they want so that spirit provides guidance and wisdom through the inner knower and meaning and purpose through relationships. Energetic Coaches work deliberately through practice to gain spiritual connection to create the space for all things to work together for the good.

SPIRITUAL PRACTICES

MEDITATION

In meditation it is possible to dive deeper into the mind to a place where there is no disturbance and there is absolute solitude. It is this point in the profound stillness that the sound of the mind can be heard.

A. E. I. FALCONAR

Meditation takes many forms in doing as well as in the stillness of pure being. Meditation is the quieting of inner thoughts and outer diversions to leave an opening to experience the presence of spirit as a melding into oneness. Between thoughts, there is a gap where spirit dwells. People meditate to develop an inner calm and quietude that opens to spiritual connection.

Those who create such an opening for spirit listen to their inner voice through intuition, flashes of insight, a sense of knowing, feelings of peace and tranquility, and experiences of oneness and balance. They can meditate while sitting, walking, running, listening to music, or conducting routine, repetitive, mundane tasks. Depending on their ability to recognize and remain unattached to thoughts, people can meditate almost anywhere because their awareness remains beyond thought. Meditation allows individuals to consciously and objectively observe their mind and emotions. It enhances their power to let go of thoughts in the stillness of the moment. People conduct meditation in many ways—through observing the in and out breath, chanting a mantra or other repetitive sound, mindfully walking, or observing the flickering flame of a candle. Whatever moves people from thinking thoughts to observing thoughts to letting go of thoughts creates the space for spirit to enter.

Meditation opens the door to spirit by removing the barriers of preoccupation, worry, stress, and rumination. If, as some say, praying is talking with God, meditating is listening to God.

Here is one example of a meditation practice:

Set aside 10 to 20 minutes a day. Many people find meditating on waking to be a beneficial way to process morning insights and to foster inner peace for the coming day. Sit quietly in a comfortable position. Observe the breath, the rhythm of exhaling and inhaling. Also observe the thoughts. As thoughts pass through the mind, imagine them to be like leaves floating on a river of consciousness. Let the flow of the river allow the thought-leaves to drift out of view. Get in touch with the part that is observing your thoughts. This is the place of connection with spirit—where the Big I lets go of the incessant thoughts of the little i. Whenever distracted by a thought, return to inhaling and exhaling the breath and letting go of the thought. With practice, releasing gets easier. Do not judge or condemn yourself for having so many distracting thoughts. The practice of letting go is what is important, so the more thoughts, the more practice.

Those who release their thoughts without attachment to them experience a profound freedom of choice and personal empowerment. The "monkey mind" no longer plays them like puppets. Observing thoughts without attachment often reveals petty and repetitive patterns. The mental barrage serves a purpose by keeping people from the present moment of awareness. It creates the illusion that they cannot control their thinking. The stimulus-response being who habitually harbors thoughts bars spiritual connection. Once people learn to observe and release thoughts, they cultivate an automatic ability to produce inner calm and openness.

Lea: *I just talked with a coaching client who broke up with her boyfriend. She was distraught. I inquired if she could stop thinking about him for now. She could not believe that was possible. I explained about the neuronal nets and how the brain has been hardwired to think a certain way and how important it is to replace habitual thoughts with something new to break the relationship addiction. Then I realized it was probably easier for me to change my thoughts to something more desirable because I had been practicing letting go of thoughts for many years through meditation.*

Deep Breathing

Developing an awareness of the breath through deep breathing provides an immediate way to connect with spirit. Spirit is often equated to the living breath, which sustains and activates the body. When humans focus on the act of breathing, their mind stills and their body relaxes. Attending to the breath connects with spirit.

John: *I attended a workshop led by Jack Schwarz, founder and president of the Aletheia Psycho- Physical Foundation. At that time, I learned a breathing pattern called "paradoxical breathing," which Jack describes in his book, Voluntary Controls. The breathing pattern is primarily abdominal and thoracic. I have practiced paradoxical breathing almost every day for the past 10 years to enhance my physical and spiritual abilities.*

To begin paradoxical breathing, inhale deeply while pulling in the abdomen. On the exhale, push the abdomen out. Maintain a sequence to the breathing in and out as follows:

- *Inhale: Count 1 to 8*
- *Hold: Count 1 to 4*
- *Exhale: Count 1 to 8*
- *Inhale: Count 1 to 4*
- *Hold: Count 1 to 4*
- *Exhale: Count 1 to 8*
- *Inhale: Count 1 to 4*
- *Hold: Count 1 to 4*
- *Exhale: Count 1 to 16*
- *Inhale: Count 1 to 4*
- *Hold: Count 1 to 4*
- *Exhale: Count 1 to 32*

With so many years of paradoxical breathing, I have learned to follow the sequence without needing to count. I have enjoyed cumulative benefits. My practice has become a habit that I would not want to do without. I know that regular, conscious breathing has put me in a state of health and connection with spirit.

PROGRESSIVE RELAXATION

Herbert Bensen outlined the benefits of deliberate relaxation of the body in his best-selling book, Relaxation Response. Letting go of bodily tensions is a wonderful way to reduce stress and provide an opening for spirit.

John: *I have found that when I tense, I block the energy of spirit. Generally my body is the first indicator that I am caught up in negative thoughts and anxious feelings. To let go of depleting energy, I use a combination of paradoxical breathing and progressive physical relaxation. My purpose is to relax my body completely while maintaining mental alertness and openness to spirit. Here is a description of physical relaxation I practice:*

Assume a comfortable position in a chair or on the floor so that the body does not require muscular effort to maintain the position. Begin with deep breathing, and on two successive naturally occurring exhalations say, "My crown will relax; my crown is relaxing." Repeat for forehead, ears, eyes, face, jaws, neck, shoulders, arms, and wrists, all the way down to the feet. At that point, on seven successive exhalations say:

I am relaxing,

I am relaxing,

My mind is calm and clear, awake and aware,

My mind is calm and clear, awake and aware, I am re-
laxing,
   I am relaxing,
   I am relaxing.
   Move back up the body from the feet to the crown say-
ing "My feet are relaxed; my ankles are relaxed," and so on.
After coming back up to the crown, say on seven successive
exhalations:
   I am relaxed,
   Deeply relaxed,
   Deeply,
   Deep,
   Deep,
   Deep,
   Deep.

This practice takes a few minutes. You can do it silent-
ly and mentally at anytime and any place where you can
maintain a comfortable position and attend solely to the
body for that period of time. You may want to make a re-
cording with your own voice leading you through the steps.
The rejuvenating effects rid the body of blockages of "chi"
(life force) to allow spirit to move through.

Note: Many people use deep breathing and progressive relaxation during meditation to quiet thoughts and open to the expansiveness of spirituality. All three practices can work separately or concurrently, depending on what people prefer.

AFFIRMATIONS

Whether you believe you can do a thing or believe you can't,
you are right.
HENRY FORD

People use affirmations to create what they desire in life. Repeating affirmations during meditation or throughout the day, out loud or mentally, engages positive thinking. Connecting them to the breath, people might silently say, "I breathe in love; I breathe out peace." Affirmations have to be congruent with beliefs, life purpose, and ideals. What the heart and mind believe together, the body will perceive and manifest. When people state what they want in present tense, they have already created it at some level. By using the affirmations with confidence that they have already begun to achieve their desires, people generate positive energy to produce "this or something better."

Energetic Coaches encourage clients to create affirmations from statements of intention, life purpose, and personal desire. Clients may choose to post them where they encounter them throughout the day. Affirmations remind people of what they are already bringing into existence.

Here are a few examples:

- I am a joyful, peaceful person, making the world a better place one instant at a time.
- I am in the moment, practicing love and appreciation, enjoying this with others who do the same.
- I am a teacher and a learner of life's greatest lessons, practicing kindness and wisdom for the sake of the greatest good.
- I am healthy and prosperous, experiencing the best life has to offer.

People can develop affirmations for specific purposes such as to achieve a desired weight, to gain confidence, or to create and receive abundance. When composing an affirmation or a goal, allow spirit to co-create the details by adding "this or something better." Examples of wording follow:

- I weigh 150 pounds or less and feel light, strong, and healthy.
- I sleep eight hours a night or what my body requires for optimum health and well-being.
- I earn $ (fill in the blank) or more with satisfaction and self-realization.

Because spirit does not recognize negative qualifiers, positive affirmations must be used. To say that something is not wanted actually attracts what is not desired. For instance, "I do not want to be broke anymore" is charged with negative energy. Such thinking concentrates on broke, causing polarity and imbalance. The negative energy of even low-grade resistance or fear is enough to block the positive energy people need to attract what they want. Like a vicious cycle, negative energy generates negative energy. Negative thinking detracts from the positive focus that people need to pursue their vision and values. Negative emotions block spirit; positive emotions attract spirit.

It may be easier for people to decide what they don't want than what they do. They can move spiritual energy in the direction of what they do want by deciding upon an affirmation. Practicing affirmations builds the positive feeling that it takes to overcome a habit of thinking negatively. Optimism tends to dissipate worry and fear and make room for learning. By directing positive energy to what they do want, people can gradually change habits of thinking from the stimulus- response negative to the proactive positive.

Along with the words of the affirmation, it is important to create the positive feeling of what it will be like when what is wanted is received. For instance, someone who wants to lose weight must feel what it will be like to be thinner and lighter, wearing different clothes, enjoying exercise and savoring a healthy diet. The experience of the desired state in advance creates what is wanted in the invisible before it gets to the visible.

VISUALIZATION

The secret of making something work in your lives is first of all, the deep desire to make it work; then the faith and belief that it can work; then to hold that clear definite vision in your consciousness and see it working out step by step, without one thought of doubt or disbelief.
EILEEN CADDY

Some people prefer to orient to the world visually. When they want ideas to appear, they see symbols, drawings, pictures, collages, or movies. To discover their value system and desired goals and imprint on their subconscious mind their desired future, individuals can create pictorial representations if they have trouble visualizing.

Visualization is painting an affirmation. Some people find it helpful to build a collage and hang it on the wall for imprinting their dreams and goals. Others draw pictures or create symbols of what they desire. Still others write key words on Post-It notes to remind them to focus on chosen ideas. Many like visualizing their powerful future in their mind's eye. They can also combine their mental image with emotion and feelings. The more people visualize what they want in detail with congruent thoughts, feelings, and perceptions, the more they charge it with energy to create it in form.

Lea: *I find it difficult to see a vision of what I want to create, so I feel the sensation that I am experiencing. Dawna Markova, in her book The Open Mind, calls what Kinesthetics do "feelages," in parallel with the term "images" for the visually oriented. While writing this book, I had to overcome the initial sense of the intangible nature of my undertaking. I could not visualize the book at first, so I imagined what it could be like in my mind's eye. I saw and experienced what it would feel like to hold the book in my hands, complete. After John and I had been writing for a year, I got the distinct feeling that the book had been born, as a tangible entity separate from me, almost like a living being that we had given breath. John said he had experienced something similar. Because of visualizing the book mentally and putting emotional and physical feeling into it, it had become real to us before it was a reality. When I finally held a bound copy in my hands, it looked familiar, as if I had seen it before. I know the feelings of appreciation and accomplishment were the same.*

Visualization can be combined with meditation and affirmation to create the inner world people desire, which then energetically manifests in the three-dimensional form. Affirmations, visualizations, and meditation join emotional, physical, and mental realms with consciousness to create a psychic imprint of what people desire. When they focus their inner knower in congruence and balance with deliberate intent, they direct spiritual energy to co-create for the highest good.

RITUAL

Arranging a bowl of flowers in the morning can give a sense of quiet in a crowded day—like writing a poem or saying a prayer. What matters is that one be for a time inwardly attentive.
ANNE MORROW LINDBERG

Rituals are the conscious process of investing an outer activity with inner significance. Any act can become a ritual if people focus their energy on investing what they are doing with meaning. They can create their own rituals or adopt ones that carry ideas from the past. Some believe that rituals no longer apply to modern-day life. Rituals are not just relegated to religion, witchcraft, shamanism, paganism, or such. They have practical applications today for people who want to connect with their inner self and spirit.

Lea: *I grew tired of the daily task of getting dressed—rolling out of bed, taking a shower, combing my hair, applying body lotion, doing a few stretches, putting on clothes, and bolting out of the door to work—usually behind schedule. Routine had become a bore and a chore. Then it occurred to me that I could transform my daily routine into a moving ritual.*

Now, before I get out of bed, I offer thanks for the gift of another day. As I leave my bed, I say thanks for the comfortable bed. As I shower, I appreciate the warm water. I tell myself that I am cleansed and healthy. As I comb my hair, I figuratively comb out the entangled thoughts that have already started to enter my head. As I apply lotion, I give thanks for my body that allows me to act in the world. As I put on my clothes, I offer thanks for the clothes I have to wear and for the people who made them. As I eat breakfast,

I express thankfulness for the food that nourishes me and for the earth and the people who helped bring it to my table. As I leave my house, I say thanks for the dwelling that shelters me. I start my day with an attitude of gratitude: I am blessed as I am dressed.

It's not the ritual itself that provides meaning. People provide meaning while consciously and intentionally performing whatever they choose to honor. Rituals focus attention to bring meaning to the preseat moment. They integrate mind, body, and emotion; and shared with others, rituals connect and focus community energy. Whether danced, sung, performed, or enacted, rituals bring the meaning of an event or intention to conscious awareness, giving expression to holidays, rites of passage, religious observances and life transitions. People create and practice rituals to express their inner being and intention to join spirit, individually and with others.

NATURE

There can be no very black misery to him who lives in the midst of nature and has his senses still.
HENRY DAVID THOREAU

The ancient alchemists celebrated "Lumen Naturae," which means the "light of nature." The light that exists in nature shines for everyone and connects all people. Nature embodies spiritual characteristics and expression. As fellow creations, humans connect with the natural environment and with spirit through awareness of this common light. Nature can exist without people, but people cannot exist without nature. Nature illustrates the qualities of spirit in an immediate and accessible example of the vastness, power, majesty, abundance and sustenance of it.

Individuals can create a peaceful, meditative calm with a mindful and appreciative walk in nature. People derive inner clarity, completeness, and balance when they commune with the natural world. In modern society many disconnect from nature, which sets them adrift in a form of spiritual rootlessness. Mass production, merchandising, and marketing detach them from the source of life through an illusion of separation from the earth. There is even the concept of "nature deprivation.""Biophilia," the love of living things, describes how people in general prefer natural landscapes to manmade because they derive a good feeling from nature. Some thinkers speculate that humans are genetically wired to need to commune with nature. Most people report feeling physically and emotionally restored after spending time in nature.

Nature provides sustenance; water to drink, food to eat, and air to breathe. It provides healing medicine through natural herbs and pharmaceuticals derived from natural blueprints. People are so intrinsically connected with nature that some take it for granted without realizing how dependent they are. Now more than ever in the history of human life on earth, people need to appreciate, respect, and preserve nature for present and future generations. The Law of Reciprocity works through nature. Humans must nurture what nurtures them and act to ensure good food, water, and air. They need a healthy natural world to support healthy people. This is obvious truth, but many people and organizations oppose natural laws through incongruent actions that disconnect from nature.

From a spiritual perspective the word nature has significance. In the Hebrew alphabet, letters, each with a numerical value, have a connected relationship if different words share the same sum. The Hebrew letters for nature and the Hebrew name for God equal each other in numerical value. Various religions and cultural belief systems give places and characteristics of nature special spiritual meaning. Native Americans have spirit animals that represent characteristics of significance. Different religious and secular groups perform rituals involving stones, stars, scents, the four seasons, the four directions, and other elements to create meaning and connection.

The life essence of the earth is called Gaia. The common life force of people and nature is intrinsically woven into the fabric of the visible and invisible worlds. But there are still those who exploit the earth, taking for granted what is freely given. They deny the negative impact people have on nature and the corresponding effect on personal health and well-being. People have overpopulated the earth, polluted the air, devitalized the soil and the food it produces, and contaminated water all over the world. Human waste and over consumption are taxing natural resources to their limits. Now we are dealing with consequences of environmental abuse. Individuals who develop an I-One relationship with nature rather than the I-object utilitarian perspective of today find wholeness.

As they grow in spiritual consciousness, people's interconnection with nature becomes apparent. Those on the path of spiritual growth develop a natural motivation to protect and sustain the earth as an important connection with themselves. They form communities to protect the environment for themselves and for future generations. Physical connection with nature provides a vehicle for spiritual connection. When tended and appreciated, nature reflects the characteristics of spirit through providing equally for everyone.

Because all individuals are connected through nature, it provides common ground for building relationships and communities. The practice of intentionally appreciating nature and conserving and protecting natural resources for future generations is something that can mend differences, bridge racial and socio-economic gaps and bring people together in appreciation and respect for their common ground.

Service/Volunteering

I don't know what your destiny will be; but one thing I know: the only ones among you who will be really happy are those who will have sought and found how to serve.
ALBERT SCHWEITZER

It is one of the most beautiful compensations of this life that no man can sincerely try to help another without helping himself.
RALPH WALDO EMERSON

As people experience personal wholeness and interconnection, they sense a call to service. As they attune to their inner world, they become sensitive to their outer world. The call to service is a practical opportunity to allow spirit to work through individuals as the instrument of Source. There are limitless ways in the larger world and in the intimate details of the day to act in service with spirit. Different people have different strengths, interests, and talents. Therefore, they have different callings to serve. The inner knower helps individuals find what service suits them. Some like working with their hands and building things. They might be attracted to Habitat for Humanity projects. Some feel a special affinity for children, so they might volunteer for the Court Appointed Special Advocate program or after-school programs. Others work diligently to promote environmental causes or help maintain the local parks. Still others connect to their immediate community by sponsoring neighborhood clean-up projects. Some politically- oriented people help in campaigns and legislative matters. Others become missionaries to help provide food, health care, education, and spiritual nurturance for those in need.

There are large and small causes to serve, but all are the same according to spirit. It is the quality and pureness of the intention that creates spiritual connection. Whether serving a neighbor or working with thousands, whether the results are noticeable on the outside or not, people gain intrinsic satisfaction through an act of service without attachment to egocentric outcomes. Because humans are all connected, what they do for others, they do for themselves. Quoting from the Winter 2006 Institute of HeartMath newsletter:

Research shows that altruistic people are healthier and live longer. In one study that followed 400 women for 30 years, researchers found that 52% of those who did not engage in volunteer work experienced a major illness—-compared with only 36% of those who did volunteer. In a British poll of volunteers, half of those surveyed said their health had improved over the course of volunteering. One in five said that volunteering had helped them lose weight. Another large research study found a 44% reduction in early death among those who volunteered—-a greater effect than exercising four times a week. And a recent investigation conducted by the University of Michigan's Institute for Social Research found that older people who are helpful to others reduce their risk of dying by nearly 60% compared to peers who provide neither practical help nor emotional support to relatives, neighbors or friends.

Those who serve as an instrument of spirit do so without the need for social recognition or self-promotion. They are content to work behind the scenes to further their cause. The intention to act in service to others provides greater meaning and purpose than any egocentric motive. Serving sustains energy and commitment even when the results may not show or when the job seems overwhelming. Those who serve for the sake of their spiritual practice are motivated from within. They know that a particular calling is part of the spiritual path.

People who serve in connection with spirit give not because the other is needy or inferior but because the other is equal and connected to the whole. The energy of the heart-centered choice to act on behalf of others is the practical expression of the I-One relationship. People serve without expectation of reward, recognition, or compensation. Pure service for the sake of serving is spirituality in action.

There is too much need and opportunity not to respond to some calling, large or small, to give back to the world. Each person is a liability to the earth because of consumption and waste production. Individuals have a need to give back because of their impact and the importance of leaving the world a little better place because of having lived within it.

Reading and Contemplating

You must understand the whole of life, not just one little part of it. That is why you must read, that is why you must look at the skies, that is why you must sing and dance, and write poems, and suffer; and understand, for all that is life.
Jiddu Krishnamurti

The saying "You are what you eat" is true for the physical body. For the inner self "You are what you read." If people consume truthful, uplifting, divinely inspired writings, they nourish their spiritual connection. Readers grow spiritually from a regular diet of inspiring texts and reminders of what their inner knower already knows. Reading provides validation and inner support as well as a special relationship between the reader and the message. Words powerfully affect thoughts, feelings, and perceptions. Reading and contemplation pull attention inward in relationship with the self. The choice of what to read and contemplate can open to spiritual energy. The inner validation that flows from spiritual writings helps people along their spiritual path. Reading truth from throughout the ages connects them to their own inner truth.

Lea: *My friend Mary studies the ancient texts of the Nag Hammadi Library and the Dead Sea Scrolls. Over the past three years I have observed her develop an inner calm and serenity that has come from reading and contemplating the scrolls. Although she encounters frustrations and setbacks in her outer life, she stays spiritually connected through the reminders of the ancient teachings of Jesus, his disciples, and other masters. The intuition and insights Mary has from reading the texts has put her in touch with her inner knower. Reading and contemplating inspired writings keeps Mary's mind tuned to her ideals. In turn, she inspires others when she shares what she has learned. Mary consciously applies what she remembers from her study to her belief system. She reflects goodness and grace in her behavior.*

Mary and I think of ourselves as "book-aholics" because we love browsing in a bookstore or library. We share stories with one another about how spirit speaks to us through books. In fact, oftentimes, when one of us has a question, a disconnection, a heartache, or a time of trial, the right book seems to fall open in our hands. We read and find spiritual solace because we are seeking it. Reading and contemplation convey the connection to us. I am least alone when in the companionship of a good book.

To move close to spirit through reading, people need to consciously choose what informs and inspires them. Reading tabloid trash, and negative, sarcastic and cynical writings separate people from spirit. Negativity breeds negativity. People absorb words on a mental and emotional level. Messages affect them in subtle and obvious ways. As they connect with their inner knower through reading and contemplation of inspired writings, individuals experience reminders and reflections needed for spiritual growth and direction.

MUSIC AND DANCE

Music has been said to be the language of the soul. It connects people with spirit through the words, rhythms, and melodies that play to the body, mind, and heart. It catalyzes people with its creativity and divine inspiration. Uplifting music connects people with themselves and others through listening, singing, and dancing to music together.

There is something about the crescendo of an orchestra, the perfect pitch of the soprano, the rousing rhythm of a marching band, or the heartfelt words of a hymn that enriches and nourishes spiritual connection. Music engages people and focuses their senses on the present moment to provide an opening for spirit to enter. The words of songs often speak to spiritual qualities such as love and reverence.

Lea: *Caught in a traffic jam on the Eisenhower Expressway in Chicago, I grew more restless by the moment—until I glanced at the car beside me. My impatience vanished instantly. I saw the driver with a baton, intently directing the invisible orchestra in his car, obviously enjoying himself immensely. I smiled and turned on my radio. Immersed in music, my neighbor had served to remind me to stay in the moment and change my attitude. What a pleasant lesson. Here was someone who had transcended traffic through music so he could experience a world of beauty and grace while others stood still. I was glad that I had happened to stop next to someone who could put me back in touch with the moment and turn unwanted downtime into a communion with spirit.*

Dancing connects the body with music and spirit through movement. Outer movement synchronized with inner connection balances mind, body, and emotions. When people let themselves go in dance, they release stress to be in the expansive and enjoyable moment.

Lea: *My living room is a popular dance hall. I dance alone, I dance with my husband, and when we have a party, I dance with friends and neighbors. If a good song comes on, someone—I'm usually the instigator—decides to move to it. We turn up the volume, and everyone who feels the tug starts wiggling. We laugh, bump, twist, and shout to a few tunes, then float back down to visit some more. I enjoy seeing those who have not been exposed to such in-home rowdiness join the dance. They begin to act like children, cavorting and laughing unselfconsciously. I find energy, fun, and connections in my mix of music and dancing.*

ART AND WRITING

A man who works with his hands is a laborer; a man who works with his hands and his brain is a craftsman; but a man who works with his hands and his brain and his heart is an artist.

LOUIS NIZER

Throughout the ages people have expressed and experienced spirituality through art and poetry. Whether from the hands of children with new crayons or accomplished masters, art has a way of touching the soul and making spiritual connection tangible. Children instinctively appreciate the pleasures of self-expression and creating works of art to proudly display on the refrigerator. Writing a poem connects people through words and the feelings they convey. Creating and appreciating art and poetry are important ways to express identity, ask questions, convey longings, and share insights. Drawing and verse go beyond words and pictures to reach the inner self and to connect with spirit.

Lea: *I spent a great deal of time by myself as a child. When I felt lonely, I would sit at a small table in the basement, pen and paper in hand. I wrote from the depth of my spirit, creating company for myself by writing about my little world. I remember emptying myself of frustrations and childhood concerns and filling myself with rhymes and prose.*

As an adult I continue to turn to art and poetry for spiritual connection and solace. The night my grandmother passed over, I poured out my emotions by writing poetry about her wonderful qualities. The words flowed as the hours flew by. I found comfort through writing about her and my relationship with her. By early morning I had written several poems about what she meant to me. I shared the poems at her funeral, where others told me that they, too, took comfort from the words. The poems captured Grandmother's legacy, and I will share them with my granddaughter some day so that she can know something about how GREAT her great-great-grandmother was.

Journaling taps the inner knower to develop a relationship with self and spirit. Thoughts compel expression, but people don't always have to act on them. Journaling provides an opportunity for reflection to find truth and choose if and how to act. Sometimes journaling is all people need to express themselves to themselves and to connect with spirit. Others may not understand them, and life always brings frustrations and disappointments to deal with, so journaling is a way to communicate within and find inner knowing. When people write with loving intention to express their fullest essence, they strengthen spiritual connection and intuition through writing and contemplating personal thoughts, feelings, and perceptions. They become more connected with self and spirit.

Everyone is an artist. To be artistic means that people immerse themselves in beauty, connect with their high self, and express transcendent qualities of the soul to self and others. Each person artfully creates a life, and the world is the canvas waiting. Henry David Thoreau observed, "It is something to be able to paint a particular picture, or to carve a statue, and so to make a few objects beautiful; but it is far more glorious to carve and paint the very atmosphere and medium through which we look. To affect the quality of the day— that is the highest of arts." People may not be able to paint or write like the great masters, but all individuals hold the potential for creativity and artful expression. The inner artist connects with spirit and wants to express and share with others. The great master artist of spirit is within everyone, seeking to create and to commune.

LEARNING AND STUDY

There's only one corner of the universe you can be certain of improving, and that's your own self.
ALDOUS HUXLEY

As long as you live, keep learning how to live
SENECA

Learning is something that reaches beyond the formal educational system. In fact, some of the most important lessons—such as how to love and live authentically—are extracurricular. Life itself is the schoolhouse for individual growth, compelling people to learn or stagnate. Resisting constant learning opportunities leads to closed-mindedness, myopic thinking, and weariness. Through learning, people get opportunities and lessons to achieve purpose, values, and vision. An entrenched worldview limits consciousness and connection. Learning stimulates growth. The willingness to learn opens individuals to spirit and their inner knower.

Some of us attend school for many years, all the while resisting learning. Those who refuse to move from the past or continue destructive and negative thinking habits have stopped learning, which requires openness and willingness to discover. The defensive, embattled ego can disconnect people from their inner knower. Spirit compels expression as potential. Experience and emotions catalyze people to evolve to full being. As they sift through their lessons and what attracts them to learn about, individuals build self-esteem and self- knowledge. The more people stretch boundaries and broaden perspectives, the more apparent to them is the immensity and mystery of the universe. Those with a lust for learning never tire of life.

In Organization Development the term "readiness" means how receptive people are to learn and change. Readiness is vitally important to receiving new information, and learning depends on open receptivity. Even the best teacher in the world cannot instruct an unwilling student. Learners determine their own degree of readiness.

There are many different ways to learn. The process of growing toward spirit in goodness provides lessons to achieve personal power and sustainable energy. Opportunities to learn never end, and resisting causes a particular life lesson to persist. Personal growth and spiritual connection require openness, willingness, and receptivity to explore what lives within the self and how to open to the outside world.

Do the External (Doing) Stretch

*Unless you try to do something beyond what you have
already mastered, you will never grow.*
Unknown

*You measure the size of the accomplishment by the
obstacles you had to overcome to reach your goal.*
Booker T. Washington

Lea: *My days used to fill with things I HAD to do that crowded out what I WANTED to do. It seemed I was always being called upon, and I resisted. I resented stepping outside my comfort zone. I realized I was overworked and overstressed and decided, "If I'm going to do it anyway, I may as well enjoy it." I looked at the need and decided to make my time, ability, and resources available. I asked for help and guidance from spirit, which combined with my good intention for all things to work together for good. I found that the initial stretch I made to do what was necessary was not as much as I had projected. I overcame my inertia by choosing to dwell in the process and let go of the result, doing what I could along the way. The special energy of spirit joined me. Resentments dissolved as I observed the results and the ease with which I accomplished my work. Now I can do more than I thought I could or would want to with less effort and lots more enjoyment.*

There is a difference between people that makes them weaker or stronger as they go through life. Some have solid boundaries. They refuse to go beyond their perceived finite capabilities or to do more than they think they can or want to do. Others keep producing enthusiastically. As people accomplish their goals with greater ease because they resist less what HAS to be done, they become more powerful. Because they live in the moment, operating with spirit, they are not beleaguered or overwhelmed. They enjoy the capability and confidence to rise to the call. People have the ability to deal with what needs to be done one step at a time. They can do so while relaxing so that they do not look outside of themselves wishing for others to compensate or feel ingratiated to them. There is no need to manipulate or get others to join. Instead, they go inside to self-knowing and find the resources and ability to do what needs to be done and let go of the rest with ease.

Stretching does not mean constant doing. It means rising to the occasion when necessary to attend to a crisis, lift a load for another, change habits to heal self of a chronic condition, or make strategic, long-term changes in dysfunctional systems or organizations. Whenever people face daunting odds, they can call on a special energy to put themselves over the top. In deciding to do and be more than they thought they could, individuals discover that stretching with free will goodwill attracts aid from the infinite energy of spirit.

Chapter 8 Appendix

Reflection

- Which spiritual practices appeal to me to undertake?
- What other spiritual practices that are not listed appeal to me?
- What practice most appeals to me to invite spiritual connection and energy? Why?
- What part of this chapter challenges me or invites me?
- What resistance do I have to maintaining a practice to open to spirit? How can I turn the energy of resistance into the energy of receptivity?
- How does my daily practice reflect the purest expression of my authentic being?
- How do I nurture others and myself through daily practice?
- How can I change what I have to do to something I want to do?

Intentional Imprint

- What do I know works to connect me with spirit? When shall I do that?
- Describe ways in which I have experienced spirit. How can those experiences be recreated?
- What was it like? How can I have more?

9. PRINCIPLES FOR SPIRITUAL CONNECTION

I have learned from experience that the greater part of our happiness or misery depends on our dispositions and not on our circumstances.
MARTHA WASHINGTON

Happiness resides not in possessions and not in gold; the feeling of happiness dwells in the soul.
DEMOCRITUS

People choose their attitude and perspective, whether consciously or unconsciously. Choice is an internal process that has power over the external situation as well as the internal one. Because attitude and perspective influence all experiences of life, Energetic Coaching focuses clients within for what works and to remedy what does not. A focus within as the origination point of outer experience puts people in charge of their thoughts, feelings, and perceptions. When people choose positive and energizing thoughts, feelings, and perceptions, they turn into powerful lasers rather than diffused 60-watt bulbs. As they activate their inner ability to choose, they create outer reality and external experiences congruent with inner values of being and outer visions of doing. Chapter 8, "Practice," relates primarily to doing. People can only sustain inner decisions if they want to practice rather than have to. The desire has to be for the self, not merely compliant with the wishes of others or demands of society. Making choices and exercising free will is where spiritual principles and values become real.

People act in response to an inner catalyst. They develop their awareness and activate their energy by making conscious choices. When they decide in congruence with their inner knower and spirit, they act with integrity and live in ways that express who they are. Once they have chosen, they cannot then claim to be a victim and blame others for what they decided. No longer can they abdicate and act like they had nothing to do with how things turn out. When people take responsibility for their choices, aligned with their inner knower and connected with spirit, they gain the attitude and the perspective that creates personal power.

Deciding in the Gap

Between stimulus and response, there is a space. In that space lies our freedom and power to choose our response. In our response lies our growth and freedom.
Víctor Frankl

When you live in reaction, you give your power away. Then you get to experience what you gave your power to.
N. Smith

It is not stress that kills us, it is our reaction to it.
Hans Selye

Spirit exists in the immediate moment between stimulus and response. Individuals choose how they will conduct each act, whether with energy and enthusiasm or with half-hearted, resentful detachment. Through all their doing, their attitude shows. Attitude is not fixed. People create power by practicing choice over thoughts, feelings, and perceptions. They may recognize their power intellectually; however, it remains a nice idea, not a reality, until they respond to a stimulus in a conscious, decisive way rather than unconsciously through habit. Living consciously in connection with spirit requires people to decide in the gap how they want to be while they go about their doing.

Years ago William James said, "The greatest discovery of any generation is that human beings can alter their life by altering their attitude." Some act as if they have no control. Happiness lies within. If they relinquish their power to choose their attitude, they become stimulus-response puppets to external circumstances. What they value and what they focus upon create the energy

Energetic Coaches set the example for clients to go beyond deciding, prioritizing, and directing outer goals. In addition to outer doing, we focus on and hold the space for them to express their inner self. We support clients finding ways to connect their doing with their being to live well deliberately. Certainly we coach to achieve goals, but the overall outcome of Energetic Coaching extends beyond measures of external success. True success stems from within, where people can realize their greatest personal power—the power to choose how to be in the gap between stimulus and response.

People express their internally held values and thoughts, feelings and perceptions in their very being—their attitude in the moment with presence, consciousness and choice. As with external practices outlined in Chapter 8, internal practices develop spiritual connection and habits of thinking, feeling, and perceiving that work to release energy and create personal power from within. The following are examples of spiritual principles in action that guide Energetic Coaches and clients to experience powerful inner being to make outer doing congruently reflect their energetic self.

Practice Miracle-Mindedness

To me, every hour of the light and dark is a miracle. Every cubic inch of space is a miracle.
Walt Whitman

We cannot kindle when we will The fire that in the heart resides The spirit bloweth and is still In mystery our soul abides.
Matthew Arnold

It is only with the heart that one can see rightly; what is essential is invisible to the eyes.
Antoine de Saint-Éxupéry

It has been said that either everything is a miracle or nothing is. Which way do you choose? Look around and ask yourself what you know about what affects you personally on a daily basis. Do you know how the autonomic nervous system works to regulate your heartbeat and breathing? Do you know how you were made in the womb? Do you understand how the universe revolves and evolves? Do you know how many stars are in the sky or how many galaxies spiral beyond ours? Do you know where your intuitive insights originate?

To small children new to the world, everything seems miraculous. They question with"Why?" and "How?" to learn as much as possible. Their curiosity and wonder abounds. Then what happens? Adults often lose their childlike wonderment as they begin to take the miraculous nature of life for granted. As scientists continue to uncover the secrets of the universe, many have a growing realization that some of what they are encountering lies beyond human comprehension. Each discovery leads to unanswered questions. The world appears to be made of tangible, material, solid objects, but it is actually composed mostly of what appears to be empty space. People continually find increasing information to measure and observe, break down and quantify, understand and explain, but the more they know, the more they know how much they do not know. The need to know everything and prove oneself as an expert, is not only impossible but allows the ego to block spiritual connection.

The more humans live within the gap of mystery and not knowing, the more some experience an intelligent and creative energy that keeps everything connected and working. To live with the awareness of how much is not known fosters miracle-mindedness. Such wonder creates an awareness of the transcendent qualities of life that invite spiritual energy and connection. To expect the miraculous and abide in the mysterious is to live without self-limiting beliefs and habits of doing and being that make life mundane, uninteresting, or downright boring.

Lea: *I was outside with my two-year-old granddaughter when we heard a bird singing loudly in the tree above us. She asked what the sound was, and when I told her it was a bird, she asked, "Is birdie singing a song just for me?" I laughed and replied, "Yes, you bet! The birdie is singing a song just for you." Why not?*

COUNT BLESSINGS

*The aspects of things that are most important to us are
hidden because of their simplicity and familiarity.*
PROFESSOR LUDWIG WITTGENSTEIN

*Generally, appreciation means some blend of thankfulness,
admiration, approval, and gratitude. In the financial
world, something that "appreciates" grows in value. With
the power tool of appreciation, you get the benefit of both
perspectives: as you learn to be consistently thankful and
approving, your life will grow in value.*
DOC CHILDRE AND HOWARD MARTIN, *The HeartMath Solution*

*There is more hunger for love and appreciation in this
world than for bread.*
MOTHER TERESA

Just as learning increases mental muscle and stimulates personal growth, appreciation increases spiritual "muscle" and stimulates spiritual growth. Ironically, people seem motivated less by what they have than what they want. They are always looking for something new. At first they may appreciate hard won possessions and relationships, but as they pursue new goals and acquisitions, they tend to lose gratitude for previous accomplishments. To dream and have goals is necessary, but to focus exclusively on the future and acquisition take away from what is worthwhile and valuable in the present. People can balance accomplishment and appreciation. Because of the tendency to take for granted, it takes conscious attention and intention to be aware of blessings and the basics of life, such as clean water, good food, and a healthy body.

Over- emphasizing outer doing detracts from inner being and appreciation.

Beginning each morning by counting blessings can set the tone for the rest of the day. With an "attitude of gratitude," people can imbue the little things in life that are freely available with special meaning and value. They can transition from being negative to being positive. They can turn dark and bleak into good, right, and beautiful in a split second. Appreciation is the key.

Individuals can develop an appreciative attitude over time by consistently looking for good. As relative beings in a relative universe, depending on how they compare themselves to others, people can choose to feel either cursed or blessed. There will always be those who are younger, thinner, richer, or smarter—though not necessarily happier. Individuals can choose to think that they are superior to others or inferior. They pick their standards for self-comparison and relative satisfaction without always choosing carefully.

Spiritual connection gives a standard for comparison that does not depend on changing circumstances or appearances. To continuously appreciate, people can look within to what is lasting and meaningful to them; then they can find meaning in outer circumstances and the worth in others.

Humans appear to be hard-wired to seek positive relationships with others. But, again, most people tend to take others for granted, especially those in relationship that have the greatest opportunity for closeness, such as family and close friends. Fears and projections can take over as a relationship nears its potential to be loving and appreciative. Rare is the couple or family who consistently and consciously practice appreciation for one another. Respecting and appreciating can become a way of being so that doing becomes a natural expression of love.

To consciously choose to see the best in another in sincere appreciation brings out the best in the other and in the self. Think of a particular person you know well. Think of him or her negatively, and notice how you feel. Then spend five minutes thinking of him or her positively and take stock of your feelings again. Which way works better? It is the same person from two perspectives, but one way builds a relationship and the other way destroys it. The beholder defines whether a trait is positive or negative. Shifting perspective gives people the personal power to appreciate or depreciate others in relationships.

In the same way, if people do not appreciate life itself, they find it difficult to connect with the Source of life. Those who value life have a strong connection with spirit. The creation appreciates the creator of it when they see life is good.

There can be so much outer striving for things that people neglect their relationships with self and with others. If they appreciate others while working toward a goal, they can maintain quality relationships in doing and being concurrently. They also appreciate more of what they have without the dissatisfaction of needing something more.

Future visions, goals, purpose, and results are important. But if people do not appreciate what they have in the present moment, they cannot value what they have achieved. They risk forever seeking something else to take its place. Energetic Coaching focuses on helping clients develop a deep, inner attitude of gratitude for what is now while coaching for future improvement.

DO THE INTERNAL (BEING) STRETCH

Unless you try to do something beyond what you have already mastered, you will never grow.
UNKNOWN

Believe in yourself. You gain strength, courage and confidence by every experience in which you stop to look fear in the face...You must do that which you think you cannot do.
ELEANOR ROOSEVELT

Security is mostly a superstition. It does not exist in nature; nor do the children of men as a whole experience it. Avoiding danger is no safer in the long run than outright exposure.
Life is either a daring adventure, or nothing.
HELEN KELLER

Lea: *At this time, we are going through the final editing of the book. It has been a time-crunching and soul-searching endeavor. The three of us, John, my co-author, Charlotte, our editor, and I are working together under an impossible timeline but with great joy. As I write this, it appears we will make our deadline after all, and our relationship together, although taxing and tiring at times, has become even more connected and appreciative. We volunteered to do this to-gether one last time. We didn't have to, we wanted to, and the process has proved to be arduous but extremely reward-ing. Our attitude has made all the difference.*

People grow weaker or stronger as they go through life. Those who maintain rigid boundaries refuse to go beyond what they perceive as finite capabilities. They do only what they think they can. Others exude enthusiasm and productivity. Because they accept what has to be done, they accomplish it with grace. Because they work in the moment, alongside spirit, they succeed. They have a self-knowing about their capability and confidence to rise to a calling. They have a way of dealing with what needs to be done while staying relaxed.

Life requires constant extension. The stretch to go beyond learned limits catalyzes growth, self-esteem, and spiritual connection. To see how important it is to extend, observe those who refuse to do so. Goethe said, "We must always change, renew, rejuvenate ourselves; otherwise, we harden." Rigid limits stifle creative potential. But some find old habits difficult to break and new habits challenging to assume. For those who will not step outside their comfort zone, life stagnates into boring sameness. They are not as attractive to others because of their low energy level. People who operate within confining limits never know how much they could be or do. By taking risks, people show themselves and others new possibilities. For those willing to do the stretch, even a perceived "failure" nets a positive learning experience.

John: *My body was telling me that something was missing. At first I passed it off as anxiety at having to meet a self-imposed deadline on a task or commitment. However, as the feeling persisted, I decided to go inside to inquire from my inner knower what wanted to be expressed. The answer I received was an absence of creativity in my life. I had become comfortable with training and group facilitating because I didn't need to extend myself and I was good at it. In connecting with my heart I realized I wasn't enjoying the work anymore; in fact, I found it boring. I began looking within for how to stimulate my creative juices. I discovered my answer in paper art, an activity I had some familiarity with and had been sitting on for a number of years. A stir-*

ring within to stretch and embark on artful expression gave me a burst of energy and challenge.

Difficulties are a part of life. Understandably, many wish to take the path of least resistance to avoid them, but often that choice leads away from spirit. Myla Kabat-Zinn says, "Each difficult moment has the potential to open my eyes and open my heart." Without challenges people can complacently fall short of knowing their capacities. At the end of the day, they may wonder how life might have turned out had they pursued unfamiliar territory, challenged inherited and unexamined beliefs, and extended themselves to be who they really are and create what they dreamed.

When people stretch outside their comfort zone, they can see other points of view. Flexibility allows them to recognize and integrate their shadow and manage their ego.

Lea: *It is possible to stretch too much. I have often said that whereas wise people know their limitations, I seem to need to bump against mine. Stretching provides self-knowing and self- appreciation to endure and overcome great challenges. On the other hand, there are priorities in life. Not everything needs to be a stretch. Because I love to learn, I have to remind myself to remain in repose even as I work outwardly to achieve goals and self-improvement. Stretching is a balance like everything else.*

A former client contacted me recently to confess that she resented my coaching for a period of time because she asked me to do something for her, which I declined to do. I knew my client had it in her to deal directly with her fear, and that she could overcome what she was avoiding. My client stated that it took longer and was more difficult than she would have liked, but she accomplished her objective and feels much better about herself for having done so. My client did the stretch and learned that she could handle more than she thought she could.

People and circumstances that trigger judgment, rejection, or dislike offer the greatest opportunity to stretch. Just as physical stretching benefits the body, spiritual stretching energizes the being. The inner knower serves as a gyroscope for choice: It challenges people to stretch when they do not want to and alerts them when they are exceeding their limits.

We Energetic Coaches remind clients to find the centerpoint between stretching and habit so they can integrate learning with convenience and comfort. There are times in life that require greater flexibility than others. Having explored new territory makes future stretches easier. As clients release how things have always been or how they would rather have had them, they open to possibilities. People's personal power remains unknown and unrealized until they stretch to realize courage and strength in the face of challenges. Inviting new ideas and experiences allows spirit to create opportunities beyond imagination.

LIVE IN THE MOMENT

To a happy person, the formula for happiness is quite simple: Regardless of what happened early this morning, last week, or last year – or what may happen later this evening, tomorrow, or three years from now – now is where happiness lies.
RICHARD CARLSON

> *There is surely nothing other than the single purpose of the present moment. A man's whole life is a succession of moment after moment. If one fully understands the present moment, there will be nothing else to do, and nothing else to pursue.*
>
> HAGAKURE

Attending immediate awareness and experience means releasing incessant, preoccupied thinking that takes away from the only instant in which humans exist—now. Although they can only live in the moment, people continually put the past or the future into the mix. By examining what keeps them from the present moment, people can let go of what they can do nothing about. While ruminating on what is not now, they cannot simultaneously experience the fullness of who they are and what is present. It takes a quick decision to shift perspective to now. By consciously focusing on being and appreciating the present, people connect with spirit. Certainly, they need goals to direct their lives toward ideals and dreams, but the visualization, affirmation, and action that it takes to manifest a desired future can only happen in the immediate moment.

Lea: *While writing this chapter, I realized that I had spent most of the day thinking about past and future things. I decided to dwell in the moment to practice what I was preaching. I listened to the birds singing outside and gazed at the beautiful blue sky and green trees. Then I noticed my thoughts and how preoccupied I had been. By getting into the now, I realized I was hungry after sitting so long. Relaxed, I remembered to take my car to the repair shop for the next day's appointment. As a break, I delivered it and returned to writing. Then I enjoyed getting back to work.*

With my thoughts open and clear, I experienced being in an expansive present.

The still moment increases space for spirit to enter. With awareness of now, people can realize how their immediate being contains the essence of life. Making now the time in which to be and do ensures that the future will take care of itself. Moment-by-moment living becomes natural with practice. Time expands.

John: *As I continue meeting with clients as an Energetic Coach, I am naturally more often present in the present. I seem to bring clients into the now by being in touch with my current thoughts, feelings, perceptions, and intentions. Instead of letting them go unnoticed and unexamined, I bring an additional dimension that shows up as an expansive and inclusive connection, which I call spirit. Some of the insights and inspiration clients have "received" during coaching demonstrates the power of the present moment to increase consciousness and open to the inner knower. The inner focus of Energetic Coaching in the present reveals gaps between inner being and outer doing that clients need to resolve. They connect with thoughts, sensations, and feelings that they might have overlooked or dismissed before. With coaching, they increase their awareness of an expansive state of being. They learn how to be fully present in the now.*

Energetic Coaches intentionally remain in the moment with awareness when meeting with clients. Using now, we can evoke a powerful presence, which clients perceive as connection. In- the-moment awareness creates a spirited coaching relationship as we open and accept clients in the infinite present.

LET GO

What worries you, masters you.
HADDON W. ROBINSON

If we don't change, we don't grow. If we don't grow, we are not really living. Growth demands a temporary surrender of security.
GAIL SHEEHY

When I let go of what I am, I become what I might be.
LAO TZU

People can choose to let go of resentments, bothers, distractions, and worries. It is the practice of releasing that renders individuals powerful and relaxed. Of course, some things are easier released than others. Energetic Coaches assist clients in letting go of what holds them back and drains their energy, including limiting beliefs, habits, disappointments, relationships, melodrama, ego-based desires, or grudges. As well as asking questions to help clients release, we show by example.

John: *In coaching, I have experienced many instances in which clients have had unrealistic expectations of others and an unbalanced external focus on doing. Often they sought something externally that could only be found within themselves. I directed them inward to identify what they wanted.*

If they want love in relationship, they must first fall in love with themselves. As clients let go of outer expectations or wishes for others to change, they release their energy to focus within. Then they can do what they think best without looking to the past or the present situation to change. By letting go, clients create the freedom for others to be them-

selves. Then both parties can respond authentically to each other. The situation may or may not change, but by letting go, clients can move to different situations and experiences with different others or simply be different themselves within the same context or relationship.

There are times in which the only way people can free themselves to grow is to let go. To do so they need to release hurts, resentments, attachments and disappointments. As coaches we might suggest they ask themselves, "What can I do to improve this situation or solve this problem now?" Sometimes there is nothing apparent. By exploring options in coaching, clients can decide what is within their sphere of influence and release what is not. Choosing to release empowers people rather than disappointing and diminishing them.

Even though life presents difficulties, coaching does not focus on pain, lack, or shortcoming. We support people's ability and strategies to transcend. If clients refuse to release what holds them back, then there is some kind of payback in their staying where they are, no matter how seemingly undesirable it may be. Through our choice to let go of our own agenda on behalf of clients—or to release the coaching relationship itself, we model ethics and boundaries in a safe environment. Authentic being and forthright behavior create a dynamic that allows relationships to grow. Energetic Coaches know that spirit is always available to fill the gap, replacing what no longer serves with something meaningful and desirable.

The practice of letting go frees energy for what people can do something about. Even though there may be a perceived loss on the outside, what they take in as a replacement compensates a hundredfold over time.

Lea: *A client asked me if it were possible to let go too much. I asked her if she had an issue with letting go, perhaps a way in which she did not trust herself to decide when to stay or when to leave. Judy told me that she still regretted a time when she had let go "too" readily. I explained to her how the pendulum could swing to overcompensate but that somewhere in the middle between holding on and letting go was a point where she could rest. She recognized that overcompensating by clinging was not necessary to make up for the past. To serve her in the future, Judy began releasing and holding on with decision and discernment. Judy realizes that relationships are two-way streets and chooses those that are not one-way streets or dead-ends. She trusts herself more and knows that every ending is also a new beginning.*

Releasing the past often means forgiving. People cannot forgive others unless they can forgive themselves. Some people are hard on themselves, second-guessing decisions without recognizing that they did the best they knew how at the time. By letting go of "mistakes" or"failures" (if there are such things), people may let go of "mistakes" or "failures" they perceive in others.

CREATE YOUR IMPACT ON THE WORLD

If you think you're too small to have an impact try going to bed with a mosquito in the room.
ANITA KODDICK

All appears to change when we change.
HENRI AMIEL

Energetic Coaches observe the energy of clients. By their resisting what they do not want, are they creating what they have? From the inside out, clients learn to see how they manifest their own reality. They discover that they can either escalate problems or innovate solutions. We ask them to decide what impact they want to have on the world and then support their developing thoughts, actions, emotions, and spoken words to achieve their desired outcomes.

A way for people to assess their impact on the world is to look at the quality of their relationships with others. Are they being in relationship in ways they would like others to be with them? Does each relationship benefit them and others? Are their relationships growing and respectful? Are they equal and reciprocal? Are they positive and supportive? To create more of what they want, people can teach others how to treat them. When they observe their impact on others in relationship, they see by reflection what impact they have on the world. It takes conscious effort and choice to decide how to live and what to leave as a legacy.

The role of parent is usually the longest, most important relationship. The health of society depends on the health of the family. If children grow to responsible adulthood, they create goodness for themselves and others. They learn by example from their parents and significant others how to be and how to relate. It is not easy to parent, but the growth it entails because of helping another grow is personally rewarding. A relationship with a child is the most impactful relationship anyone can create. For this reason, when coaching those who have children at home, Energetic Coaches focus on the family relationships and keep in the forefront the importance of the influence and example significant others set for children.

There are no perfect parents or childhoods. Most people are continuously building from their foundations to become whole adults. Energetic Coaches hold the space for clients to release what no longer works from their past belief systems and stories. We encourage them to set their sights on things that release them from negatives of their past and create positives in their present and future.

Relationships are key to where people are on their path. At each level of progress, people grow together or apart. Especially in close, one-on-one relationships, the other serves as a mirror. Partners can determine who they are and the impact that they have by examining their relationships. Clients may be unaware of their effect on others. By looking at the big picture, coaches help clients appreciate their impact. Once aware of their potential, they are likely to act consciously to create good relationships one at a time.

Lea: *Sally told me how she had spent three months planning a retreat, only to have her idea "squashed." I asked why she wanted to work with groups only. Although she said that she preferred one-on-one work, she said that it didn't seem "big" enough. I consulted rather than coached with her and shared that from my perspective and background in OD, system change happens one person at a time. One is as "big" as it gets.*

Take a Time-Out

Renew thyself completely each day; do it again, and again, and forever again.
Chinese inscription cited by Thoreau in Walden

Stop talking, stop thinking, and there is nothing you will not understand. Return to the root and you will find Meaning.

SENGTSAN

Overwrought and out-of-control children may balk at timeouts as punishments. Adults, on the other hand, can appreciate timeouts to calm and refocus, decrease stress, and increase clarity. Anyone can benefit from making space to settle down. As a discipline or practice, taking a break offers rewards by interrupting what is unproductive. Redirecting energy to the present moment, people can enjoy being without doing.

John: In coaching, a "pattern interrupt" can focus clients on the present. Sometimes in the flurry of speaking and dialoguing, they lose track of their mission. Although I enjoy friendly interchange, if I sense our conversation is not serving their stated purpose, I redirect them to intentional dialogue. If clients seem scattered and unsettled, I ask them to reflect on what they are sensing, which brings them into the present. Clients automatically slow their breathing and begin to introspect during timeouts. Usually they recognize that they have shifted some aspect of themselves. I remain engaged and attentive as the change in pace brings them insights. The ensuing silence and reflective space can be powerful. In the quiet awareness of the space of the shared moment, they connect with themselves and their desired outcomes in real and open ways.

Energetic Coaching helps clients see how constant doing is not necessarily productive. Because there is a tendency to appreciate others and themselves for the external doing more than internal being, they create an imbalance. Energetic Coaching puts the emphasis on being so that clients do not always have to do something except show up in openness and receptivity. A timeout makes space between stimulus and response so that people can deliberate. Before unconsciously reacting, they can experience the moment from a high-level perspective. During a timeout they can consciously choose to objectively observe themselves and ask, "What can I do right now to improve this situation?" Because high-level awareness opens channels to spirit, the information they receive may be spontaneous and surprising.

Taking a timeout during a stressful or hectic period helps people avoid mistakes or accidents. They can choose their words, consider options, imagine possible outcomes, breathe deeply, and decide the next step. Timeouts diffuse stress and bring calm awareness to the present moment.

Lea: *When I was teaching, I used timeouts to bring the class to the present moment. If I sensed a disconnection from the students, I would stop my lecture. I would allow others to speak followed by complete silence. The energy in the classroom would shift, and the students would turn their attention and receptivity to the front of the room. By pausing, I would return to the present moment and connect with the students rather than solely focusing on what I thought I had to teach.*

CHANGE YOUR FOCUS

Each of us literally chooses, by his way of attending to things, what sort of universe he shall appear to himself to inhabit.

WILLIAM JAMES

The secret of happiness is not in doing what one likes, but in liking what one has to do.

J. M. Barrie

To achieve a goal or vision in the outer world, people must first image it. Then the mind works to match the present picture to the desired future. To accomplish the goal requires faith— belief without evidence—that people possess the ability to create what they want. By focusing on the vision or the goal, they direct their energy toward achievement and engage the senses before the ego can judge. Imagining overarches the step-by-step process of doing to focus on the outcome. When people experience their desired future in the present tense as though they had already accomplished it, they begin to realize the desired experience, almost magically transforming it into their new reality. This is what is sometimes called the Law of Attraction.

There is a part of the brain called the reticular activating system that acts like an efficient executive assistant. It sifts through incoming data, sorting for what is crucial. Associated with the sleep-wake cycle, it is the center of arousal and motivation. The RAS alerts humans to information associated with what is valued while screening out nonessentials, distractions, and clutter. Like tuning a TV, the antenna of the RAF picks up desired frequencies even though many other programs are available.

If people focus on the negative even without conscious awareness, the RAF tunes to what they don't want, such as fear and powerlessness. Ironically, fear and avoidance of what people don't want attracts the negative because of their focus. A fundamental coaching protocol aims to change negative belief systems, attributions, visions, and projections into positive language and perceptions. Those who focus on the positive are likely to create more of what is wanted instead of what is not.

People select what information they attend to. If they live in fear, they operate on a low frequency and activate negative energy. When the media shows negative aspects of world events, they slant viewers' focus to the difficult and despairing. Even so, people can avoid negative energy by turning off horror, murder, exploitation and human depravity on screen, on radio, and online. They need to focus on the good and positive input to offset so much negative. Prime time programming may appeal to some, but not everyone. Despite real or imagined tragedies, fears, dire warnings, and red alerts, positive people in balance can offset the negative effects of the news, television programming, and negative people in their lives. Individually and collectively, people can choose positive focus and actions in spite of what is wrong in the world.

Negativity has an attractive force. An unhappy person can influence others who do not hold a positive vision. People can disconnect from negativity by focusing on the positive. Concentrating on goals and reframing negative messages, individuals invoke the power of faith. To some, projecting goals may seem like pretending, but envisioning is not child's play. This kind of confidence in things unseen requires an inner knowing that all things do work together for good when that is what is intended.

Modern medicine acknowledges that there is often a psychological or emotional connection to the onset of disease. Stress and negativity deplete the body's immune system. Because people can make themselves sick through negative thinking, stress, and worry, they can also use positive energy to heal.

Energetic Coaches notice where clients put their energy. What they focus on means they let go of everything else. Some people naturally maintain an optimistic outlook, but others turn to the pessimistic instead. We can redirect focus by asking clients about the positive aspects of a perceived negative belief or result. Choosing a positive outlook is a reframe and not a Pollyanna projection. There is never a positive without a negative and vice-versa so, it is important to choose where to send energy. Energetic Coaches continually help clients notice where they are focusing and how they are labeling an event or a feeling. We challenge them to direct themselves where it will be the most beneficial.

TAKE OWNERSHIP

Our ultimate freedom is the right and power to decide how anybody or anything outside ourselves will affect us.
STEPHEN COVEY

As long as you can find someone else to blame for anything you are doing, you cannot be held accountable or responsible for your growth or the lack of it.
SUN BEAR

To achieve wholeness, people take responsibility for their actions through knowing their intention. When they excuse themselves or blame others, they diminish their sphere of influence. Separated from self and others, they lose spiritual energy. Through self-pity they abdicate power to create something good. As related beings, individuals can use the same standards for themselves as they use for others. Ownership means looking at what is on the outside and seeking a connection from within. By contemplating the learning opportunities in events, people can achieve personal power by creating what they want out of it. Without claiming ownership and personal responsibility, some become stimulus-response puppets instead of powerful creators of reality.

Through developing our own sense of ownership, Energetic Coaches readily respond if clients blame others or look outside themselves for causes. Some abdicate personal responsibility by blaming themselves first to deflect others from holding them accountable. Many refuse to change inside. Their plight renders them powerless. Energetic Coaches maintain the focus on what the client wants. Blame, projection and avoidance, excuses and defensiveness drain energy and block spirit. We help clients bring to the surface and examine their excuses or abdication of personal responsibility. We also balance for those who have a tendency to blame themselves or take too much responsibility for others or unforeseen events. We help clients build positive, balanced belief systems and take action on what they can do in responsible ways.

Lea: *When clients reject and condemn themselves or others, I ask, "What can you do to change the other person or the situation?" Usually clients conclude that they cannot change others. Often they can think of something to change the situation, including letting go, which they may not want to do. When they find fault or blame themselves or others, I sense a downward spiral of energy that leads nowhere. But even if they can do nothing to change the outside, they can always change their perception of the situation. By choosing their own attitudes, people claim their power. It is rewarding to watch power build as clients name and claim what they want rather than complain about what they don't want.*

My client, John, was highly focused on another person in his church group. No matter what John wanted to do, this person had a criticism and another idea how to do better. I witnessed John's hyper-focus on the other person and asked if he was able to shift his focus to others in the group. John was startled when he realized that there were 15 others in the study group he led, but he gave all his energy to just one. This drained his energy and his enjoyment of the group. Once John removed his focus from the person, that person appeared to become less problematic.

LIVE THE GOLDEN RULE

A man's feeling of good will towards others is the strongest magnet for drawing good will towards himself.
LORD CHESTERFIELD

You haven't learned life's lesson very well if you haven't noticed that you can give the tone or color, or decide the reaction you want of people in advance. It's unbelievably simple. If you want them to take an interest in you, take an interest in them first. If you want to make them nervous, become nervous yourself...It's as simple as that. People will treat you as you treat them. It's no secret. Look about you. You can prove it with the next person you meet.
SIR WINSTON CHURCHILL

Almost everyone is familiar with the Golden Rule which instructs people to treat others as they would want others to treat them (or not do to others what they would not want done to them). The law of reciprocity works in relationships. If all people practiced this one rule, they would make the world a wonderful place.

Why don't they?

Anything other than one is an illusion. What is done to the other is done to the self. People hear their own wisdom and see the effect of their actions through how others respond. The inner knower monitors who a person is, and the collective consciousness reflects the current state of society's awareness as a whole. For spiritual connection and energy, relationships with self and others must be congruent. Spiritually-connected people take responsibility for what they exhibit and what they choose, knowing that they are related to others like mirror and reflection.

Living the Golden Rule means practicing kindness, caring, and goodwill toward others. The rule also entails caring and good intentions toward self. Incongruence in thought, word, or deed makes knowing, accepting and loving the self difficult if not impossible. Unless people practice the Golden Rule within and treat themselves kindly, compassionately, and lovingly, they cannot treat others accordingly.

Dealing with the challenges of life creates a common ground for connectedness. Adversity teaches empathy and understanding. After individuals experience pain and suffering, they are often more compassionate about the pain and suffering of others. Life is short. It can be so difficult. Those who do not want to add to the difficulties inherent in the world can act to lift the load for others, thereby lifting their own as well.

People do not normally talk about pain and difficulties in polite company. Ashamed of sorrow, disappointment, or grief, they hide their wounds behind silence or bury their problems below consciousness. Many want to avoid being a downer in front of others. Some live superficially in pseudo-happiness with eruptive anger over the smallest things. Others become depressed by repressing anger and disappointment. By burying hurt, people isolate themselves in grief. Seemingly oblivious to how much their cynicism and disappointment show through, some hold so much resentment that they do not know how to be kind to others. Or, they may not care. When people least want to extend themselves to others is the most propitious time to give what they would like to receive. When there is nothing a person can do to make themselves feel better, he or she can always do for someone else—which returns to make that person feel better.

When clients deal with people who are unkind, Energetic Coaches seek to get their clients to understand what part they play. We facilitate clients in their growth to see difficult others in an expansive context. Usually the ones clients are dealing with have gone through some difficulty or grave disappointment. People who retaliate, belittle, or wrongly assess the intentions of others are good examples of how not to be. Instead of perpetuating the negativity with a response in kind, clients can choose sympathetic options instead. Oftentimes, hurtful behavior stems from a hidden or repressed part of the past. Our clients do not need to know in detail the reasons for unfair projections or unkind treatment by others. Those people alone have their issues to resolve. Clients are coached to let go, realize that it's more about the other person than it is about them, and refrain from trying to rescue or compensate for poor behavior. What works for the good of both parties is to show kindness when there is none, to care when it is difficult, and to exercise goodwill toward all. Energetic Coaching is a calling to use the Golden Rule in relationship with self and others. There is perhaps no greater opportunity when others have a negative self- judgment than to fully accept them without condemnation and without trying to change them. Then a good example is set about how one expects to be treated in return

Clients in the presence of the Energetic Coach as compassionate witness may project negative attributions, anger, resentment or disappointment. We know that they are struggling with issues that they have yet to address and assimilate. We hold a space for clients to learn about themselves and accept themselves. As instruments of spirit, we know that we cannot stand in judgment, condemnation, or separation from others. Instead of giving energy to the painful past, the sad story, or the current difficulty, Energetic Coaches choose to emphasize potential. Holding the vision of who clients want to be, we assist them in finding value in themselves and their experiences. Because we honor the spark of spirit within them, we can mirror for clients what counts: We are all infinitely powerful, lovable, and valuable. Despite our best efforts, there may be some clients who refuse to see their own goodness and how they have created their present situation. If there comes a time when it is obvious that more coaching will not help the client get unstuck, therapy is recommended. All the while, the coach intentionally practices the Golden Rule.

To Choose or not to Choose

To talk goodness is not good—only to do it is.
CHINESE PROVERB

Spiritual principles and practices are only ideas until people adopt and apply them. It takes a conscious choice to be and do differently. Whether people admit it or not, the inner world of thoughts, feelings, perceptions, and intentions are

subject to their dominion. Individuals choose how to express themselves in the world. There is an innate drive to growth and goodness. However, it does not come easily or even naturally all the time. Because of the challenges of life, people must choose daily how to be. Doing branches out as the manifestation of inner choices. Through consciously deciding to achieve goodness and connectedness, oneness and wholeness, people invite the guiding light of their ideals joined by the bursting sun of spirit to illuminate their path. They become beacons themselves. Not easily, of course, but how else is there to validate and reflect human potential? How else to demonstrate one's true character? How to be as a person is a choice—the most important choice that people can make. Energetic Coaches choose how we want to be, and what we want to reflect. We right ourselves through our inner knower when our path takes a turn and intentionally serve as a beacon to others to connect with the light of Source.

CHAPTER 9 APPENDIX

REFLECTION

- What positive changes in perception and attitude do I resist? What can I learn from my resistance? What do I need to allow to achieve my ideals?
- How do I practice what I preach?
- What is my challenge in being an Energetic Coach?
- What other spiritual principles provide energy and connection to serve my highest good?

CONTEMPLATE THE FOLLOWING

Personal transformation can and does have global effects. As we go, so goes the world, for the world is us. The revolution that will save the world is ultimately a personal one.

MARIANNE WILLIAMSON

We put ourselves to all sorts of inconveniences to satisfy our guilty passions, but when it is a question of overcoming them, we will not lift a finger. It is just this penny's worth of suffering that nobody wants to spend.

ST. LEONARD OF PORT MAURICE

INTENTIONAL IMPRINT

- What spiritual principles do I want to embody to make the world a better place?

10. SPIRITUAL VALUES

Intelligence is derived from two words – inter and legere – inter meaning "between" and legere meaning "to choose." An intelligent person, therefore, is one who has learned "to choose between." He knows that good is better than evil, that confidence should supersede fear, that love is superior to hate, that gentleness is better than cruelty, forbearance than intolerance, compassion than arrogance, and that truth has more virtue than ignorance.

J. Martin Klotsche

Spiritual values form the core of Energetic Coaching. We know that consciously adopted inner values catalyze individual growth and spiritual connection. In this chapter we outline some of the inner values clients may choose as ideals to guide thoughts, perceptions, emotions, intentions, words, and actions. Clients bring their own values to coaching whether they are aware of them consciously or not. Most unconsciously held values originate in childhood and some may no longer work for the adult. We support clients' reviewing their values and deciding what they need to revise or replace with what will serve them better now. Although not a comprehensive list, we offer insight into some important spiritual values for cultivating inner and outer congruence to create inner knowing and spiritual connection.

PURPOSE AND MEANING

*So many people walk around with a meaningless life. They
seem half-asleep, even when they're busy doing things they
think are important. This is because they're chasing the
wrong things. The way you get meaning into your life is
to devote yourself to loving others, devote yourself to your
community around you, and devote yourself to creating
something that gives you purpose and meaning.*
MITCH ALBOM, *Tuesdays with Morrie*

Purpose and meaning are not to be found or discovered as if
they had been hidden or lost. Humans don't have to seek what
they are here to do or who they are here to be. Rather, they
decide the purpose and meaning for life. As Carl Jung said,
"It all depends on how we look at things and not how things
are in themselves. The least of things with a meaning is worth
more in life than the greatest of things without it." People give
things importance through their choices and inner guidance.
They may not realize their unique gifts and talents until they
make conscious choices to recognize and use them. Many
search as if purpose and meaning could be found "out there,"
but until individuals decide their purpose, they cannot sustain meaningfulness and motivation. Those without purpose
and meaning in life are those who have not yet chosen.

Positive purpose is an internally directed human drive
that creates a seamless connection with spirit. There is a tendency to assign purpose and meaning to outside events, but
any value that people give to externalities comes from inside.
Meaning in life ranges from no awareness on a conscious level to exquisite connection in every aspect of day-to-day experience. With choice, people can set their intention so that all
life experience has meaning. As people connect with spirit,

minute details magnify in importance. Serendipity abounds and synchronous events happen.

Once basic survival needs are met, people naturally seek meaning and purpose in life. With maturity, many review their lives for threads of significance. Energetic Coaches meet clients who have achieved outer success but who have come to experience external achievement as ultimately dissatisfying. Material acquisition no longer motivates them. Possessions possess the possessor with constant obligation and demand for maintenance and attention. Many seek coaching to achieve success but for different reasons. They want to base their efforts on inner spiritual values instead of outer ego-based needs. Energetic Coaches help ensure that clients speak and act in alignment with spiritual values as stated by their life purpose, meaningful intention, or vision statement. They create sustainable inner energy through an overarching reason to do what has significance to them. It's not so much the details of the goals, but the meaning the goals hold that provide significance.

As Peter Senge wrote in *The Fifth Discipline*, "We often spend so much time coping with problems along our path that we forget why we are on that path in the first place. The result is that we only have a dim, or even inaccurate, view of what's really important to us." Rather than firefighting whatever issue arises in life, people with purpose and meaning give a strategic perspective on priorities. They give weight to lasting values.

Lea: *I was talking with a former client, Sandy, who had just started back to college to become a nurse. She was struggling with Biology, so I asked if she intended to continue in the nursing program. Sandy said she had gone back to college to get a degree to help people. She wanted to end up with something in the helping professions. She recognized that she enjoyed the challenge of school. Doing the stretch to get through the classes helped her to build her character and self-esteem. The desire to help others and grow as a person provided the purpose and meaning Sandy needed to change careers and work hard to pursue her dreams. Even though not totally certain of the outcome, the purpose and meaning sustain the effort.*

Having a purpose for being gives meaning to life and helps overcome depression, hopelessness, and a sense of uselessness. Have you ever met a depressed person who has a strong purpose and meaning for his or her life? Purpose and meaning call people to work for good. In return, they reap rewards through inner satisfaction and growth. A purposeful, meaningful life creates mental health, emotional stability, and physical gratification. Energetic Coaches have chosen and created our own meaning and purpose. We encourage clients to do the same for themselves, individually and in relationship with others.

LOVE

It is not how much you do, but how much Love you put into the doing that matters.
MOTHER TERESA

Neither a lofty degree of intelligence nor imagination nor both together go to the making of genius. Love, love, love, that is the soul of genius.
WOLFGANG AMADEUS MOZART

In his famous quote Teilhard de Chardin stated, "Some day, after we have mastered the winds, the waves, the tides, and gravity; we will harness for God the energies of love, and then for the second time in the history of the world man will have discovered fire!" By now, humans have mastered potent physical energies in the universe and put them to use, but what do they know of love? How many seek love and how few find it truly and lastingly? Finding true love, like finding purpose and meaning, is a decision. It's not something that is found, per se, it is created intentionally.

Love is a basic drive in human behavior. Like purpose and meaning, people often seek it externally rather than consciously creating it internally. What many equate to love is the release of brain chemicals and temporary loss of ego boundaries. Love is not a chemical reaction and has nothing to do with initial attraction. Love is a choice. The decision to be and do love is a sure way to create it in life.

To be and do love invites the energy of spirit like no other decision that humans can make because spirit *is* love. Love is the deepest essence of internal being. Love transcends ego because love has no other desire than the best for self and others. Love recognizes the uniqueness and value within self and within others. Like spirit, love cannot be acquired directly. It must be given to be gotten. Love is selfless and unconditional. Love does not overlook the flaws and shortcomings in self and others, but rather decides to love despite human frailties and foibles.

Love, like *spirit*, is an overused and misused word. Although people experience love emotionally, it is not a feeling. Love is the direct connection with spirit that integrates the mental, physical, and emotional bodies. It compels people to act with good intent and free will choice.

M. Scott Peck, in his book *The Road Less Traveled* says, "I define love thus: The will to extend one's self for the purpose of nurturing one's own or another's spiritual growth."

This simple definition speaks volumes about the power of love to connect humans to something greater and more lasting than just a fleeting feeling from a brain burst of chemicals or a self-centered need to feel special. It requires free will goodwill and the extension of self for other.

Love's force provides the motive and the energy people need to sustain discipline and practice for spiritual growth. As with spirit itself, love is of a mysterious nature that must be experienced before words make sense. Love informs individuals about the ideal relationship with self, with another, and with the community and guides them to act to create greater good for all. As Igor Stravinsky observed, "In order to create there must be a dynamic force, and what force is more potent than love?" Love provides the energy and intention for creativity to flourish.

When people base intention and purpose on love, they open to the creative energy of spirit. By giving love, they receive love; the mirror and reflection unite. Those who want love in their lives decide to be and do love in order to have love. Because of the connection of love of self and spirit, the more humans love, the more they join spirit. True love exists at the centerpoint where spiritual energy connects with the inner knower. Even though love does not seek self-fulfillment through others, lovers experience enhancement and growth when two become one. They experience expanded wholeness and self-love in an ever-widening circle of self-perpetuating energy. Once people consciously create love from within, they experience it in lasting and satisfying ways everywhere else.

Psychoanalyst Erich Fromm describes love in his book, *The Art of Loving*. Observing the tendency to be externally oriented in a materialistic way, he says, "The world is one big object for our appetite, a big apple, a big bottle, a big breast:

we are the sucklers, the eternally expectant ones, the hopeful ones and the eternally disappointed ones." Humans cannot sustain love solely for personal gratification. Love cannot be acquired like a possession. If people orient externally, they see others and the world as separate and self-gratifying. The I-object relationship blocks love and spiritual connection.

Love requires consciousness and effort. Doc Childre and Sara Paddison in the HeartMath Discovery Program say, "Love is not automatic. It takes conscious practice and awareness, just like playing the piano or golf. However, you have ample opportunities to practice. Everyone you meet can be your practice session." People can express love everywhere in every moment of the day. The more they do, the more naturally they love and the more love returns to them. Love for others is only achieved when individuals know and love themselves. By deciding to love others despite their shortcomings, people come to love themselves. Love becomes a self-replicating force of energy; what people give returns to them in kind.

Lea: *I don't know how I found my husband, my true love. All I know is I was not looking. Jaded about "finding" love because of "failed" relationships over many years of trying, I had given up. I had let go and let God, so to speak, and decided to love myself best of all. I became the type of person I would want to have in my life. I practiced being loving, trustworthy, kind, and open. I released past baggage and did lots of personal development. My work on myself kept me so busy and focused, I almost failed to recognize Steve as the kind of partner I had been seeking right along.*

Energetic Coaching seeks to help clients understand love and choose it for themselves. As coaches we must first know and be love in order to help others know and be what they want. We need to know and express love in relationship through first loving ourselves, warts and all. The spiritual energy of the I-One relationship redirects clients who are seeking love outside of self. Energetic Coaches keep them focused within to decide to love—to be and do love rather than to get and have love. As the greatest expression of authentic being, Love lies within everyone at the centerpoint of spiritual connection.

GOODNESS

Keep a good heart. That's the most important thing in life. It's not how much money you make or what you can acquire. The art of it is to keep a good heart.
JONI MITCHELL

Goodness is our nature. There are very few people who don't want to be and do good. Even if not, no one would admit so, because goodness is a given as to what we should be. Even those who commit evil acts justify and rationalize to themselves that what they are doing is good. Evil disguised as goodness has done much harm in the world (witness a "holy" war), but true goodness always prevails. People can never sustain creating hardship and harming others. They will always, ultimately, be overcome by goodness.

People desire for others to see them as good, and even though they are born into goodness, they often struggle with feeling good about themselves. Being and doing good are choices. Goodness is available to everyone. To have a good heart requires that people choose internally to create goodness externally. It is our rewarding work in Energetic Coaching to intentionally promote goodness in ourselves and hold the space for clients to choose to be and do good.

Some things seem inherently good. Those connected with spirit are likely to make something good out of things that others perceive as bad or undesirable. People who find the good during challenging times transcend the present situation. They can imagine something better and work toward it. The intention to find goodness overrides judgment and separation of "not that" and joins spirit in creating something good out of something "bad." Just as what people desire appears to be "good" and what they don't want appears "bad," their perceptions form their opinions.

Lea: *My coaching client, Carolyn, was wrestling with her attitude. She confessed to me that she felt jealous of others. She thought that jealousy was totally "bad." I asked her, "What if jealousy was a good thing?" My question changed her pattern of thinking, opening a learning opportunity. By looking at others as possible examples of what she could be and do, Carolyn began to embrace jealousy as a positive motivator to decide what she wanted in her own life. Carolyn used jealousy to remind her to look within and redirect energy to find a positive strategy to achieve what she wanted for herself...*

Even though there is goodness at the core of everyone, negative thoughts, feelings, and perceptions remain until people acknowledge them and change them. In relationships a connecting channel exists between people in which they convey their inner thoughts, either spoken or unspoken. Most can readily tell the difference between people with a positive or a negative attitude. There is a natural aversion to those who harbor ill will. There are ways to discern goodness, even unconsciously. People look into the eyes and smile for proof of sincerity. They listen for the intent behind the words. They believe actions more than declarations. They can tell when others are of good heart, and they respond automatically in kind. People sense when they can trust and open to others or when they need to put up their guard. Energetic Coaches demonstrate good heart in words and actions and expect that clients will follow suit. Whenever we sense anything less than goodness, we share our perceptions, ask questions without projection or judgment, and anticipate that the good will prevail.

COMMITMENT AND PERSONAL RESPONSIBILITY

Don't wait for a light to appear at the end of the tunnel, stride down there…and light the bloody thing yourself.
SARA HENDERSON

There is an obvious difference between those who accept personal responsibility and hold themselves accountable and those who go along for the ride; between those who wait, second- guess others, or abdicate personal responsibility, and those who step to the plate. Some go above and beyond the call of duty, and some ignore the blaring bugle. As with all noble and worthwhile values, commitment, personal responsibility, and self-accountability require making conscious decisions, sometimes in the face of obstacles and daunting odds. Marie Curie stated, "Life is not easy for any of us. But what of that? We must have perseverance and above all confidence in ourselves. We must believe that we are gifted for something and that this thing must be attained." Energetic Coaching helps clients to decide on commitments according to their inner guidance and intention as outward expressions of their self.

Some take responsibility for too much and some for too little. Because people cannot possibly commit to everything, their purpose and intention help them to prioritize. Energetic Coaches guide the processes so clients can choose how to balance their commitments. For instance, in relationships, one person may try to compensate for the lack of commitment by the other. Those who don't commit avoid making priorities and taking action. Those who commit, on the other hand, may allow others to shift blame and abdicate their personal responsibility onto them. Equitable relationships are a two-way street with mutual effort and responsibility.

To maintain balance in commitments and take personal responsibility for outcomes means people consciously choose what is theirs and what is not. As they take ownership, sometimes they have to make tough choices of when to commit for the duration, when to participate temporarily, or when to stay entirely uninvolved. People demonstrate commitment by maintaining personal responsibility even when the situation gets difficult and despite whether the choice is easy or popular. Whether committed in relationships or to a cause, people demonstrate strong character and inner value system by taking personal responsibility decisively and staying with it.

Individuals' lives reflect the commitments they make. Those who find committing difficult base their lives on a shifting foundation of stimulus-response behavior. Associates know that they cannot be depended on to do what they promised. No one can take them at their word, and those in relationship with them often have to over-commit to compensate. Actions prove what people value and what they have committed to and give others a strong sense of who they are. People demonstrate integrity and authenticity by their ability to commit in a balanced and thoughtful way.

John: *When I meet with new clients, I discuss their commitment to getting the results they say they want with a sense of well-being. Some clients think that I'm suggesting that they will have to put in a lot of effort without realizing the energy they will receive in return.*

When I commit to a task or a way of being, I let go of everything associated with what I am supposed to do or how I am feeling while I'm doing it. To me, commitment means being in the moment with whatever shows up as I set about achieving my outcome. There is no place for all the illusions about why the project won't work or the fact that it's never been done before. Neither is there angst about whether I will succeed or fail or if the outcome will be good enough. I feel joy in being with whatever shows up, open to guidance from spirit, and reveling in the creative part of ME. I admit there are times when the energy of spirit is necessary to remind me how simple a commitment can be. My commitment defines me and demonstrates to others what is important to me. This distinction sets priorities and frees time and energy for me to act on what I committed to. Others know me by what I commit to and my dedication to seeing it through to the best of my ability. Through my experience and personal example, clients see that commitment is worth the effort as a positive way of expressing who they are.

By making commitments (without over-committing) and taking personal responsibility for outcomes, over time people create a legacy of trustworthiness. Remaining at the centerpoint, they persist through their chosen commitments. As Energetic Coaches we aim to make strategic commitments and take personal responsibility for inner growth and an ongoing contribution to a better world, helping others to do the same. When people take personal responsibility for their intentions and the outcomes of their efforts, they create a strong identity. We demonstrate that identity, willingness and resolve to others in our coaching relationships. Spirit adds strength and courage to follow through as clients choose positive, prioritized, and balanced commitments while assuming personal responsibility for their actions and results.

Lea: *Commitment and personal responsibility are greatly valued. With perseverance as my greatest signature strength according to the scale found at www.authentichappiness.com, I have sometimes been called stubborn. No matter how much effort or how long it takes, I see projects through to their completion. Perhaps that is why two different former employers called me back to work for them after a long absence to help them out. I am known for going all the way with what I say. That seems to be very rare and valued by others, especially employers, who are sometimes surprised when people do what they say and follow through on their assignments to completion.*

ACCEPTANCE

Lord, grant me the serenity to accept the things I cannot change, the courage to change those things I can, and the wisdom to know the difference.
The Serenity Prayer

When people accept situations they cannot change and others for who they are, they demonstrate nonjudgment, forgiveness, and understanding. Acceptance means letting go of what is outside the personal sphere of influence of the inner self. That sphere of influence may appear limited, but inner space is much more vast than outer space. By looking within for direction and making conscious decisions to release what is outside personal control, individuals empower themselves. Respecting their own free will and boundaries, they also respect the free will and boundaries of others.

Energetic Coaches help clients determine what they can do something about and what they can't. Some have a great deal of letting go to do because they are hooked on judging, blaming, rejecting, and condemning. Many seek coaching because they have been focusing on things they could do nothing about. The situation or other person may or may not change, but individuals can choose to accept and allow. Some many need to forgive others. According to Joan Borysenko, Ph.D., "Forgiveness is not the misguided act of condoning irresponsible, hurtful behavior. Nor is it a superficial turning of the other cheek that leaves us feeling victimized and martyred. Rather it is the finishing of old business that allows us to experience the present, free of contamination from the past." Releasing through forgiveness and acceptance signals that people have chosen to be and do according to spirit. They create space and energy by accepting what they can do nothing about; then they can focus their laser-like energy on what can be accomplished. By accepting and letting go, they allow others the same rights to be and do according to their sphere of influence. In a universe based on free will, others have the right and responsibility to choose for themselves. If their actions affect others negatively, those affected can let go of the relationship without resentment. Releasing empowers much more than trying to change someone else. Remaining in negative relationships causes people to lose power and behave inauthentically.

Even if people cannot understand a situation, they may choose to accept it. To accept without good reason or knowing outcomes may be difficult. Human ability to be nonjudgmental, forgiving, and understanding is limited, requiring practice throughout life. Letting go of appearances and desire with faith that all things work together for good invites spirit. When people choose to let go and remain open to this or something better, all they can do is wait and watch with hopeful expectation. Sooner or later, they can see that acceptance has opened to spirit and allowed everything to work out in unimaginable ways. If they open to it, their perceived bad may have shifted into good.

The following story is adapted from classical Taoist literature modified to reflect Native American culture by Raymond Reyes, PhD, Associate Mission Vice-President for Intercultural Relations at Gonzaga University:

MAYBE

Once there was an elder who was very poor but content and happy. All he had in the world were a small parcel of land, his humble lodge, an old horse and a strong, young warrior grandson. One night the horse ran away. When the elder's neighbors heard of this, they came as a group to give their condolences and said to him, "This is indeed a great misfortune." But the elder only replied, "Maybe," and smiled. The neighbors were surprised and thought him to be a bit strange as they departed for home.

The next night, the elder heard a great racket outside his lodge. His horse had returned, but not alone. It had returned with several other young wild horses and led them straight into the old man's corral. The next day, the neighbors returned. This time, they were very joyous and said to the old man, "Surely good fortune shines upon you and the

Creator has truly blessed your family." The elder smiled as before and again replied, "Maybe." The reservation community thought him ungrateful and perhaps a bit disturbed and muttered among themselves.

Soon it became time to tame the wild horses and the elder's grandson tried to mount one to begin the process. He was immediately thrown and he broke his leg. The neighbors, upon hearing of this and being a genuinely concerned tribal group, once again returned to the grandfather's house to offer their condolences. Once again, in spite of the hardship this would undoubtedly bear upon the old man, he merely smiled and said, "Maybe."

This time the neighbors left in disgust, thinking the grandfather to be a fool or perhaps insane. The next day, however, a group of experienced warriors poured through the village, forcing all the young men to join them. The tribal chief was going off to war and these young men were to be his pawns. When these warriors came to the grandfather's lodge, they found the grandson to be unable to walk and therefore of no use as a warrior. They left him behind.

Soon the neighbors came to the elder again, some weeping because their sons had been taken, perhaps never to return. They saw that the elder's grandson was still in his bed, his leg with a splint and bandaged. They said to the old man, "You are indeed a lucky man." The grandfather smiled gently and said only, "Maybe." The neighbors stood quietly for some time. Gradually, they, too, began to smile and nod their heads. And as they slowly departed, they, too, could be heard saying to one another, "Maybe."

Acceptance means going from judgment and resistance to an open "maybe" stance. Opportunities to accept present themselves over and over in life. Every situation that someone would like to change contains the opportunity for acceptance. Acceptance presents little challenge when the outer situation or people agree. When they disagree, Energetic Coaches propose that clients ask themselves these questions: "What can I do about this situation"? and "What do I have to release"? Acceptance does not mean abdicating personal responsibility. It means that individuals identify where their responsibility ends and where other people's begins. Acceptance allows people to detach from what lies beyond their personal sphere of influence so that they can maintain their energy and personal power even though they would prefer things to be different on the outside.

Clients expect coaches to accept them as they are. Acceptance can be a challenge. What about the times when clients miss appointments or when their first words are "I didn't have time to prepare for our meeting"? Acceptance assures clients the safe space of the compassionate witness. Because people judge themselves with little self-acceptance, the ego tries to compensate. Reflecting acceptance to the client along with expectation for something better neutralizes excuses and ego defense mechanisms. We support where clients are in their progress, outcome, and commitment. Through nonjudgment and acceptance that they are perfect as they are, we draw the positive energy of spirit into the coaching relationship. We demonstrate acceptance while challenging clients to reach for their goals. Humans achieve best by expecting success.

Energetic Coaches demonstrate characteristics of spirit through patience and acceptance. Our acceptance of clients fosters their acceptance of themselves. Empowered, they seek answers from within, make decisions, and trust in themselves. Energetic Coaches take personal responsibility for doing what they can within their boundaries to help clients fulfill their purpose and achieve their goals. We possess confidence that clients are in the perfect place and that we are all living a process of perfection that will never be complete.

EQUALITY AND BALANCE

It is the heart that makes a man rich. He is rich according to what he is, not according to what he has.
HENRY WARD BEECHER

We cannot be happy if we expect to live all the time at the highest peak of intensity.
Happiness is not a matter of intensity, but of balance and order and rhythm and harmony.
THOMAS MERTON

People are balanced when there is equality without judgment of superior or inferior. Energetic Coaches accept that there are two equal sides to the coin of life and that there can be no good without bad and no shadow without light. We realize that the outer world reflects the inner, and that despite separate appearances, we are all one. This balanced perspective leads to openness through acceptance. It puts people at the centerpoint of their inner knower where they connect with spirit. They no longer have to resist or respond with ego defense mechanisms. They can be and do freely and allow others the same opportunity.

Humans are all created equal, of course, but the tendency to judge and separate disconnects them from one another and spirit. Equality means accepting others as they are without judging them or placing them in a hierarchy. Each person possesses different traits, strengths, outer appearances, capabilities, and skills, but all go back to the same Source at the centerpoint. Ego may want us to think otherwise to justify its existence, but by choosing equality and balance, we create the clear mirror with the congruent reflection of how things really are. Allowing the benefit of the doubt provides insights about why others behave the way they do without the need to judge or separate. At the centerpoint of congruent being and doing, it is easier to accept what is. By choosing equality and a balanced perspective, individuals value self and others as equal parts of the one. No matter what our social status, intellectual capability, or relative standing compared with another, people are all intrinsically equal.

There is equal worth in all despite how people appear or behave. As individuals on a particular growth curve, people operate on different frequencies and naturally attract and connect with those on a similar wavelength. This can cause a tendency to tune out and separate from those on other frequencies. Through the conscious choice to maintain equality and balance despite the immediate attraction or reaction to another, people relate with others as equals. They know perceived differences are superficial, and at the centerpoint, everyone's the same. Through experience and example of accepting the minor (and illusory) imperfections in others, people come to accept themselves for who they are. Once they truly know themselves and their great potential to transcend differences, people can be who they are with self-acceptances and allow others to be the same. Even if the other chooses to be in judgment and separation, people can maintain the opening to connect, knowing that there can be no real separation in this lifeboat called Earth.

Knowing oneness and the inane illusion of status created by ego, people want for others what they want for themselves. Inner peace and happiness are inalienable human rights. By letting go of the self-seeking and self-promoting tendencies of the ego, people achieve oneness through equality with others and inner balance with self.

As relative beings in a dualistic world, people tend to compare themselves with others. In the externally-oriented world of appearances, people cannot possibly find happiness. Individuals can never be young enough, beautiful enough, smart enough or rich enough. When people look to others for a standard of being, they lose their sense of connectedness and equality. The inner knower is silenced through judgment of someone else, either as lesser-than (building oneself up in relation to them) or as better-than (putting oneself down in relation to them). Without being conscious of comparisons or being co-opted by them, people lose awareness that calls them back to the centerpoint and lose balance. Once they experience the peace at the center, they value it so much that comparisons and judgments are no longer appealing. The polarity produced by judging others good or bad, inferior or superior disconnects people from spirit. Through growing awareness, people can regain balance by choosing not to judge. When they realize that false separation has created an unbalanced condition, there is a desire to recover the happier state of equality and connection.

When being and doing are congruent in the balance of oneness, the holographic nature of life is comprehended. It is realized that the one is all, and that the all is in each one. The big picture with its grand perspective is seen. The larger perspective helps people let go of labeling others "good" or "bad," "black" or "white." Shades of gray stretch from one end of the spectrum to the other so that there is no contrasting black and white that judgment creates. As Energetic Coaches we help clients realize that all may not be as it appears, that maybe they can choose to remain outside of judgment of self, others and the situation. By gaining the larger perspective, we maintain equality and equilibrium without the encumbrance of judgment that blocks spiritual connection.

SENSE OF HUMOR

A sense of humor keen enough to show a man his own absurdities, as well as those of other people, will keep him from the commission of all sins, or nearly all, save those that are worth committing.
SAMUEL BUTLER

Closely related to faith; (humor) bids us not to take anything too seriously.
FULTON J. SHEEN

John: *George describes himself as outrageous. I met him in a spiritual community. When he walked up to me, he told me his name, saying, "I came here to visit for two days and stayed 32 years." I felt drawn to George and could sense spirit radiating from his presence.*

I made inquiries of people who had known George for a long time. They agreed with deep affection that, yes, he did behave outrageously. In his younger days he had been a Methodist minister. He had traveled widely, representing the community in world conferences and spending time with influential people.

As a fascinating storyteller, George will share his stories with anyone who will listen. He amused my friend David and me while we were on a 6:00 am trek through the hills outside Denver, Colorado. Alongside a waterway, over rocks and through brush, George shared some of his life sto-

ry along with witty affirmations and animated mantras. I'm sure much of what we heard will be in the book that he and a friend are writing, George, By George. I experienced George as an open, playful human connected with his inner knower and effervescent about his life. It was no wonder to me that he has attracted many individuals to his community. George speaks from the heart about his 71 years of living. What I heard and felt was the energy of a man who knew who he was with a humorous perspective. George has the capacity to touch the lives of people, sometimes outrageously, from a loving place. I felt the grace of spirit mostly through his boundless sense of humor.

As the ego becomes less necessary for protection, a closer connection with spirit creates a light-hearted perspective that naturally results in a spontaneous and eruptive sense of pure humor. By transcending ego, people learn to laugh at themselves and with others in healthy and happy connection. They have fun without making fun of anything. When the inner knower reveals a hidden aspect of self, a sense of humor brings a winking recognition rather than a recoiling rejection. An inner smile arises because of catching ego in its tricks. The work of self- reflection and self-knowing becomes exploratory and playful as a sense of humor spontaneously grows from within.

A close connection with the inner knower and spirit develops the ability to lighten up and recognize humor in everyday life. People can soar high enough to see the big picture with less ego attachment when they take themselves lightly. They trade self-consciousness and fear of embarrassment for fun. Public humiliation is an opportunity to laugh at oneself before others can. With self-acceptance of warts and all, the warts become amusing. Humor invites the energy of spirit.

Lea: *One of the reasons I chose John as my coach was because of his ready sense of humor that was conveyed when I first talked with him on the phone. His spontaneous laughter and fun-loving perspective made our coaching meetings light-hearted, a great balance for my heavy stuff. Even when I would be frustrated to the point of tears, John kept a glint in his eye that signaled he did not give additional negative energy to what was happening. John's wit and humor are always present and ready. Not to say there's no difficult conversation at times, just that there's a lighter aspect that is given weight. John moderated the eruptive emotions and quiet despondency that came forward in coaching with the wisdom that to "go there" with me would not do any good. It has been a pleasure knowing John over the years. Interspersing our meetings with smiles, chuckles and eruptive laughter at times creates a contagious tendency to laugh at my own seriousness. John's sense of humor is one of acceptance for self and others. I can tell John would never laugh AT anyone – only with them. A sense of humor is an attractive energy that compels one to it. Laughter is contagious. I found myself enjoying my work at self-betterment more because of John's humor.*

Self-awareness and spiritual growth create a healthy sense of humor. A sense of humor does not mean that people cannot be serious when needed, but it does mean that they do not allow cynicism in others or themselves to go unchecked or entertain negativity and melodrama. The light-hearted perspective is valued too much to give it up easily. Maintaining a sense of humor fosters the tendency to see things in terms of what is working rather than what is not. Those who have a funny bone can stay above the fray and allow events to play out, doing what they can to improve a situation. Energetic Coaches possess a positive, natural, spontaneous humor based on a persistently optimistic stance gained from the endless task of self-knowing and self- improvement without attachment to results.

With clients we need to be sensitive to the tone of what they find amusing and how they express it. If clients use gallows humor or belittling sarcasm, we can use powerful questions to explore the shadow behind the dark humor, negative projections and false separation. Energetic Coaching helps clients determine what humor is at someone else's expense and what spontaneously arises from knowing one's self, growing into potential and appreciating the grace and goodness (and humor) behind appearances. The ability to laugh at one's self and to lighten up on self-judgment allows a person to fully embrace the self and let go of ego. We sense when a client's humor is authentic or not. A dismissing chuckle, superficial smile or fake laugh means further exploration is needed in the moment. The coach cannot be co-opted into avoiding tricky territory the client would rather shrug off or laugh away. We don't buy it when someone makes a cutting remark and excuses it as "just kidding." If it hurts, it's not humor. Energetic Coaches work to develop a sense of humor that is spontaneous, true and real.

Aprendizaje, apertura y humildad

Asking yourself these deeper questions opens up new ways of being in the world. It brings in a breath of fresh air. It makes life more joyful. The real trick is not to be in the know, but to be in the mystery.

Fred Alan Wolf

I'm now running through a list of famous people who have claimed that something is the final word, and I can't think of a single one who hasn't been proven wrong.

JEFFREY SATINOVER

Spiritual connection reveals how much is known yet how much will never be known. Even the accomplished Michelangelo admitted, "I am still learning." The more people are open to the many different ways and experiences of spirit, the more they realize how vast and mysterious life is. By being open to learning with humility, egocentric tendencies are balanced. The wonderment and appreciation for life grows as individuals become permeable to new information. They realize that the more that is known reveals how much is not known. Life offers limitless opportunities to learn and is the ultimate university. If learning ceases, the world becomes dull, lifeless and boring. If people resist learning thinking they already know enough or don't want to know differently, they miss the next lesson coming that will challenge a static world view and stimulate new growth. Humility provides greater openness for more learning by letting go of the ego's need to be "right" and in the know. Humility creates the readiness to accept learning as it comes, knowing the lessons bring with them even more lessons. Openness and humility can be the most difficult spiritual values to cultivate because people are so tied to their stories and world view, even if they don't work or hold them back to being more of whom they really are. Once again, to be open and humble are traits that are cultivated through conscious choice.

Lea: *I have taught many courses at the local community colleges. A few of my classes I have started with the statement, "I cannot teach you anything." The students are confused until I explain that no one can teach anyone anything unless that individual decides to learn. I take responsibility for teaching the class, but the responsibility for learning belongs to the student.*

Most people come to coaching because they are open to new learning. That does not mean that there won't be "stuck" points along the way in which new learning is resisted because it reveals different ways of being and doing that are challenging. Coaching holds the space for new and necessary learning to be chosen and adopted. Wisdom comes from applying new and challenging information. The ego may resist the toughest and most important lessons. Energetic Coaches sponsor learning by asking questions instead of pronouncing answers for clients. Those who come to coaching most likely have a value system that includes learning, openness, and humility, but clients usually present issues they are wondering how to resolve. By helping clients get in touch with their inner knower, we encourage readiness and receptivity to more authentic ways of being and doing. When clients resist learning, Energetic Coaches challenge them to investigate the nature of the resistance. Usually it has to do with a worn out paradigm that no longer works. Energetic Coaches realize that clients have to choose what new information might benefit them and decide if they are ready to learn it. Clients learn when it is no longer advantageous to resist and because they have an overriding will to grow. The accepting and open space held by the compassionate witness of the coach allows clients to be open and humble, ready for new growth.

COMPASSION

A person experiences life as something separated from the rest - a kind of optical delusion of consciousness. Our task must be to free ourselves from this self-imposed prison, and through compassion, to find the reality of Oneness.

ALBERT EINSTEIN

NBA basketball coach, Phil Jackson, commented about the game, "Once you've done the mental work, there comes a point you have to throw yourself into the action and put your heart on the line. That means not only being brave, but being compassionate towards yourself, your teammates and your opponents." Competitive compassion is rare. There are more exhibits of unsportsmen's like conduct. More examples of compassion in action in our world are needed. Energetic Coaches exhibit compassion and encourage compassionate choices in helping clients become better people creating a better world.

To have compassion for others, people must first have compassion for themselves. Individuals cannot give what they do not have and cannot have what they cannot give away. All inner human values must be adopted by free will choice and cultivated from within to be expressed without to others. People naturally feel greater compassion for others as they develop compassion for themselves. Like everything of lasting value, compassion comes from within through choice and naturally arises by putting oneself in another's shoes. This creates the connection of oneness that is so necessary to bring out the best and create the willingness to work together for the common good.

Compassion stems from heartfelt empathy. When individuals allow themselves to experience the same feelings as another, egocentric boundaries are dissolved. Having compassion does not mean pitying another or projecting onto another one's own hurts. Both are ego manifestations to be separate and superior, self-referent and self-centered. Others automatically sense pity from another and consciously or unconsciously reject it. Only those who have self-pity want pity from others, but that is disempowering and disabling. True compassion is powerful being manifested in powerful doing. Compassionate people recognize the common threads of human experience. They know life is difficult and want to help make it less so. Because of its ability to connect and build bridges, compassion brings high consciousness and awareness of the interconnection of all things. It makes it possible for people to be fully open to what is happening without judgment. Spirit is experienced through compassionate thoughts, words, and deeds.

Lea: *I was coaching a client through a difficult relationship with a person who was once a close friend. Because of something that was projected upon my client, her friend accused her of being less than honest. Knowing my client in her efforts to be truthful, I questioned if she had been, in fact, less than up front with the other person. As the story unfolded, the client and I examined any gaps in integrity that she could have created. As it turned out, it appeared that the former friend had made a false projection upon my client in regard to my client's true motives and intentions. Once my client could see that she had not deliberately or knowingly misled anyone, she could let go of her need to self-critique and defend her actions. Then she was able to look objectively at the other person and wonder why such a projection would be made. Once my client realized that her friend had been hurt by others who were not truthful, my client could see why the false projection was made.*

My client examined her part in the relationship and decided she was a good person with good intention. The mirror did not have to distort to accommodate the projection, and my client could let go of the relationship without guilt and with compassion for self and her hurting and hurtful friend.

Compassion naturally arises when the oneness at the center of a life of connected wholeness is realized. Thomas Merton says, "The whole idea of compassion is based on a keen awareness of the interdependence of all these living beings, which are all part of one another, and all involved in one another." Compassion reveals the reciprocal nature of the universe. What is done for others returns in kind. During difficult times, people tend to isolate themselves. It is ironic that people separate and feel alone when a connection with others is needed. Peace, comfort and strength are found by giving and receiving heartfelt compassion. Developing compassion creates more self-acceptance, which leads to inner peace within self and outer peace in the world.

Compassion is a decision to connect with the world that clears the channels for spirit to work. Christina Baldwin says, "Spiritual energy brings compassion into the real world. With compassion, we see benevolently our own human condition and the condition of our fellow beings. We drop prejudice. We withhold judgment." Energetic Coaches hold the space as the compassionate witness so clients develop greater compassion for self and as a natural outcome of that, for others, also. Oneness becomes evident as compassion manifests and connects.

KINDNESS AND CARING

Let no one ever come to you without leaving better and happier. Be the living expression of God's kindness: kindness in your face, kindness in your eyes, kindness in your smile.
MOTHER TERESA

Forget injuries, never forget kindness.
CONFUCIUS

Some say that civility is dead, and it certainly seems that way at times. Many homes and organizations show disregard for others. On the highway, road rage is rampant. Behind the isolating mask of unkindness are people who are not kind to themselves. Kindness and caring connect us with self, others and spirit. Consistent kindness comes from deciding to be so.

Practicing acts of kindness creates more kindness "in kind." Whenever an unkind or uncaring act is experienced, the best that can be done is to give kindness in return. The vicious circle of an eye for an eye is broken. By seeing the lonely disconnectedness behind unkind behavior, people develop compassion for the other and give back something much better than what was received. Instead of the natural human response to retaliate, showing kindness reverses the downward spiral of negative energy. Good deeds and kindness turn the spiral upward with positive energy. As the wise Sophocles once stated, "Kindness begets kindness."

Lea: *Kindness is not something I specifically coach toward, but I can see that if it is missing in self or in relationship with others, there is a huge gap to be bridged on the way to wholeness. I listen to the words, but mostly the tone, body language and other nonverbal behavior. I cue in when clients judge themselves and one another disparagingly. When that happens, I make an invitation to be more open and accepting, even kind, to oneself and the other. With a shift in perspective, there is usually an instantaneous knowing of what to do or how to handle difficult people or situations.*

This invitation to kindness I use with my four-year-old granddaughter, and she gets it, too. She responds to kind words and actions very positively. By setting that tone and example, my granddaughter becomes more calm, gentle and kind herself. I am intrigued by the contagiousness of kindness and how it automatically evokes similar responses in others.

Sometimes kindness is perceived as a weakness. Manipulators try to take advantage of "nice" people, but the greatest strength lies in the decision to be kind, especially when others are being insensitive. It is easy to reciprocate rude behavior with more of the same, but choosing kindness offers an example to others of a better way to be. Kind actions interrupt a negative pattern and diffuse destructive emotions. Those who practice unkind behavior can usually justify their actions for whatever reason, but there is no benefit to it. Any retaliation or"stooping to the same level" only makes people feel worse about themselves. Reflecting kindness, especially in the face of rudeness, shows others a different way of being. In Energetic Coaching we hold that there is never a good reason to be unkind. Unkind thoughts and actions artificially separate us from others and disconnect us from the inner knower, silencing intuition and blocking spirit.

> *Unless someone like you cares a whole lot,*
> *nothing is going to get better. It's not.*
> Dr. Seuss, *The Lorax*

Kindness is a natural expression of caring. Caring is at the root of commitment to self and world improvement. When caring is practiced continually, energy is renewed through being connected, one and whole. Leo Buscaglia, author and teacher, notes how important it is to care stating , "Too often we underestimate the power of a touch, a smile, a kind word, a listening ear, an honest compliment, or the smallest act of caring, all of which have the potential to turn a life around." To care is the greatest gift we can give oneself and others.

Energetic Coaching is a care giving profession. Because caring is not always easy, we must be able to renew our ability to care by remembering our original reason for committing to a caring profession. Heartfelt caring for self and others causes acts of kindness and compassion, even courage, to arise spontaneously. Others sense when we care about them and when we don't. We decide to care, and it shows. Even when it appears easier to not care, it is usually not possible to abdicate our responsibility without losing an important sense of who we are and why we are here. Caring is more than "taking care of." It involves engaging in a positive relationship that maintains congruence within and in connection with spirit. When it appears that it would be easier to ignore someone's need or when the situation appears daunting, caregivers make a conscious decision to act on their commitment to care whether it's convenient or not. It may be frustrating and painful to care at times, but to be involved and act without caring disconnects from spirit.

The quality of caring demonstrated in being and doing is obvious to others. Look at the difference between those who care about the work they do and those who don't. Those who don't care increase the workload for others and make the work environment more stressful and difficult. What they may not realize, however, is that their attitude influences others to respond in the same ways to them. It is much more difficult to care when a boss or coworker doesn't, but without caring, individuals become part of the problem. The inner knower knows when being and doing is less than our potential, and energy is depleted.

Lea: *I asked my husband, Steve, about his ability to achieve results. Steve stated that he attributed his success to his relentless inner drive to excel. I believe it came from his being a caring person. As Steve described some of his most gratifying achievements in the workplace, I realized that he cared about the company, even when others did not. This caring for the company's success came from his sincere care for others who worked there – not from a personalized desire to succeed or get ahead. Eventually, Steve's caring commitment to achieving goals became a part of the culture of excellence. People came to care more about one another and their jobs because of his example. Those few who did not care became noticeable and either had to leave or get with the program to fit into the culture. Steve had a saying, "If you can't get out, get in; if you can't get in, get out." The level of caring that was demonstrated and expected of others did not allow for anything less than one's best effort to do the job.*

The opposite of love and caring is not hatred but apathy. When people discharge apathy by replacing it with caring, they realize what can be done to change things for the better. Even when it appears that no action can be taken presently or directly, focusing the caring heart with silent prayers for something better can work in miraculous ways. Those who don't care abdicate personal responsibility for the relationship or situation that they are in. Energy is drained in the presence of those who do not care. Some believe that to care is draining, but it is the opposite. True caring is an expression of what it is to be human and creates energy and motivation to act.

Apathy shuts down spirit and depletes the person and drains those around him or her.

To care does not mean to self-sacrifice or to be overly invested in results. The decision to care and act within one's sphere of influence is all that is needed. Individuals can care while letting go of immediate results or specific outcomes. If caring becomes draining, inner and outer congruence need to be restored to return to balance. People first have to care for themselves to have the ability to care for others or work to improve a situation. Energetic Coaching helps clients maintain caring while weighing options, evaluating outcomes and remaining patient and hopeful while the planted seed germinates.

Because the coach truly cares and silently transmits to clients their worth and value, the client is given a good example of how to be and do the same. Such a relationship gives an example of the ability to sustain kindness and caring despite changes in other people or the outer situation. This is an example of how to be that is needed in the world today. To function as one interconnected global community requires each person to make long-term commitments and personal investments to preserve our environment and humanity. Even though the problems faced today appear overwhelming and even insurmountable, Energetic Coaching encourages clients to care to make a positive difference one person at a time. We improve the larger world through improvements incrementally made in each individual life. It requires true caring to sustain that process.

COURAGE AND STRENGTH

What the superior man seeks is in himself;
what the small man seeks is in others.
FRANÇOIS LA ROCHEFOUCAULD

All of the significant battles are waged within the self.
SHELDON KOPP

Energetic Coaching is inner work. Courage underlies the ability to self-reflect and make choices of how to be. Strength gives us the ability to see decisions through. It takes moral bravery to stick to values, which can mean losing relationships, being ridiculed, being left out or being blamed or mistrusted by those who do not like the reflection in the mirror. It is a challenging undertaking to connect with spirit and follow the inner knower's guidance. The commitment to do so often requires a loss of what is comfortable and known. Looking within to the source of what needs to be changed rather than projecting upon the external and placing blame on others is difficult to say the least. The process never ends. As British writer Joseph Conrad observes, "Facing it, always facing it. That's the way to get through it. Face it." Many do not want to do that. Inner self-reflection is difficult. Looking at the outer world and hearing its messages is scary, too. On a daily basis people are exposed to fear provoking messages, images, and even advertisements designed to get them to buy something to protect themselves from some unknown, dreadful possibility (which could be as awful as not keeping up with the Jones'). Without even knowing it, people become seduced into a sense of false security by accumulating goods or living in a gated community. The only true security comes from within, but finding it requires courage to look inside and strength to do what needs to be done to create self-reliance. Some have been under such tremendous pressure to toe the party line, be in with the in crowd, or just to get along that they feel they have to let go of who they are and what they want just to be in relationships. Little pieces are parceled off and individuals become smaller and fragmented. People become externally-oriented and act in stimulus-response ways as a result. The inner compass swings wildly, and it's hard to find true North. People stay in relationships that bring out less than who they are because of fear: the devil that is known appears better than the devil that is not. People lose themselves piece by piece, and the ego is needed more and more as the false protector of the smaller, fearful self.

For little children external guidance and lots of "no's" are needed. Children are socialized and instructed in the patterns and norms of culture. People start life being externally-oriented and directed, but can no longer afford to be so as adults if they are to become the fullest expression of their authentic being. Courage and strength are required to look within to know one's true identity in order to express oneself fully. Each decision to do so in the face of resistance, false projections or coercion by others and systems of command/control, threats and punishments and party line politics make individuals stronger and more courageous. It can't be easy. Reflection, intention and decision are required to know oneself and withstand challenge. People wouldn't become strong and self respecting without challenges to overcome. Being authentic reflects one's powerful and positive identity back despite the outer pressures of being labeled, marginalized, ostracized or threatened by others. All things are put in perspective when people are courageous and know their inner strength. Losing a job is not the same as losing a life, and even losing a life may not seem as threatening when compared to the prospect of not living in truth and integrity.

Lea: *I am repeatedly challenged by those who want something of me they should be finding in themselves. I risk relationships by not being co-opted into compensating for others. The relationships I have are based upon strength rather than weakness as we challenge one another to our personal best. My career has presented many challenges to my authentic self, also. I never was good at playing politics or pretending not to know. I was fired once from a workplace that resorted to threats and silent warning tactics to keep me from speaking and being my truth. As a single mom, I lost my house because of the resulting loss of income. From the time in elementary school when I took on the playground bully to now as I am working on child protection system changes, I sometimes feel alone and a bit weakened by the challenges. The difficulties are not only created by huge, cumbersome systems that don't work, but by individuals within them who are overly invested in maintaining the status quo and securing their position of illusory power. I am committed to not being like that and find myself often on the fringes. I don't fit in, but I wouldn't want to, either.*

I went into coaching during a period of intense self-questioning, wondering how I had created my history of "failed" relationships and career. Even in my volunteer positions, I could not abide the systems of political trades and personal favors or how people disrespectfully treated one another and talked behind backs. Through John's Energetic Coaching, I was put more closely in touch with my inner knower. John's confidence in me and belief in my positive intentions bolstered my resolve to continue to be myself, not seeking confrontations, but not backing down when the gauntlet is thrown. John has helped me see how my chal-

lenges have made me stronger and supported my difficult decisions to follow through on my truth.

Energetic Coaches help clients get in touch with their inner knower and realize their inner power. We encourage clients to claim the courage and strength to make themselves congruent. This means doing whatever it takes to match outer doing with inner being to become the fullest expression of one's authentic self. Then clients can look out into the world for their life purpose and pursue it by conscious choice from within. These conscious decisions provide the remembrance, renewal and resolve when ridiculed and labeled as troublemakers for stepping outside the box to tell the truth and express high ideals. It requires strength and courage to do the work of inner growth and consistently express values in outer language and action. Values compel us to remain congruent in the face of enormous obstacles and pressures to conform. Energetic Coaches help clients make tough decisions and take action, even in the face of perceived danger, threat, or loss.

Lea: *My family culture, good in many ways, included a shadow aspect of being "better than" someone else. As a child, I tried to go along with this paradigm, but always felt "less than" instead (funny how the need to be better than others actually creates the polar energy of less than). As I grew older, I had to let go of the need to be better than – it was much too much work. Then I became sensitive to the demeaning remarks made about others. It got so I could no longer tolerate the negativity and could not laugh at put-downs or ethnic jokes. I have had to change conversations, ignore and even request more respect. This has offended people, and there has been some retaliation (Oh, Lea thinks she's better than), but eventually my wishes have been respected. I believe my stand to not listen to gossip or tolerate demeaning jokes has helped others self-reflect and eventually see that they feel better about not being so negative and disparaging. Then there is not such a need to put others down to feel better about oneself.*

The most insidious fear is low-grade anxiety about unidentified, potential consequences. A decision is required to not react from fear and instead examine a continuum of possibilities from the worst that could happen to the best. Enlightenment means to shine light upon, to understand.

What the shadow energy of fear needs most is courage to look at it. With the courage to remain true to self and the strength to acknowledge inner fears, spirit assists through inner direction and resolve. Once action is taken in the face of fear, outer validation comes but not before. This is required in order to preserve the universal principle of free will. The universe waits for a decision and then responds. People won't know the outcome until free will is shown. That way, people become more fully empowered by having ownership for their decisions and results. They see how they are joined when aligned with universal principles that often call them to make tough decisions or step outside the party line. Even if feared consequences are experienced (which rarely happens), it is better to act authentically than suffer the stress of avoidance or false compliance. People know when someone "sells out" and respect is lost.

Because we have personally experienced and overcome difficult situations and continue to learn from the shadow teacher, Energetic Coaches help clients build strength and courage. We believe naming a fear is first. Once named, it is much easier to put a fear out into the open and objectively examine it. Usually, it is not so fearsome from that point forward. We do not allow ourselves to run from fear; that only makes the fear stronger. We know that overcoming challenges builds great strength and courage in the long run. We may have clients who are facing extreme difficulty but, through inner knowing gained by demystifying our own fears and facing our shadow, we support clients in taking appropriate action even when it appears that significant others and systemic dysfunction apply pressure to conform. We help clients change jobs, careers, location, relationships and themselves to embark on the new and unknown. Sally Ride, the first female astronaut says, "All adventures, especially into new territory, are scary." Life is an adventure, and growth more often than not requires courage to create something new. Energetic Coaches hold the space in expectation that clients have the courage and strength to follow their inner knower. No matter where it leads, Energetic Coaches know that by making the decision to be true to self, spirit joins with that special energy that causes all things to work together for the good. Courage and strength grow by acting in ways that are true to self. Energetic Coaches help clients decide who they really are and what they really want and to go for it.

Energetic Coaching for Values

I will conduct myself in a manner that reflects well on coaching as a profession and I will refrain from doing anything that harms the public's understanding or acceptance of coaching as a profession.
International Coach Federation *"Standards of Ethical Conduct"*

Society governs by rules, regulations, and guidelines such as the above, which automatically create resistance through outer constraints on inner will. Externally mandated rules of conduct describe broad generalities using threats and penalties to assure compliance. That such an immense, contrived, complicated and expensive system of outer laws had to be created is a sad commentary on the lack of inner values that can be relied upon to consistently direct human behavior. To be fully empowered, people need to be able to express themselves free of external dictates. Following society's rules out of mere compliance is not the path to human wholeness. Individuals achieve wholeness by acting on freely chosen values that express who they really are. At that core is goodness, expressed in an infinite variety of ways through unique self-expression.

When the internal state is egocentric and incongruent, people tend to act in self-serving ways that disconnect them from spirit. A fundamental requirement for human transcendence is making free will choices. People are hardwired to resist constraints on freedom. They cannot sustain inner motivation unless they can choose from viable options. When outside authorities or laws force compliance by coercing, cajoling, or commanding, people resist. Force crushes inner empowerment, rendering adults children again, defiantly resisting or resentfully acquiescing.

A two-year-old child requires consistent, external rules for growth and personal safety, but even a small child responds better to offered choices within limits rather than being told plainly, "No." A teenager rebels automatically against outside influence until assuming adult responsibilities that go with the rights of independence. For self-empowerment and self-respect individuals require the right to make their own decisions. Adults who demand freedom without taking responsibility lose balance. A grown up is one who accepts the responsibilities implicit in freedom of choice and does not need to be told what to do from the outside. Internal direction given by the inner knower always points in a good direction. Spiritual energy joins as people choose freely to align with the divine that they are.

Passive spectators can criticize the game, but the player on the field performs in the moment. By suiting up and taking the field, people demonstrate to self and others that they can perform. There can be no authentic being without congruent doing and vice versa. Because society cannot command inner being, it focuses rules and regulations on doing. But people cannot not express what is inside. If people governed themselves instead through high-level consciousness centered in spiritual values, society would not require a cumbersome and costly legal system that has not been shown to make anyone a better person.

Deciding to live by freely chosen values and building internal and external congruence is difficult, especially considering all the external temptations to get ahead at the expense of others—to"work the system," to"sell out,""cover up,""take the path of least resistance,""cop out," or "play it safe." Individuals are often tempted to try to "get away with" something they know in their hearts not to be good and right. Even negative thoughts take their toll on the psyche. What may not seem to have a detrimental impact externally, however, takes its toll internally. People lose self-respect and the connection with the inner knower because of the ensuing need to rationalize and justify anything other than the truth.

Spiritual energy and connection arise when truth and congruence are sought. The reward is inner peace. With practice, living congruently with high-level values becomes a habit. Once consciously aligned with spiritual values, external constraints and commands are not needed. People empower themselves to act in ways that naturally follow manmade laws because they want to do the right thing. They challenge systems and regulations that do not make sense. Relationships that mirror each person's high-level system of values influence the community as a whole so the effect becomes exponential. Energetic Coaches seek this end, beginning with creating a congruent relationship with self and branching out to relationships with all others.

Energetic Coaching is based on the principle of "reciprocal determinism," which means that we have the ability to exercise control over our thoughts, feelings, and actions through conscious choice. We want to do so because we know that all of life is connected, and what we do to others comes back to us for better or worse. The challenge for Energetic Coaches is to practice our inner values and outer vision in daily life. We aspire to live in the moment with spiritual values to achieve wholeness and oneness and to assist our clients to do the same. We coach clients to be adults, taking direction from within with full responsibility. This is not easy work, so we may not have the most clients or the most lucrative coaching career, but that is not the desire. It is something much greater. We want to be better people creating a better world and coach others who want to be and do the same.

CHAPTER 10 APPENDIX

REFLECTION

- How does my ego keep me from getting to know my true self?
- How do I need to better express my true self?
- What are my most deeply-held values? How do I demonstrate those values to others?

- Where did my values originate? How do they serve me now? Are there values that need to be updated to serve me better?
- Are there values that I need that are missing in my life? If so, how can I act in ways that are congruent with those values?

CONTEMPLATE THE FOLLOWING

I have never given very deep thought to a philosophy of life, though I have a few ideas that I think are useful to me: Do whatever comes your way as well as you can. Think as little as possible about yourself. Think as much as possible about other people. Dwell on things that are interesting. Since you get more joy out of giving joy to others, you should put a good deal of thought into the happiness that you are able to give.

ELEANOR ROOSEVELT

INTENTIONAL IMPRINT

What values would others say I have? How do I express those values? How can I apply my value system to become the fullest expression of my authentic being? How do I make myself a better person creating a better world?

11. WHOLENESS AND ONENESS

*To be what we are, and to become what we are capable of
becoming is the only end in life.*
ROBERT LOUIS STEVENSON

Coaching with spirit comes full circle, back to the individual in relationship with self. People expand their consciousness through making choices. By acting intentionally in the outer world to become better people, they co-create a better world. Expressing themselves in words and actions as congruent beings, they invite spiritual energy. People invoke the principle of reciprocity by putting out what they desire to get back. By consciously choosing inner values, principles, and visions along with outer practices, individuals unite mind, emotion, and body: Mind— through choosing thoughts and perceptions; Emotion—through choosing feelings that are positive and energizing; Body—through expressing thoughts, perceptions, and emotions consciously and congruently in actions. Individuals balance and align the three areas of human experience according to inner being reflected in outer doing. Once they achieve congruence, the triad becomes the circle of wholeness in which the three aspects of human experience blend into one. The spiral of spiritual energy blends into wholeness.

Triad & Sphere

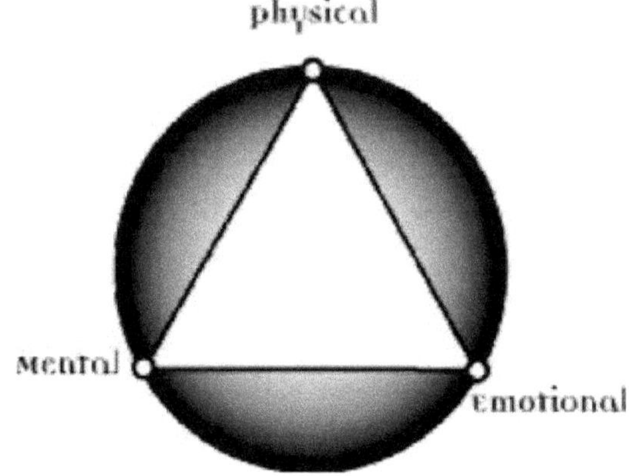

To achieve individual wholeness and connection, people use free will goodwill to express who they are in relationship with self and others. Energetic Coaching helps clients open channels to spirit from within to be mirrored in positive and equal relationships without. In Energetic Coaching we refer continually to the"inner knower." We reinforce what works to create inner and outer congruence for spiritual energy and connection. Energetic Coaching supports inner principles and outer practices that have been demonstrated throughout the ages to create personal power and peace.

Through their values and vision, people create their reality. They forge a lasting legacy, their individual imprint on the world, by expressing who they are in their relationships. Through their inner choices in congruence with who they are, individuals create meaning and purpose. They decide to what extent they want to manifest their potential. Spirit aids when individuals choose positive thoughts and actions and grow by connecting with the divine in all of life. Because

Energetic Coaching creates a relationship based on spiritual values, principles, and practices, clients learn how to open to their inner knower for spiritual energy and connection.

With vision individuals direct their energy toward desired outcomes. What they want reflects their inner values. Through creating and achieving their vision, individuals reflect their inner being in outer doing. If vision is the destination, values are the North Star and principles provide the power to get there. Personal vision changes with growth and achievement, but values remain constant. Consistency and congruence build trust in relationships. People develop authenticity in relationship with others, and most importantly, in relationship with self.

By deciding and defining inner relationship with self, individuals can relax about who they are. They do not constantly have to seek external validation to test their identity. Because they know their inner self, they do not need outer attention, recognition, or reward to validate their worth and power. Inner values add meaning and significance to the outer accomplishment of vision. Even when people are not conscious of their values, they guide and motivate resulting in observable actions and outcomes. Through self-reflection, examination of relationships with others, and determination of their intentional legacy, people imprint the world through values. Energetic Coaches help clients choose their values rather than unconsciously inherit them from family, culture, social influences, and organizational systems. Clients decide which values express their life purpose and align with principles that work. Energetic Coaching encourages clients to become the people they want to be instead of reacting habitually or merely complying with outside influences.

Individuals sense each other's values in relationship. Those who doubt their own values tend to capitulate to the values of others. Choosing values and principles frees people from inner conflict and the push/pull of outside expectations. It releases their energy to pursue their visions. Maintaining a strong value system allows people to withstand challenges from others. Especially when confronted or pressured, individuals benefit from secure self-knowing. Their authenticity is apparent when they do not have to question their motives, their worth, and their identity. Maintaining a high-level perspective creates and conserves energy, no matter the outer situation. Spiritual values such as equality, connection, goodness, and love provide Energetic Coaches with energy, guidance and motivation to serve others. Having chosen and cultivated such values, we demonstrate them in coaching behavior that expresses our nature with authenticity and integrity. The client benefits through a growing self-knowing created by experiencing the mirror of another's congruent being and doing. As spiritual beings living in a material world, such reflection bridges the gap between inner and outer duality and dispels the illusion that we are separated and isolated beings in a disconnected world.

LIVING VALUES, PRINCIPLES AND VISION

I have spent my days stringing and unstringing my instrument, while the song I came to sing remains unsung.
RABINDRANATH TAGORE

Character may be manifested in the great moments, but it is made in the small ones.
PHILLIPS BROOKS

Energetic Coaches know that we can only speak about spiritual energy and connection by consciously choosing our being and doing in alignment with spiritual values, principles, and practices in daily life. Our inner knower provides guidance that maintains congruence with our inner values and outer vision. Ignoring or denying the inner knower when our values are tested disconnects us from spirit when we need it the most. As the bridge between the visible and invisible worlds, we make the inner real in the outer world through our conscious choices. Spirit responds to our conscious intention to be and do to our full potential.

Lea: *Recently John and I had the wonderful opportunity to attend a talk given by the 14th Dali Lama, Tenzin Gyatso, in Washington, DC. He chuckled very slightly as he relayed that he had been asked what was the "best" religion to follow. He answered that it was only important to choose what one wants to follow, and then to do so continuously and deliberately. He pointed out that we choose food and clothes to wear, but we do not consciously choose how to be as a person. Through choice and intention, the Dali held that any religion would do if practiced consistently with good heart.*

The Power of Principles

If there were in the world today any large number of people who desired their own happiness more than they desired the unhappiness of others, we could have a paradise in a few years.
Bertrand Russell

Relationships reflect the characteristics of those within them. The mirrors of others show people directly if they are being true to themselves. To the extent that people deny or repress true being, they attract relationships that do the same. The closer the relationship, the better the mirror, because those who are closest reflect best. The inner knower provides the compass to align people with their desired values and the guidance to act according to their principles and ideals. As the keeper of life purpose, it registers any difference between values and vision and how individuals think, feel, and behave. It compels people to resolve discrepancies in order to experience integration, wholeness, and spiritual connection with self and others. Relationships reflect gaps between who people are and how they want to be. If they ignore the inner knower in order to be in relationships that do not support them to be the fullest expression of authentic being, they risk compromising themselves in relationships that do not work for them.

People realize their spiritual values, principles, and vision by speaking and acting with intention for the highest good. Inner intention drives outer expression. Although external situations change, intention anchors a consistent internal direction. Spiritual energy expands in ever-increasing frequencies, attracting similar intention from others back to the sender. Even when the external situation appears bleak, people can balance and restore energy through good intention. By maintaining inner congruence during outer chaos, they transcend a temporary challenge and retain inner peace.

When individuals choose to live honestly and authentically with good intent in thought, word, and deed, they no longer need command-control laws and external mandates of ethics and codes of conduct. They develop a personal relationship with spirit that is free of religious dogma, literalist fundamentalism, or personal autocracy. Individual spiritual commitment frees people of cumbersome, costly, inefficient external systems of rewards and punishments or culturally imposed and socially dictated standards of behavior. People express their authentic being based on their innate drive to inner goodness and outer pursuit of personal potential. Individuals become mature grownups rather than rebellious children, attracting what they want rather than resisting what they don't want.

Those who honor themselves honor others. Those who do not violate themselves cannot violate others. Inspired by spirit, people let go of negative and depleting relationships, instead opting for positive and replenishing ones. Those who know the truth do not have the compelling need to impose their will on others to compensate for inner doubt. They can live out their own visions and values because they work for them. There is no need to buy into flawed systems that don't work or kowtow in order to get along.

Without high-level personal principles, values, and vision, people tend to rationalize actions and outcomes by blaming something outside of self—but the inner knower knows better. Consciousness calls individuals to deal with whether they are lying, cheating, denying, slacking, or withholding. Anything less than honest self-expression and personal responsibility chafes and grates on self and others. No outside attempt to discern intent and reward or punish behavior can compensate for those who do not will to be and do good. To connect with spirit and the inner knower, people must choose positive inner ideals and hold to them without needing external threats or rewards to do so.

Individual choice guides outer action to create relationships based on laws of attraction and reciprocity. Imagine what it would be like if everyone intentionally aligned with high-level values and maintained a connection with their inner knower and spirit. We could co-create heaven on earth.

Consciousness calls people to grow and envision how to improve. Values compel them from within to demonstrate possibilities through personal example. Values evolve as consciousness grows. History has demonstrated that injustice and authoritarianism are not sustainable and that goodwill does prevail over those who would seek to do harm. Humans are phototrophic beings: they grow toward the light. As the world grows smaller through the global economy and interconnected communication and partnerships, it is clear that what benefits the whole benefits the individual and vice-versa. Once people realize the interconnectedness of the whole, they are compelled to be better people creating a better world. Even when it is not easy, most desire to be and do good. People grow through continuous improvement in self and in relationships with others. Energetic Coaches assist clients in their efforts to increase consciousness and connect. We may never fully arrive, but free will goodwill sustains our drive.

TWO-WAY RELATIONSHIPS

If each of us sweeps in front of our own steps, the whole world would be clean.
GOETHE

There is reciprocity in the universe. Because people are a connected whole, the Golden Rule serves as a modus operandi of personal conduct; it works to enhance self and other. Realizing oneness, the need to judge others becomes unnecessary.

Guided by the inner knower, people act in congruence. Although another's expression of self may be different, people can accept such differences knowing that at the core of being people have the same desire to be known and accepted for who they are. Energetic Coaches assist clients to become the fullest expression of their authentic self through the freedom gained by self-acceptance and love and the experience of being accepting and loving to others as they are. Recognizing the oneness of mirror and reflection, individuals self-reflect rather than project on others. Individuals are no longer separated and isolated but connected and whole.

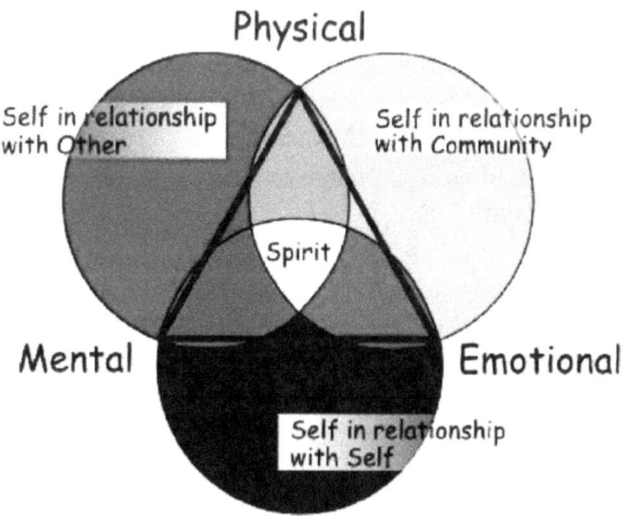

In congruent relationships people experience spiritual connection and energy. As people choose the inner-outer relationships with self, others, and community as a combined expression of growing consciousness, they manifest greater connection and oneness.

John and Lea: *Creating this book has been a joy for each of us. Although collaborating, writing, and editing has required a great deal of time and energy over three years, the process has increased our connection with self and one another. Because the work of the book has challenged us to walk our talk, our work has compelled us to connect with others, work with spirit, and live consciously. The book has spilled over into our daily lives, enhancing our relationships and validating our values.*

We have experienced spiritual energy throughout our collaboration. As equal and esteemed partners doing meaningful work, we have found that our regard for one another serves as an example for how we want to be in all other relationships. We have attracted people who helped us with this writing, such as our fellow coach and editor, Charlotte, and other friends and acquaintances. In our coaching business, our experience of collaboration and connection has served as an example of how to be with clients, holding the space of equality and esteem for the other's self-reflection, self-discovery, self-expression, and self-acceptance through expanded inner knowing.

Daily life and work have become opportunities to live the process we have written about: First working on our own inner congruence, then expressing it through our relationship with one another, and then offering the book as a connection with the larger community. Throughout the process, we have tested our statements, our principles, our values, and our actions to make sure they work as written.

Through our writing relationship we have connected with spirit. Our work has been effort, but through our free will goodwill, it has drawn us to spirit for energy and guidance. Time for study and reflection has materialized without a feeling of "Have to finish." Surprisingly, we anticipated a loss at the end of this project—as if we might have to search for energy and balance without our work calling us back to center. Then we realized that we could not lose energy and balance unless we allowed it. We have created something to connect with the whole. That something is the work of Energetic Coaching in which our individual growth into wholeness expands into our relationship with one another and into the community.

THE GROWTH OF CONSCIOUSNESS

As human beings, our greatness lies not so much in being able to remake the world—that is the myth of the atomic age—as in being able to remake ourselves.
MAHATMA GANDHI

Everyone stumbles over the truth from time to time, but most people pick themselves up and hurry off as though nothing ever happened.
SIR WINSTON CHURCHILL

IN OUR HOLOGRAPHIC UNIVERSE THE OUTER WORLD REFLECTS THE INNER STATE OF THE INDIVIDUALS WITHIN IT. ENERGETIC COACHING SEEKS TO FACILITATE INDIVIDUAL EVOLUTION OF CONSCIOUSNESS DELIBERATELY AND DYNAMICALLY, WHICH IN TURN WILL IMPACT THE COLLECTIVE WHOLE FOR GOOD.

EACH PERSON HAS A PART TO PLAY.

There is a continuum in the growth of consciousness. Energetic Coaches meet clients where they are on the continuum. The different stages of growth have to do with upbringing, life experiences, innate wisdom, and desire to learn. Some people come to coaching with an aware and open stance. Often called "sensitive" or"intuitive," they appear automatically to be conscious. Others may have avoided the necessary work to go within and self-reflect. They may still cling to externally imposed rules, dogma, beliefs, and prescriptions. They have a story, and they're sticking to it. When their story no longer works or when the rewards no longer satisfy or when the consequences become too difficult to ignore, they may open to coaching. At first, such clients may cling to what has worked in the past and want the coach to support the unsustainable world view that drains energy and diverts attention from the inner self. Energetic Coaching holds the space for inner examination. There is no place that clients should be other than where they are. They may grow into high consciousness and self-awareness—or not. We provide the fertile ground and the seeds, just as nature does. Like nature, we can only offer the opportunity. It is up to clients to plant the seeds and nurture them.

CONGRUENCE

This above all things: to thine own self be true, and then it must follow, as the sun the moon, thou canst not then be false to any man.
WILLIAM SHAKESPEARE, *Hamlet*

Congruence ends duality and the need to contrast and judge. When people balance and include at the still centerpoint, the apparent two become the actual one. Inner and outer congruence closes the gap that separates them from spirit and from self and one another. What is within is also without, and vice versa. Inner and outer congruence with self and others connects people and dispels the illusion of being isolated, separated, and alone.

External experiences reflect individuals' inner state. The world may appear to have the power to change people but only if they allow alteration. Spirit connects at the common core of humanity. The motives, projections, wants, and needs of ego and others continually challenge people unless they are connected to their inner knowing and spirit. Spirit and inner knowing serve as protection against manipulation, influence peddling, and external enticements. People who desire wholeness need consciously to maintain congruence between their inner being and their outer doing. Empowered adults create themselves by inner motivation based on spiritual principles and values—not by outer inducements based on transient attractions and desires. Practice enables people to stay the course, especially when it is not easy or convenient to do so. Incongruence not only separates individuals from their inner knower and spirit but also casts the illusion of a struggle within self and with others. People lose energy in the push/pull of stimulus and response and maintaining separate inharmonious parts. Few realize the toll of thinking, speaking, and acting in inconsistent ways. One incongruent act erodes trust others have that a person will be true and consistent in his or her dealings. It is hard to regain trust so best not to lose it. It takes a choice to stay congruent and remain positive in the downdraft of flippant, insincere, thoughtless, or hurtful words and actions. People stay congruent by demonstrating their practiced ability to be and do according to how they decide rather than reacting unconsciously.

Consistency in behavior and responses conveys honesty, integrity, and authenticity. Consistency creates trustworthiness. Trust is the bonding agent of relationships, improving communication, cooperation, and connectedness. Congruent people are consistent. They know who they are, retaining their being no matter what happens on the outside with others. They know what is theirs and what is not, and they take ownership of what they have created. Equally important, they let go of what is not theirs. Such people know that they must first be true to themselves in alignment with their inner knower, and then all else unfolds from the centerpoint. They bring warring inner factions to peace, which allows the inner knower to come through to help make tough decisions, provide discernment, and give guidance for the conscious choices that must be made regularly to maintain inner alignment.

The inner knower points to the true self. People learn to trust themselves because they know themselves. Individuals trust others to the extent that they are able to trust themselves. Relationships with others become complimentary as individuals grow to know themselves. By being able to trust themselves, individuals expect trust in relationships, even though others may not be trustworthy. If not, self-respect compels them to let go of relationships with incongruent others without blame, regret, or self-recrimination. They see that if they are betrayed, it is more a reflection of the other than of the self. All relationships serve as good examples, either of how to be or how not to be.

CONGRUENCE IN ENERGETIC COACHING

*You cannot tread the Path before you become the Path
yourself.*
ZEN SAYING

Energetic Coaches play many roles, using flexible approaches in coaching clients to congruence. By staying present, open, and authentic while coaching, we behave and speak with integrity. We depend on our inner knower to maintain the compassionate witness stance while we pose powerful questions to clients. We mirror what clients project, challenge what appears incongruent, and then ask them to summarize what they discovered and decided. By being congruent with good intention ourselves, we do not have to rely on external tools and cookie- cutter techniques. Freedom allows us to let go of self-reference and be present and real with clients as they do their work.

John: *Adele wanted to become a certified SUN Coach. The first part of our agreement was that I would coach her for eight meetings. Our work together proceeded nicely as we approached shifting into certifying her as a coach. A key element of that training deals with marketing and client development. Concurrently, we were working together toward her signing up the three full-paying clients required for SUN Coach Certification.*

I became aware that Adele was conflicted about marketing, even though she had developed plans in our coaching meetings. Her body language did not match her words. When I asked about her stated outcome, she realized that she was not yet ready to take the client development step. She decided that she wanted to redefine her outcome—"gain confidence in my coaching skills." At the time, feeling con-

fident about her coaching skills was of greater value than marketing. If I had stayed with the program and not been receptive to Adele's inner knowing, she might have complied to market rather than be true to what she wanted at the time. Adele grew in her coaching abilities as she grew in being true to herself. Now she has a successful practice due in part to a unique and customized marketing strategy that is an authentic expression of who she is.

Congruence requires people to make a continual, in-the-moment choice aligning their thoughts, words, and deeds with who they want to be. They move from responding to external forces to consciously guiding themselves from within. As inner-directed, consistent, self- motivated actors, they achieve spiritual connection through congruence with spiritual values and principles. By coaching for congruence, Energetic Coaches encourage self-reflection for inner knowing to develop visions. We deal with clients' shoulda-woulda-coulda's. By addressing them, clients release energy and focus on the present and future. We hold the space for clients to discover their innate goodness, inner guidance, and powerful ability to carry through on decisions. Energetic Coaching brings forward the inner knower—the ultimate life coach.

CLOSING THE GAP

Everyone thinks of changing the world, but no one thinks of changing himself.
Leo Tolstoi

There is only one corner of the universe you can be certain of improving – and that's your own self.
Aldous Huxley

Humans are spiritual beings in a material world. By freely choosing values and acting from their authentic inner being, they create wholeness and connection with spirit through their inner knower. When spirit receives the conscious choice to connect, it joins people's efforts and intentions. Individuals combine thoughts, feelings, and perceptions in their inner reality before they create their outer reality. Then it is just a matter of time before they manifest what they want or something better because they have calibrated themselves and their intentions to a high- level frequency that attracts spiritual energy and connection.

To live in close relationship with self and spirit, people are compelled to respond by being and doing authentically. As their consciousness grows, they desire congruence and connection. Life demonstrates a rhyme and reason and synchronicity abounds. What people manifest provides individual meaning. Congruence alleviates the alienation created by the illusion of separation and judgment of good/bad, right/wrong, like/dislike, this/not that, and so on. Individuals become their own best friend, in close relationship with themselves. As they experience creativity, passion, and purpose, they dispel loneliness.

Egocentricity separates; spirit connects. In separation, people lose track of their immense and powerful inner self. The ability to create more of what they want comes from choosing to be fully who they are. What they want calls forth inner orientation rather than outer acquisition, which can only serve as a temporary substitute for self-knowing and acceptance. All relationships become important, especially their most difficult ones, as they use the mirror and reflection to learn about themselves. Energetic Coaches facilitate clients' relationships, starting and ending with the relationship they have with self.

People experience spirit through relationships between their inner and outer selves and with the inner and outer selves of others. As they learn, they also grow in their relationships. At times, they may disconnect within self and with others because of incongruence and confusion. In order to stay the course, Energetic Coaches provide clients with a positive, validating relationship that reflects the common core of goodness and positive intention in everyone.

To achieve what they want in life, people must make decisions for themselves. If they do not, someone else will make them instead. Whereas people cannot achieve total control over external events, they can maintain their preferred inner state and purposeful vision based on their chosen values. For those seeking practical ways to be as the fullest expression of their highest self, Energetic Coaches aim to serve as examples and support when others, invested in the status quo, may challenge clients' "new you." Our support and confidence is vital when clients are making changes and others sense that the control and influence they once wielded is diminishing.

Many people orient externally. Some clients may feel "lost" as they switch to their own inner direction. Although people create their experiences from within, they may not realize the untapped power hidden inside. When they decide to be who they want and to express themselves in the world guided by values and inner-directed vision, Energetic Coaches support their decision. The outcomes clients achieve may differ from what they originally expected. It may take time and effort, persistence and patience to orient inward. It may seem that nothing is happening, even when clients are proceeding with the work. Energetic Coaches know the process because we have gone through it to discover that everything is in divine order. Who clients are and what they want they have already created within, and it is just a matter of time before they manifest their visions.

OUR ENERGETIC COACHING VISION

Truth is hidden in the subtle nature of the heart of everything, although it is invisible. One cannot see it from inside and neither from the surface. One can only live and experience it.
Heart Sutra

Imagine the kind of world it would be if all consciously chose spiritual connection through positive vision and values. It would be a world of peace, free of judgment and full of grace. Relationships would be healed and nations would share boundaries and beliefs. All communities would honor people for making positive and worthwhile contributions in their own way. People would treat one another well and base their relationships on equality, free of false separation and ego-protecting mistrust. They could communicate openly with one another from inner essence. They would confidently state personal truth and relish being who they are. Each person would respect the other's unique self and path.

As we speak, in communities throughout the world, people are expressing and experiencing their transcendent qualities. They are connecting with spirit and one another. Free people communicate their inner qualities uniquely in relationship with others who are free to do the same. Energetic Coaching envisions a critical mass of people holding themselves accountable to be what they want to see in the world. To freely choose to connect with self and others releases energy and enthusiasm. Spirit releases energy one person at a time to become so obviously present, positive, and pervasive that those who choose to remain separate and ego driven must self-reflect rather than project on others. As all people realize enlightenment in the power and peace of connecting, the darkness will become light. Resistance will be futile. For those who would like to hide, there will be nowhere to go where the light does not shine. Ultimately, those who choose to live in darkness will be included and loved despite their intentions and actions. Energetic Coaches know that at our inner core, we are all the same, desiring and deserving love.

As the energy of goodness and love that is spirit spreads, humankind becomes kind, balanced at the centerpoint of oneness. What was once two in the illusion of duality and separation becomes one. Through achieving individual inner and outer alignment, people create congruence in the world. Self and other remain individual and unique yet connected. Relationships flourish in equality and respect. People see disconnections as the illusion that they are. They know the Golden Rule works for everyone and want to treat others the way they would like to be treated.

The light of inner knowing in each person continually burns. It is only when individuals become fooled by the illusion of inequality and separateness that the basket hides the light. When individuals take responsibility to be what they want to experience in the world, they create visions together to overcome pain and problems. Humans may never live in a perfect outer world, but the positive intention and effort to grow in consciousness and connection creates personal purpose and power. Relationships reflect who people are as they come together in goodness and love. The world as a hologram reflects inner and outer congruence in the mirror and reflection of each person within it.

IF WE CHOOSE

As above, so below. As within, so without. We know the tree by its fruit. We see a single coin rather than its separate sides. The visible external reflects the unseen internal. It takes positive intention and conscious choice every moment to connect while at the same time operating as complete, autonomous, unique individuals. The holographic aspect of individuation and integration transcends duality, melding the two into one.

Each person as an individual completes the whole. Spirit manifests in the external world through the quality of individual relationships building upon one another. Ancient Confucian philosophy dealt with creating a community. Christ stated that the kingdom of God would be manifest when the two became one. There is no longer stimulus/response, desire and resistance, or labels of good or bad. There is no gap between who people are and how they present themselves to others. They work on themselves to become the person of their potential to produce congruence and inner peace. Energetic Coaching helps them to use the mirror and reflection of relationship to achieve dynamic oneness.

Creating wholeness and oneness through intention and invitation to spirit is the work of Energetic Coaching. We create inner and outer congruence when we decide wholeness is what we want. As spirit and inner knower connect through our values, principles, and visions, our outer experience reflects our inner self. The self reflects as true in the worldly mirror. Assuming personal power and taking personal responsibility, we become what we want to see in the world—free will good will for all. In this moment, the one becomes One.

We are the ones we have been waiting for.
ORAIBI, Arizona Hopi Nation

WITH GRATITUDE

As co-author in writing ENERGETIC COACHING, Being and Doing With Spirit, I have come to appreciate the wisdom and power of my inner knowing. My deepest gratitude is the awareness of the work of spirit over the course of time it took in completing this book. This awareness started when my coach trainer and mentor, Teri-E Belf planted the seed for me to write a companion workbook to her book, Coaching with Spirit, Allowing Success to Emerge. Although the workbook never materialized, I am grateful to Teri-E for igniting the spark for this book and writing the book's Foreword. A second awareness came about when my wise inner knowing made it quite clear that I was to partner with my coach-in-training client, Lea Harper as co-author. This book would not have been written without her valued and dedicated contributions and unwavering loving support over the years of writing. My gratefulness for this unique experience with Lea is profound. A third awareness was the insight to invite my colleague Charlotte Ward to be the book's editor. I am grateful to Charlotte for her expertise as an editor, and her willingness to convincingly challenge us to keep the reader in mind as we wrote. Gratitude goes to my coaching peers and the coaches in training that inspired me to demonstrate and, with Lea's input, refine the concepts and applications contained in our book. I want to acknowledge my family and friends for their generosity in reading the myriad of drafts so necessary to achieve the final product. Their encouragement and cheerleading, along with a little prodding, made this journey most enjoyable.

JOHN COLLINGS

When I found John and asked him to be my coach, my inner knower knew before I realized how
beneficial, positive and empowering our relationship was to be. On the outside, we are contrasts; John with a successful career in Organization Development and a Master Certified Coach, well known in his field. I was on the fringes, trying to find a fit in my chosen field of OD, but not as an external expert as we were taught. I found coaching to be a hopeful fit, but not quite, until John and I collaborated on this book. Now I find something that will be a reflection of who I am and what I find to be most worthwhile in life. It is with gratitude, most of all, to John who made real to me what I had believed, provided validation for my fullest expression of self, and joined me in wanting to be and do for the greater good. My husband, Steve, is a key ingredient to the reality of this endeavor. Steve always believed in me and my projects, from going back to graduate school, to starting my own business, to writing this book. Steve has been my mentor, my friend and my confidante, always supportive and never questioning, even when the payback is not immediately there. I go back even farther to the beginning of this quest for truth. It's my mother I find at the root of it all. She taught me courage to be myself. She taught me that no one was any better than anyone else. She taught me truth, she taught me consequences, she taught me the dignity of silence when others were disparaging. She showed me that whatever the outcome, I cannot fail when I try my best. I would like to thank my dad and my siblings for teaching me how to let go, and my daughter and her family for helping me grow. I know John and I would both like to thank our grandchildren for their wide-eyed wonder and simple wisdom of the world that reminds us of what we forgot long ago. I want to acknowledge my friends, who are now truer friends than I have ever had. They provide a good

mirror for me; I like the reflection of myself I see in them. They challenge me, but also give me a safe place to land. I must also acknowledge Charlotte Ward, who somehow made my writing readable with a poetry and grace that is uniquely her own. With Charlotte's patient tutoring, I have learned a great deal. I would like to thank Word Association Publishing who recognized the importance of this work and gave it the attention it deserved. Also, to be honest and not knowing how to say this, I must acknowledge the spark of this endeavor, the Source that brought it together, the energy that kept it going, the seedbed of consciousness from which it came, joining us to create that which is most meaningful. Finally, there is great appreciation for you, dear reader, for the opportunity to connect within the fullness of the whole.

Lea Harper

Knowing that there's this interconnectedness of the universe, that we are all interconnected and that we are connected to the universe at its fundamental level, I think is as good an explanation for spirituality as there is.

Stuart Hameroff, MD

BIBLIOGRAPHY

- BELF, TERI-E (2002). *Coaching with Spirit: Allowing Success to Emerge.* San Francisco, CA: Jossey-Bass/Pfeiffer.

- BENSON, HERBERT; KLIPPER, MIRIAM (1975). *The Relaxation Response.* New York, NY: HarperCollins.

- BUBER, MARTIN (1970). *I and Thou.* New York, NY: Touchstone.

- CHILDRE, DOC L.; PADDISON, SARA (1998). *HeartMath Discovery Program Level 1: Daily Readings and Self-Discovery Exercises for Creating a More Rewarding Life.* Boulder Creek, CA: Planetary Publications/HeartMath LLC.

- CHILDRE, DOC; MARTIN, HOWARD (1999). *The Heartmath Solution.* New York, NY: HarperCollins.

- FRANKL, VIKTOR E. (1955). The Doctor and the Soul: From Psychotherapy to Logotherapy. New York, NY: Random House.

- FRANKL, VIKTOR E. (1959). Man's Search for Meaning. Boston,- MA: Beacon Press.

- FROMM, ERICH (1956). The Art of Loving. New York, NY: HarperCollins.

- JUNG, CARL G. (1938). *Psychology and Religion (The Terry Lecture Series).* Binghamton, NY: The Vail-Ballou Press.

- JUNG, CARL G. (1972) *Collected Works of C.G. Jung, Volume 8, The Structure and Dynamics of the Psyche.* Princeton, NJ: Princeton University Press.

- LABORDE, GENIE Z. (1997) *Influencing with Integrity: Management Skills for Communication and Negotiation.* Redwood City, CA: Syntony Press.

- MARKOVA, DAWNA (1996). *The OpenMind: Exploring the 6 Patterns of Intelligence.* Berkley, CA: Conari Press.

- MASLOW, ABRAHAM H. (1999). *Toward a Psychology of Being.* New York, NY: John Wiley and Sons.

- Peck, M. Scott (1978). *The Road Less Traveled: A New Psychology of Love, Traditional Values, and Spiritual Growth.* New York, NY: Touchstone.

- Peck, M. Scott (1987). *The Different Drum: Community Making and Peace.* New York, NY: Touchstone.

- Piedmont, Ralph L. (1999). *Does Spirituality Represent the Sixth Factor of Personality? Spiritual Transcendence and the Five Factor Model.* Journal of Personality, 67, 985 – 1013.

- Ryan, Kathleen; Oestreich, Daniel (1998). *Driving Fear out of the Workplace: Creating the High-Trust, High-Performance Organization.* San Francisco, CA: Jossey-Bass.

- Seiling, J.G. (1997). *The Membership Organization: Achieving Top Performance through the New Workplace Community.* San Francisco, CA: Davies-Black.

- Seiling, J.G. (2001). *The Meaning and Role of Organizational Advocacy: Responsibility and Accountability in the workplace.* Westport, CT: Greenwood Publications.

- Senge, Peter M. (1990). *The Fifth Discipline: The Art and Practice of the Learning Organization.* New York, NY: Bantam Doubleday Dell Publishing Group.

- Wheatley, Margaret J. (1999). *Leadership and the New Science: Discovering Order in a Chaotic World.* San Francisco, CA: Berrett-Koehler Publishers.

KOLIMA
BOOKS

9 788418 263385